Stefan Buczacki plant problems

Stefan Buczacki
plant problems

"My guiding principal in this book is that understanding is the key to the prevention and control of garden problems – and ultimately, therefore, to better and more enjoyable gardening."

David & Charles

Note: Throughout the book the time of year is given as a season to make the reference applicable to readers all over the world. In the northern hemisphere the seasons may be translated into months as follows:

Early winter - December	Early summer - June
Midwinter - January	Midsummer - July
Late winter - February	Late summer - August
Early spring - March	Early autumn - September
Midspring - April	Mid-autumn - October
Late spring - May	Late autumn - November

Page 1: Adult cranefly
Page 3: Gooseberry sawfly
Right: Red deadnettle

A DAVID & CHARLES BOOK

First published in the UK in 2000

A catalogue record for this book is available from the British Library.

ISBN 0 7153 0963 3

Book design by Ian Muggeridge
Photographs supplied mainly by
Professor Stefan Buczacki, B&B Photographs (see page 224)

Printed in Italy by LEGO SpA
for David & Charles
Brunel House, Newton Abbot, Devon

Contents

	6	Introduction
Part one	10	**Understanding plants and their problems**
1	12	What is a plant?
2	24	The plant kingdom
3	32	Life forms
4	36	The merits of mongrels
5	44	Pathogens – organisms that cause disease
6	50	How pathogens grow and feed
7	56	Attack and defence
8	66	Viruses and plant diseases
9	70	Pests and plant damage
10	80	The nature of ecology
11	86	The influence of climate
12	98	Understanding soil
13	106	Other problems
14	112	Weeds
15	118	The spread of plant problems
16	124	Prediction of plant problems
17	128	Control: physical and cultural
18	146	Control: biological
19	150	Control: chemical
Part two	162	**Problem identification and treatment**
	164	100 common problems
	184	Keys to plant problems
	214	Indexes to plant problems
	220	Index
	224	Acknowledgements

Introduction

"The general belief has long been that if you look after yourself, then you will be less susceptible to ailments. Get your feet wet or go out in the rain and you will be more likely to catch a cold. Neglect your plant, fail to feed and water it, and it will be more likely to be affected by disease. Clubroot, however, seemed to belie this maxim."

Several years ago, while engaged in research on clubroot, a particularly important plant disease, I consistently found one concept difficult to convey to some of my colleagues. The notion that I put forward was that the better growing (or the more healthy, if you like) the plant, the more severely it was likely to suffer once clubroot had gained a hold. This seemed to fly in the face of much of the information that their own researches with other problems had taught them; it seemed to fly in the face of much logic; and it certainly flew in the face of the advice promulgated by countless generations of mothers and nannies. However, my experience and my experiments all told me that the better growing, more vigorous plants succumbed soonest.

The explanation (or at least, the explanation that satisfied me) lay in the nature of the disease and the way it reveals itself. The cause of clubroot, which affects only the Brassicaceae (the cabbage family), is a curious species of fungus known as *Plasmodiophora brassicae.* The symptoms of clubroot are dramatic and unmistakable: the roots are distorted to form massive and grotesque galls, sometimes in the form of a single club-like structure, sometimes in the form of finger-like swellings that give the entire root system the appearance of dahlia tubers. In consequence, the conducting and other functional tissues of the roots are distorted and fail to function properly. The plant then suffers a serious reverse in its fortunes and declines quickly in vigour, although, significantly, it isn't generally killed.

The impressive outward manifestations of clubroot are brought about by increases in both the size and number of the root cells. Like all tissue growth in plants and animals, this is under the control of chemicals popularly called hormones. Plants belonging to the Brassicaceae also contain chemicals that are the precursors of hormones, or of substances very like them. In ways still not understood, the presence of *Plasmodiophora* in the tissues causes the precursors to change to the real thing, with consequent tissue proliferation. And it's here, too, that clubroot is rather unusual; not many diseases result in an *increase* in the growth of at least part of the host plant (the plant being attacked). More usually, the entire plant grows less, and is smaller and enfeebled.

This story demonstrates that plant pathology (the science of the study of plant diseases) contains few golden rules, and that even experts can be surprised by the behaviour of a problem with which they are personally unfamiliar.

Diseases are only part of the difficulties that can befall plants. Like people and animals, plants are also prey to attack by pests.

Hosta 'Frances Williams' finds good company with hardy ferns

And here again, the reverse of what's traditionally expected is the more common: in general, pests behave like clubroot (but unlike most other diseases) and prefer to attack the bigger, more lush, better growing individuals.

All of this makes life difficult for gardeners trying their best to keep their plants healthy so I would like to convey the notion that if a plant is grown 'correctly', it will be less likely to succumb to problems. However, as will be evident already, 'correctly' isn't easy to define, and, as I shall also demonstrate, there will always be the unexpected situation that can confound all and any logic.

So how is a plant to protect itself against pests or a disease like clubroot? Should it do so by growing feebly? This seems unlikely as it will then fall prey to those pathogens that would be unable to attack it while it was growing vigorously. Clearly, if we can understand the ways that plants defend themselves, and how and why some plants in some situations are more prone to problems, we can then capitalize on this knowledge and enhance the defences. This in turn will make cures less necessary.

To reach this level of understanding, it's important first to step further back and discover how diverse are the problems ranged against plants, how a normal, healthy plant functions and how each type of problem achieves its ends.

DEFINITIONS

Let us begin with a few useful definitions. I've already referred to diseases and pests; they are popularly linked with a third category of problem – disorder – and there's widespread confusion between the three. My definitions, at least in so far as they relate to plants (clinical and veterinary, as opposed to plant, pathologists, might view things slightly differently), are as follows.

Black spot (*Diplocarpon rosae*) on the climbing rose 'Blairi No 2'

A **disease** is an impairment of normal function brought about as a result of infection (invasion, if you prefer) of the tissues by a micro-organism. The micro-organism may be a fungus, a bacterium or an actinomycete, which are all readily visible with a light microscope and commonly visible at least *en masse* to the naked eye; it could also be a virus, a phytoplasma or some other self-reproducing entity, which is only rendered apparent with electron or other forms of high-magnification microscopy. Any organism that causes disease is called a pathogen.

Aphids massed on the young shoots of an aquilegia

below: Blossom end rot, a symptom of calcium deficiency, on tomato

My definition of a **pest** is much simpler: a pest is an animal that causes damage to a plant. Most groups of the animal kingdom, from some of the smallest (eelworms), to some of the biggest (mammals), contribute at least a few. Nonetheless, one group, the insects, outweighs all others in importance.

A **disorder** is anything else that goes wrong with a plant. It's always caused by the effect or action of something non-living.

Understanding plants and their problems

Part one

This section covers all aspects of pest and disease management in plants. It outlines how, by following good gardening practice and maintaining high standards of garden hygiene, you can avoid many of the worse problems that so often confront gardeners. It also explains why many problems occur and dispels a number of gardening myths.

If you are faced with an invasion by a serious pest, or your plants are succumbing to disease and it becomes necessary to resort to chemical or biological control methods, all the information you require for effective and rapid treatment is also included here.

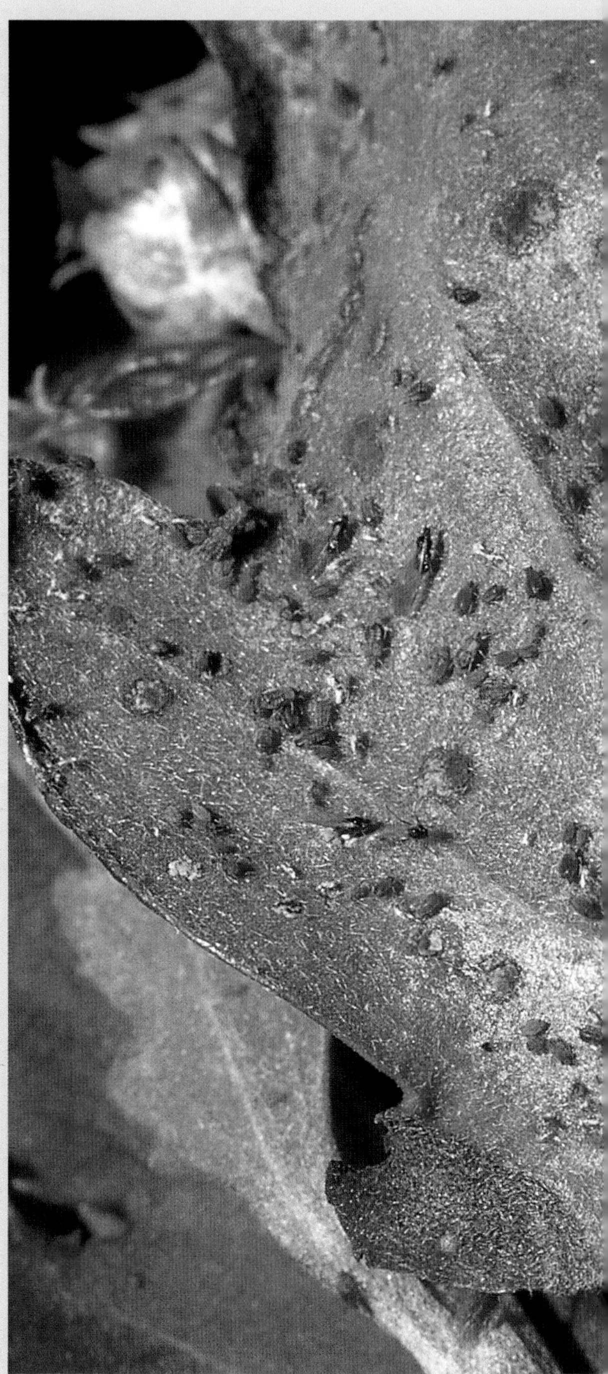

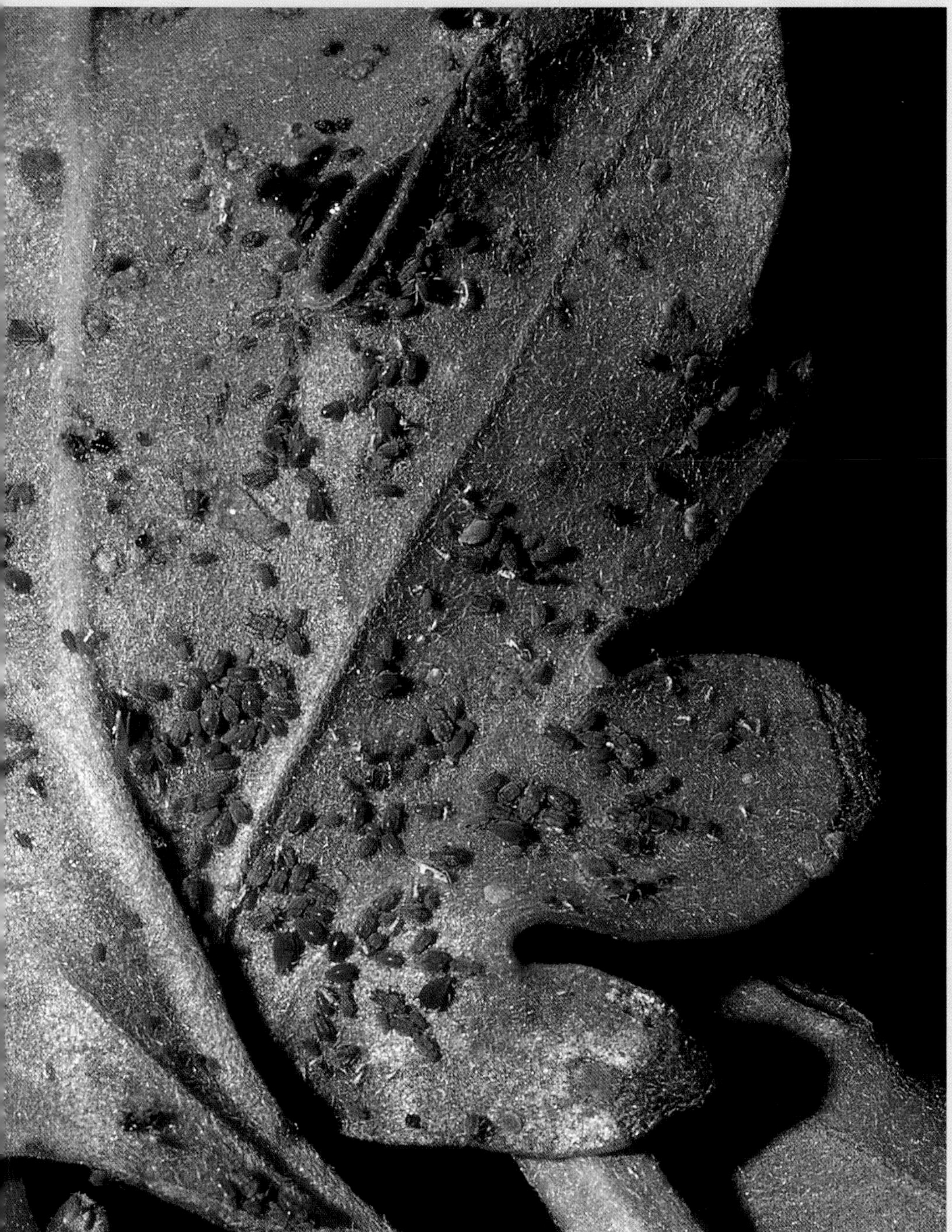

White rust (*Puccinia horiana*) and aphids (*Aphis gossypii*) on a chrysanthemum leaf

1

What is a plant?

"A plant is a living organism that synthesizes its food from inorganic substances, possesses cellulose cell walls, responds slowly and often permanently to a stimulus, lacks a nervous system and has no powers of locomotion."

The definition of a plant is almost the antithesis of the definition of an animal which is a living organism that cannot synthesize its own food (and must, therefore, eat), doesn't have cellulose in its cell walls, produces fairly rapid and temporary responses to stimuli, does have a nervous system and can move from place to place. There are, of course, exceptional examples for which these definitions must be 'bent' slightly, but overall they are pretty acceptable and wide-ranging.

I've implied that plants and animals are, in a sense, opposites and I think this is fair. I should add, however, that modern science divides the living world into more than the original two kingdoms – plants and animals – and has five kingdoms, fungi and other microscopic organisms, to which I've already referred, making up the others. But more of these anon (pages 24–31).

Plants are the key to the success of all life on earth. As a botanist, perhaps I might be expected to say this, but I say it with some justification. For it is the plants' ability to synthesize their own organic food that forms the basis of most food chains: no matter how many sequences exist of 'bigger fleas' biting 'smaller fleas', somewhere further down the line something will have bitten a plant.

The hairy leaves of *Genista hirsuta*

"Plants are the vital conduit for transforming the inorganic atmosphere into the multitude of different organic molecules that make up living things."

A green pigment called chlorophyll is the key to this extraordinarily important process. It's unarguably one of the most significant molecules on the planet. The process itself is called photosynthesis; during photosynthesis carbon dioxide and water are combined to produce carbohydrates, using energy from sunlight that has been absorbed by the chlorophyll. This is a simplification: the process is complex and entails several quite distinct chemical stages, some of which take place in the dark.

Photosynthesis occurs in any plant cell that contains chloroplasts. Each chloroplast is a microscopic body with a structure rather like a pile of loose sheets of paper; the chlorophyll lies on these 'sheets'. Interestingly, chlorophyll requires light in order to be produced. It also requires the mineral element iron: the reason why some plants turn pale green or yellow in alkaline soils (a condition called chlorosis) is because they are unable to absorb iron correctly. And the variegated plants that attract so much gardening interest are generally less vigorous than forms with all-green leaves because they contain less chlorophyll.

In considering photosynthesis and chlorophyll, one thinks, inevitably, of the green parts of plants: the leaves and to some extent the stem. These are, however, but two of a plant's complement of organs. Because many types of problem characteristically attack some but not all parts of the plant, it is now appropriate to look in rather more detail at the overall structure of an individual plant. (This will be of help later in the book, pages 187–213, where the diagnostic keys require you to concentrate on one part of a plant at a time.)

Every part of every plant is made up of tissues, which are in turn made up of cells. Some cells contain chloroplasts but many do not. Few cells are individually visible to the naked eye, and, although there's rather a wide range in size, the typical plant cell is an irregularly shaped bag of watery fluid approximately one-tenth of a millimetre in diameter, confined by a boundary or wall. It's a sad fact that generations of school children and not a few biology students, used to looking at cross-sectional diagrams in their textbooks, have grown up imagining that cells are two-dimensional objects and that they join together to produce something akin to wire-netting. In fact, every cell is very much a three-dimensional vessel that is full of fluid. Within the fluid, called cytoplasm (or, in a broad and non-specific sense, sap), float a nucleus, which has overall control of the cell's functions, and various other microscopic bodies, such as chloroplasts, responsible for particular vital processes.

Most of the damage that is caused to plants by pests and pathogens is brought about by some disruption of the cells, most particularly by damage to their boundary walls. Cell walls may be more or less modified, depending on their particular purpose and this can have a major bearing on their susceptibility to damage. The cells of a petal, for instance, require the colouring pigments within to be clearly visible to pollinating insects. Hence, they are thin, translucent and physically extremely weak – a major reason why flowers so easily fall prey to damage. By contrast, the cells that make up wood are considerably strengthened to support the huge physical bulk of trees and shrubs; the ability to attack and degrade wood is, therefore, limited to organisms with particular physical or chemical weaponry.

The needle-like leaves of *Pinus*

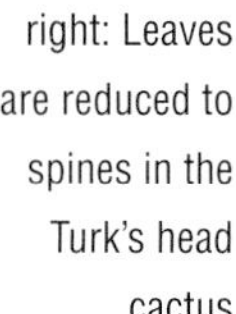

right: Leaves are reduced to spines in the Turk's head cactus

For a plant to grow, it must increase in size. This is performed, not by individual cells becoming much larger (although this may happen as a response to attack by certain pests and some pathogens, like *Plasmodiophora*, pages 6–9), but by new cells forming as a result of the division of existing ones. This new growth occurs in particular regions called meristems, or growth points, and the position of a plant's meristems has some important implications for pests and pathogens. In the majority of plants, the meristems are at the tip of the stem, and anything that damages this will seriously disrupt the development of new tissues overall and could result in major distortion. By contrast, grasses have their meristems at the base of the stem and so damage to the shoot tips causes them no harm: this is, of course, the reason why lawns can be mown.

leaves

In addition to photosynthesis, leaves have another important function: they are a medium for gaseous exchange. All leaves possess pores or stomata through which air (containing the essentials of carbon dioxide for photosynthesis and oxygen for respiration) passes inwards, and water,

"The structure of a leaf is a compromise between presenting a surface that maximizes the capture of solar energy, with one that minimizes water loss."

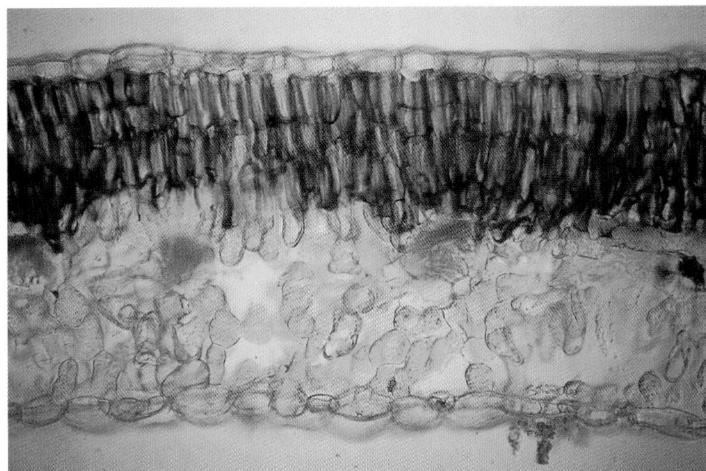

Transverse section through the living leaf of a lupin

taken in from the soil, passes outwards as water vapour. Not surprisingly, the pores through which gas exchange occurs have been utilized by some pathogens as a convenient entry point to the inner leaf tissues.

Generally, the size or, more precisely, the total surface area of the leaf (or the total number of leaves per plant), tends to reflect the energy-trapping function; rather like a solar panel on a house roof, a large, flat surface facing the sun provides the greatest efficiency. The shape of the leaf, however, together with the thickness of the outer covering to the epidermis, tends to be an adaptation to limit water loss. Size and shape can also have secondary functions: the needles of conifers in northern regions may be arranged to encourage the sliding off of snow; some plants have holes in the leaves to limit wind damage; and the modified leaves of cacti, reduced to spines, deter animals from browsing.

Despite the vast variation in form among leaves of different plants, they all possess the following elements: strands of conducting tissue for movement of water and dissolved nutrients, 'packing' tissue within which the photosynthesis occurs, and an outer skin or epidermis. The epidermis is often covered with a waxy cuticle; its thickness and character is a very significant factor in determining how easily pathogens or pests can enter.

The distinction between deciduous and evergreen plants (or, more accurately, between those that shed all their leaves simultaneously each year and those that retain them for longer periods and then shed them piecemeal) has little basic botanical significance. For instance, there are many genera, such as *Magnolia,* that contain both deciduous and evergreen species. And although in most groups one system predominates, even here there are exceptions; for example, almost all conifers are evergreen, but the larches are notable for being deciduous. Nonetheless, ecologically, the evergreen habit has some important consequences. In a mixed vegetation community, an evergreen species will cast shade all year round. Being evergreen makes a plant more vulnerable to the effects of winter wind or snow damage, but, conversely, gives it a head start with growth in the spring. The presence of some foliage all year round prolongs the period during which evergreens are prone to attack by leaf-eating pests and leaf-infecting pathogens; this is balanced, however, by the fact that the organisms aren't

Young apple shoot with older tissues becoming woody

active all year round. The reasons why the deciduous condition evolved from the evergreen is a matter of controversy, but it may be a complicated response to moderate, but not severe, seasonal cold, high summer humidity and other factors.

There are numerous ways in which leaves have become structurally adapted to satisfy the maximum surface, minimum water loss compromise mentioned above. It must be said that there are exceptions to almost every one, but a few examples will illustrate some of the general principles. In moist conditions with low light intensity, leaves tend to have a high surface area to volume ratio for maximum energy trapping, along with a thin cuticle or covering to the epidermis. The deeply dissected and fragile leaves of many of Britain's native woodland plants illustrate this well; in gardens the same thin cuticle means that these plants are often prone to pest and disease problems. By contrast, in dry climates with high light intensity, the need to limit water loss takes priority over the need to trap solar energy and the leaves of many desert plants are correspondingly small, relatively thick and possess a water-retentive (and problem-excluding) cuticle. Hairiness of the leaf surface is another feature intended to limit water loss but it too can have a rather sophisticated pest-excluding function.

When leaves fall from their parent plant, all of the tissues in the leaf stalk are severed, leaving behind a scar. For a short period, sometimes only a few hours, the tissues of the parent plant are exposed at this point. Opportunistic pathogens have capitalized on this and the leaf scar provides a characteristic entry point for a number of diseases.

stems

The stem is a framework or support for holding the leaves and flowers (and, ultimately, the fruit) in their correct functional positions. It grows towards the light. It also provides the channel for the transportation of nutrients and water to and from these organs. Although it may contribute in a minor way to photosynthesis, the stem is primarily a mechanical feature and endows the plant with the various shapes and modes of growth called life forms (page 24).

Despite their enormous variation in form, all stems possess the same basic structure: one or more strands of conducting tissue through which the water and nutrients move, a surrounding zone of 'packing' tissue with provision for the radial movement of these substances, and an outer skin, the epidermis. The stem tissues also have the ability to produce an extremely durable chemical called lignin and to develop what's known as secondary thickening – in other words, stems can form woody tissue – and these features are of importance in resisting pest and disease attack. A comparison between the stem of a buttercup, a year-old apple shoot and the trunk of a beech tree shows the result of an increasing content of lignin in the tissues. (Monocotyledonous plants don't produce wood in the conventional sense, but some large ones, such as palms and bamboos, do have comparable ways of strengthening their stems.)

Because lignified tissues are resistant to desiccation, they provide a plant with the means of surviving above ground during periods of adverse conditions – over a cold winter or during a drought, for instance. So, while many soft-stemmed perennial plants die down to a bulb, tuber or other underground body each winter, a perennial plant with woody tissues can remain above ground. And the ability to survive its period of dormancy above ground confers a huge advantage on the plant in that it doesn't have to start its growth from scratch each season. It can capitalize on previous years' growth and, of course, grow much larger as a result. All of the largest forms of plant life have a woody stem structure; for example, some conifers and eucalypts can be over 100m (325ft) high, with a mass of over 2000 tonnes, and *Pinus aristata*, the bristlecone pine, may live for over 5000 years.

Few small plants possess woody tissues, and those that do tend to occur in harsh climates and to be very slow growing. Conversely, the really large plants with non-woody tissues usually occur in moist, tropical climates where there's no need for a rest period and where ultimate size tends to be limited by physical instability; these plants invariably require the support of

An old beech tree with a massive woody trunk

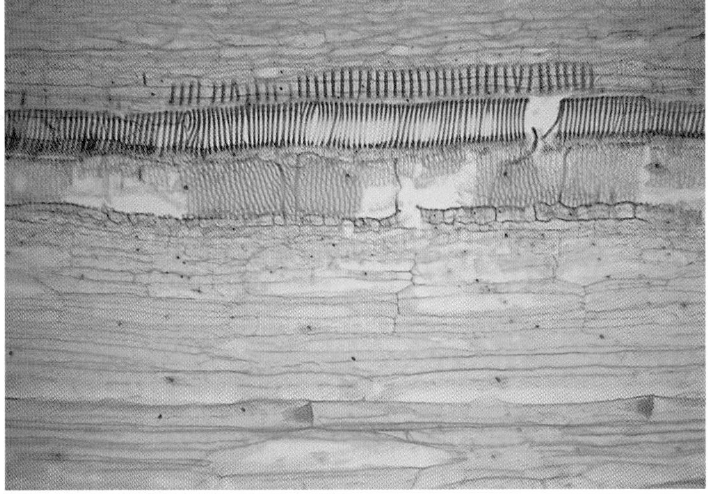

below: Longitudinal section through a stem showing the spiral strengthening of the water-conducting elements imparted by lignin

Swollen tap roots of carrots

other vegetation for their weak stems.

Because they are tough, woody tissues, especially when they are combined with a comparably thickened epidermis in the form of a layer of bark, also provide the plant with some resistance to attack by pests and pathogens. However, being above ground during the winter period, when active growth has ceased and wound-healing responses are comparatively ineffective, does, like the evergreen habit, render woody plants at some disadvantage.

roots

Whether they grow in soil, on the bark of forest trees or float on water, almost all flowering plants have roots. Roots serve the principal functions of supplying physical stability and providing the means by which water and mineral nutrients can be taken up from the soil. The internal appearance of the individual root is not, at first sight, recognizably very different from that of the stem, having central conducting tissues, surrounding 'packing' tissue and an outer epidermis. It differs structurally, however, in that none of its cells contain chlorophyll, and behaviourally in that it usually grows away from light and towards moisture. There are mechanisms by which older roots, like stems, can be reinforced, although, of course, the great physical strength of the stem isn't required below ground.

right: The fibrous root system of willowherb

The extent of a plant's root system is often not fully appreciated by gardeners. Although when a tree is dug up, it is evident that the growth in the soil isn't very different in extent from that above ground, it usually comes as a surprise that even beneath a vegetable plot, there may well be over 20km of roots per square metre. The basic distinction between, for example, a long, vertically penetrating taproot, such as that of a carrot, and the many-branched, fibrous, adventitious roots of a grass will be familiar; beyond this the extent and degree of branching of a plant's root system are influenced, among other factors, by the soil structure, texture and depth. Most gardens have a sufficient depth of soil for the development of the relatively short taproots of herbaceous plants, but in some, the soil depth may well be inadequate for the growth of deeply rooting trees – a knowledge of the nature of a plant's root system is one aspect of selecting species appropriate to your garden.

right: The newly emerging root of a maize seedling showing the root hairs

A subsidiary function of the root system of some plants is as a food reserve. Many non-woody perennials, such as dahlias or celandines, develop tubers or other root structures in order to permit above-ground growth to start afresh at the start of the season. (It should be appreciated that many of the familiar overwintering food reserve bodies, such as bulbs and corms, aren't roots, but modified stems.)

"There have been countless occasions when people have brought me small dead portions for diagnosis taken from the top of their plants, when the real cause of the problem was below ground."

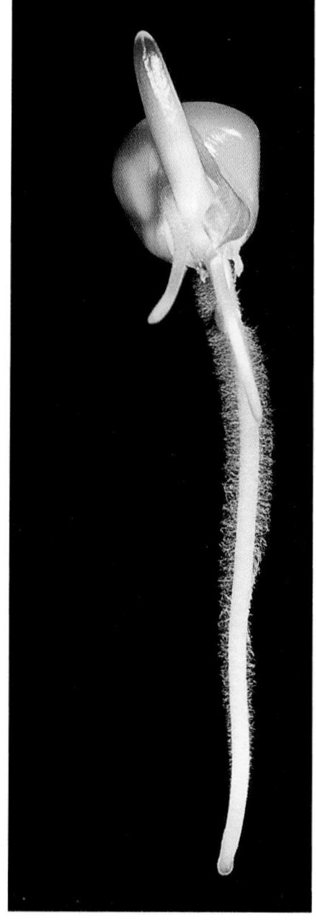

While the visible roots of a plant provide the obvious means of physical anchorage, the vital nutrient- and water-absorbing function of a root system is performed mainly by root hairs, which are tiny, finger-like extensions from cells of the epidermis. Root hairs are virtually invisible to the naked eye, although they can be seen if a seed is germinated in a moist atmosphere and the young root examined closely: *en masse*, they give the root the appearance of a minute paintbrush. Once their delicate nature is appreciated, it will be understood why transplanting is such a traumatic experience for plants. In such an upheaval, the root hairs and associated epidermal cells are irreparably damaged. Only if the operation is performed into warm, damp soil, or at a time when the plant is dormant (and thus not requiring immediate water uptake to replenish that being lost through the leaves), will there be opportunity for new root hairs to form before the plant, as a whole, suffers materially.

The fragility of root hairs suggests that they would be of considerable importance in admitting pests and diseases, but this is only partly true. Undoubtedly, in a few instances, such as clubroot and some eelworm attacks, infection or invasion of root hairs plays a crucial role. But in general, it seems that they are just too small to offer a great nutritional attraction. Roots overall, however, are immensely important targets for pests and diseases. The normally moist environment in which they live is highly favourable to microbial activity in general (and a large number of pathogens are soil-inhabiting), while some types of pest (eelworms are classic examples) are permanent soil inhabitants. And, as roots are unseen, damage to them isn't immediately evident. At several points in the keys (pages 187–213), you are advised to check the roots if you have observed a particular above-

ground symptom. Remember that, as well as conferring structural stability, the root is the first stage in a water-pumping process (in tall trees, an extraordinarily efficient one) and that if this pump is impaired, the first symptoms will appear at the furthest extremity: the top-most leaves and branches wilt before those lower down.

flowers

The fact that flowers offer such a diverse range of structure, colour and overall appearance is the reason why many gardeners garden. But it's worth bearing in mind that their natural function isn't to give delight to the human eye: the flower is a reproductive organ and its sole purpose is to ensure that pollination occurs, fertilization of the ovules takes place and, in due course, seeds form and the species is perpetuated. Every aspect of a flower's structure is directed towards this end; this is as true of flowers borne individually, like roses and buttercups, as it is of

top:
An individual lupin flower exposed to show interior structure

above:
The semi-double flower of a water lily

The composite flower heads of *Helenium* have inner tubular florets and outer ray florets

those aggregated in an inflorescence, like buddleia or wisteria.

There are two main ways in which flowers can be pollinated: by utilizing some physical feature of the environment (usually wind, although water is also used by some aquatic species), or by encouraging some form of animal life to carry the pollen. In temperate climates, insects are the most important creatures for pollen transfer although a wide range of others, from slugs to bats and humming birds, is used by some plant species. Many of the adaptations needed to aid pollination, and particularly the presence of bright colours to attract insects, mean that the flower is a delicate object. Thus, it doesn't require a great deal of sophistication on the part of a disease-causing micro-organism to breach the barrier of a petal; and few pests have jaws that are unable to chew through the fragile tissues. Evolutionarily, a flower is a telescoped leafy shoot, but in undergoing the loss of a thick cuticle and other modifications necessary for its specialized role, it has rendered itself much more vulnerable to problems.

Buds, the precursors of both flowers and leaves, are fairly well protected, primarily to ensure that the immature tissues within aren't desiccated. I always think of the unfolding of a bud as akin to the hardening-off process by which gardeners gradually accustom their plants to the rigours of the great outdoors. In offering protection from environmental factors to the young leaves or petals, the scales covering a bud also provide protection from pests and diseases – pests and diseases attacking buds are relatively few.

top:
The single flower of the hybrid tea rose 'Dainty Bess'

above:
Individual flowers on the inflorescence of lilac

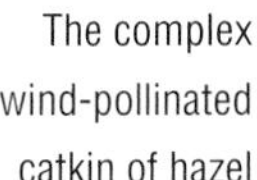

The complex wind-pollinated catkin of hazel

A range of fruit types, each adapted to a dispersal process. Clockwise from top centre: oak, sycamore, thistle, lupin, blackberry

seeds and fruits

The result of the pollination and fertilization is seed, generally contained within a fruit. Just as flowers are adapted to encourage pollination, so fruits are adapted to facilitate their dispersal from the parent plant. And, as with pollen, some fruits are dispersed by wind and water and others are dispersed by animals. The various methods of dispersal result in the many different fruit forms; in some, like nuts, it is hard and strong, but in other instances, it is soft and fleshy. We grow and eat many types of fruit, but it's their attractiveness to birds and other animals that is the primary purpose of their structure.

Being soft and fleshy, many fruit are attractive to pests and diseases and it is commonly a combination of the two that gives the problems we see. Small wounds caused by pest action allow decay or other disease-causing micro-organisms to enter.

Seeds are a different matter. Most have a tough outer covering, first to enable them to survive the dispersal process (many pass unscathed through the digestive tract of creatures that have eaten them), and

Potato stem tubers

second to survive physical damage to their contents in the soil until they germinate. This tough covering also protects them against decay organisms and, to some degree, against small pests; however, seeds do form the normal food of many bigger creatures, especially many mammals and birds, which effectively define themselves as pests in the process. In some cases, as the seeds themselves are fairly well protected, they also enable harmful organisms to survive within them to cause damage to the seedling as it emerges, or in a few instances, to the mature plant much later.

Cyclamen corm, sometimes now called a tuber

bulbs, corms, rhizomes, tubers

Botanically bulbs, corms, rhizomes and tubers are rather different and distinct plant structures: bulbs are short, swollen, telescoped buds with a flattened stem at the base from which roots arise; rhizomes are swollen roots; corms are short, fat, swollen stems; and tubers may be either swollen roots (as in dahlias) or swollen stems (as in potatoes). However, the adjective all these definitions have in common is 'swollen', and this betrays the key to their functions. They are swollen because they have a large number of cells packed with some form of carbohydrate as an overwinter nutrient storage that can be capitalized on to feed the growing plant in the following year. Commonly, the storage material is a sugar, such as fructose, glucose or sucrose in carrots, beetroot (including sugar beet) and onions, but inulin, in Jerusalem artichokes, and starch, in potatoes, are among other common forms.

left:
Bluebell bulb

The presence of storage carbohydrate is, of course, the reason why potatoes, among many other comparable plants, make such an important and valuable food crop. But the presence of large numbers of cells packed with such readily available nutrient, very often beneath a relatively thin epidermis, make these structures irresistible targets for many diseases and pests. This underlines the importance, not only of choosing undamaged storage organs, but also of keeping and handling them carefully before planting.

2 The plant kingdom

There are probably over 300,000 species of flowering plants in the world (conifers, ferns and other groups will add a few more), although no-one agrees on the precise figure any more than anyone knows how many have become extinct within recent history, or how many remain to be discovered. This figure can probably be doubled when varieties and cultivars are included. It's possible to gain an idea of how many are grown in gardens, at least in western European gardens, on anything like a regular basis, because of volumes, published annually, citing every plant currently listed in nursery catalogues. From this it's possible to say that, on average, about 12,000 species and nearly 60,000 varieties and cultivars are available to European gardeners at any one time. It's also been estimated that between 15,000 and 20,000 species are cultivated for food, ornament or other purpose somewhere in the world.

By definition, every species is different from every other but similar types are grouped together into genera, and similar genera into families. Globally, there are probably about 11,000 genera and 400 families of flowering plants, of which something over 2,000 genera and around 140 families are represented in European gardens. (No two authorities will agree on

FAMILY TREE Euphorbiaceae

GENUS Euphorbia

SPECIES Euphorbia characias

the totals because no two agree on precisely how wide or narrow a compass each grouping should embrace.) Although the use of Latin names still, unfortunately, causes irritation among some gardeners, I think that the merits of an international plant-naming system are now fairly widely recognized. What is less readily appreciated, however, is the relevance that this system has to the subject of plant problems: some of the differences that exist between various plant groups, and that are, therefore, used as the basis of naming or classification, have interesting and important implications in these plant groups' relative susceptibility to particular problems.

plant names

The naming and classification of plants is embodied in the modern science of taxonomy which serves, or attempts to serve, two quite separate purposes. The first is to give every living thing an unambiguous name, that will be immediately understandable to anyone no matter where in the world they are or what language they speak. The second is to group together organisms that are closely related. (There is, in practice, a third purpose in that most taxonomists hope that their naming and classification systems give an indication of evolutionary progressions.)

SUB-SPECIES
Euphorbia characias
ssp. *wulfenii*

CULTIVAR
Euphorbia characias
ssp. *wulfenii*
'Lambrook Gold'

VARIETY
Euphorbia characias
ssp. *wulfenii*
var. *sibthorpii*

"The naming system devised by the Swedish botanist Carl von Linné, usually known as Linnaeus (1707–1778), is now used universally and is the one that gardeners at large love to hate."

Linnaeus' system has the merit of being international through being based on one language, Latin (although in reality, many names are borrowed from classical Greek or from modern languages and converted to the Latin idiom), but, while it might be universally understood in the written form, there's no denying that variation in pronunciation when plant names are spoken can still give rise to unfortunate ambiguity.

The Linnean system groups together closely related types by giving each organism a dual name, or binomial. Examples of these binomials are given later, but to appreciate fully their usefulness, it's important to look closer at the most important of all the classificatory groups, and also the most misunderstood, the species. The species is the cornerstone both of the Linnean system and of modern classification, yet it's one of the hardest of all the concepts to define and appreciate. My preferred definition of a species is 'a group of individual organisms that are readily able to breed among themselves but not generally able to breed with organisms belonging to other groups or species'. A species, therefore, is reproductively isolated. (Note that a species is a group of individuals: the word 'species' is the same in the singular and plural, despite the persistent attempts of nurseries, who should know better, to foist the impossible singular 'specie' on us.) A group of species that display many similarities is called a genus (plural genera); in the instances when members of one species do prove able to breed with those of another, it's almost always with those closely enough related to be placed in the same genus; intergeneric hybrids are rare.

Back to binomials. The binomial of each organism comprises a genus name and a specific or trivial name. For example, the plant known to the colloquial English speaker as herb Robert is given the binomial *Geranium robertianum*. This unique combination of the generic name *Geranium* with the specific name *robertianum* conveys immediate meaning to any botanist, anywhere. It also indicates that this plant is very similar (or closely related) to such other plants as *Geranium sanguineum*, *Geranium pyrenaicum* or *Geranium richardsonii*. Often, the specific name attempts to give some brief descriptive information about the plant: *sanguineum* suggests a geranium with blood-coloured flowers or *pyrenaicum* one originating in the Pyrenees, for example. Or, as in *richardsonii*, it may commemorate someone (like Richardson) who might have played some part in its study. Sometimes, as in *robertianum*, the name is obscure: no-one seems to know who Robert might have been.

Below the species in classificatory rank lies the subspecies, a group of individuals that has developed slight (and usually morphological or behavioural) differences by evolutionary change, generally brought about by geographic isolation from the main species. Commonly, subspecies arise on small off-shore islands and they remain fertile with the main species on the nearest mainland, should the opportunity for inter-breeding arise. If the opportunity is denied and isolation is very long-term, this inter-fertility may be lost and the subspecies then becomes a species in its own right. It was his observation of this 'origin of species' on the isolated islands of the

Galapagos that played a large part in Charles Darwin developing and writing his eponymous account of evolution.

A group of individuals within a species or a subspecies that differs from the remainder in smaller or less biologically significant ways is called a variety. Many garden plants are varieties that have arisen naturally and been collected and propagated for some desirable horticultural feature; the cauliflower, cabbage and Brussels sprout are all varieties of the same species *Brassica oleracea* for instance. Even more significant is the cultivar, which is a variety that has arisen in cultivation, either by accident or by deliberate artificial hybridizing and selection. Cultivars (abbreviated to cvs.) can occur within species (*Colchicum speciosum* 'Album'), within subspecies (*Euphorbia characias* ssp. *wulfenii* 'Lambrook Gold') or within natural varieties (*Brassica oleracea* var. *capitata* 'Hispi'). In gardening they are popularly all called varieties.

Genera that appear similar or closely related are grouped in turn into families, and gardeners will be familiar with many important examples: the rose family Rosaceae, the pea and bean family Papilionaceae, the grass family Poaceae, the enormous daisy family Asteraceae and, largest of all with over 20,000 species, the orchid family Orchidaceae, are but a few of them.

classes and divisions

There are plant taxonomic groups, larger and broader than families. Most familiar to gardeners is the division of the flowering plants into the two classes – monocotyledons and dicotyledons – for which botanists now tend to use the names Liliopsida and Magnoliopsida. Monocotyledon or Liliopsid seedlings emerge from the seed with just one seed leaf or

TWO CLASSES of flowering plant

Liliopsida Plants of this class, such as this daffodil, produce just one leaf from seed. Many bulbous plants are liliopsida

Magnoliopsida Plants of this class, such as *Mahonia aquifolium*, produce two distinct leaves from seed

DNA AND PLANT CLASSIFICATION

Despite the best of intentions, there are times when the logic of Linnaeus and his modern disciples seems obscure. For example, in a vegetable plot cabbages, lettuces and spinach are superficially similar, yet all three are placed in quite distinct families, and each shares its family with some seemingly improbable companions – cabbage with shepherd's purse, lettuce with sunflower (and many tropical trees) and spinach with a bizarre mixture that includes some desert shrubs and climbers. The reason for this apparently illogical state of affairs is because Linnaeus chose not the leaves or other vegetative parts of plants as a basis for classification, but the structure of the flowers. This was largely because the flowers are much less prone to vary under environmental influences. Moreover, flowers are a plant's reproductive organs, through which and by which the overall range of variety in the plant kingdom arises.

Recently, widespread publicity has been given to new research in which, according to one popular newspaper account, 'traditional plant classification has been thrown out of the window'. Fortunately for traditionally educated botanists, this has been another instance of journalists' hyperbole. The research reported has been based on the DNA analysis of plants. (DNA or deoxyribonucleic acid is familiar as the chemical containing the genetic code. It can reveal the relationship between different organisms, such as plants, as well as positively identify criminal suspects.) In reality it has only demonstrated the relative relatedness of one plant family to another, which has always been a matter of debate. The grouping of plants *within* families, based on more traditional taxonomic methods and study, has been quite unaffected and increasingly tends to be vindicated by more modern techniques.

cotyledon; dicotyledon or Magnoliopsid seedlings emerge with two. And the two groups tend to mature into plants of fairly distinctive and different overall appearance. For instance, the Liliopsida are most obviously distinguished by their elongated leaves with parallel veins; grasses and many bulbous plants, such as irises, daffodils and crocuses, are familiar examples.

The flowering plants as a whole constitute a taxonomic division of the plant kingdom, for a long time called the Angiospermae, but now more correctly known as the Magnoliophyta. Parallel divisions are the Pinophyta (formerly the Gymnospermae), which embraces conifers and related plants, and, moving further down the evolutionary scale, the Pteridophyta (ferns), the Equisetophyta (horsetails) and the Lycopodiophyta (clubmosses and their relatives). Few gardeners seriously or deliberately cultivate any members of the plant divisions that are still more primitive – mosses, liverworts or algae.

problem specialization

To some extent the different plant taxonomic groupings do indicate or reflect differences in susceptibility to problems. This is partly because problem-causing organisms often specialize in the range of plants that they affect. Both pests and diseases can be loosely ranked as highly or less highly specialized. Woodlice, for example, aren't very specialized: they will attack any kind of plant that offers them some nutrient, whether it's a moss or a beech tree. By contrast, many aphids are highly specialized: not only do they feed on just one or a very small group of plant species, but they also need different host species to complete various phases of their life cycle. There are parallels among fungi: the grey-mould fungus *Botrytis cinerea* will attack almost any kind of plant matter, while many of the rust-disease fungi are highly host-specific, and require different host plant species at different times in their life cycle. Principally, these degrees of specialization are manifestations of nutrient requirements and the ability to utilize and digest a wide or a restricted range of nutritional chemicals.

One interesting group of sap-sucking, aphid-like pests called adelgids only attacks conifers. And, even more specifically, every species of adelgid, whatever other conifers it infests, always attacks one or more species of spruce, *Picea*. Some adelgid species are even more specialized in that they require more than one species of plant to complete their life cycle, but the second species is always another type of conifer. There are species of true aphid that attack conifers, but they only require one plant host to complete the life cycle, and in some instances that host can be one of a fairly wide range of conifer species. Conversely, the extremely common pathogenic fungus *Nectria cinnabarina*, the cause of coral spot die-back, is rare on conifers but can be present on almost every kind of other woody plant.

There are many family-, genus- or even species-specific, problems. I've already referred to the unique susceptibility of the family Brassicaceae to the effects of club-root disease (*Plasmodiophora brassicae*), but among numerous others are the preference of the Colorado beetle (*Leptinotarsa decemlineata*) for the potato family Solanaceae, the carrot fly (*Psila rosae*) for the Apiaceae, the bacterial disease fire-blight (*Erwinia amylovora*) for most woody members of the sub-family Pomoideae, which is part of Rosaceae, the asparagus beetle (*Crioceris asparagi*) for asparagus, the lily beetle (*Lilioceris liliae*) for lilies, bud-blast disease (*Pycnostysanus azaleae*) for rhododendrons and the lime mite (*Eotetranychus tiliarum*) for lime trees.

Viruses are the most highly specialized of all pathogens, and they display the two extremes: a considerable number of viruses only affect one type of host plant while others, most notably cucumber mosaic virus, infect almost everything.

Within specializations there are also occasionally apparent anomalies. For example, the cyclamen mite (*Phytonemus pallidus*), not surprisingly attacks cyclamen, but will also cause problems on the totally unrelated strawberry. Instances such as this will tempt an expert to look more critically at the pest or pathogen concerned to see if it really is a single species rather than two, otherwise similar ones. The corollary of this is that plant taxonomists have sometimes used susceptibility to a pest or pathogen as part of their evidence for plants being closely related. But, in these cases, care must always be taken to understand the reason for the particular susceptibility and then assess its taxonomic significance. An interesting case in point arises from the food plants of the large white butterfly (*Pieris brassicae*). Every gardener will have seen the voracious green, yellow and black caterpillars of this beast playing havoc with vegetable brassicas. They may also have seen it doing equivalent damage on nasturtiums (*Tropaeolum* species) and occasionally on mignonette (*Reseda luteola*). A modern plant dictionary classifies these plants into three families, the Brassicaceae, the Tropaeolaceae and the Resedaceae, and, on most taxonomic criteria (most especially flower structure), they are quite dissimilar. What they do have in common, and what renders them uniformly appealing to large white butterflies, is the presence of certain sulphur-containing chemicals called mustard oils. Although the presence of mustard oils may suggest that the plants are closely related, in this instance the mass of other evidence proves otherwise.

Among pathogens, another interesting situation arises fairly frequently in that the same species of fungus or bacterium will cause totally different symptoms on different host plants. Among common garden examples, the fungus *Rhizoctonia solani* causes such disparate effects as black scabby lesions on potato tubers, a canker of potato stems, damping off of many types of seedlings, a rot of cabbage heads and rotting of many types of fruit when in contact with soil. And quite often, two very different symptoms arise as part of two phases of the development of the same disease (something to be aware of when using the keys later in the book): bacterial canker of cherries (*Pseudomonas syringae* pv. *mors-prunorum*), for example, causes gum-exuding stem lesions and leaf spots.

specialization and evolution

There's continuing disagreement about the relevance specialization has to evolutionary advancement. One line of reasoning suggests that a rust fungus, with its

TAXONOMIC GROUPS within the plant kingdom

Bryophyta (mosses and liverworts), such as *Leucobryum glaucum*

Lycopodiophyta (clubmosses and relations), such as *Selaginella kraussiana*

Equisetophyta (horsetails) such as *Equisetum arvense*

Pteridophyta (ferns), such as *Polypodium interjectum* 'Cornubiense'

very specific requirements, is at a more advanced stage of development than the ubiquitous grey mould. The opposing view considers the life cycle of such species as the black rust of grasses (*Puccinia graminis*) and argues that the whole process is beset with inefficiency and cannot possibly represent evolutionary progress. In the life cycle of black rust five types of spores are produced; the rust also requires two specific and totally unrelated host plants, the means to survive very cold winters, and a chance meeting, in a leaf, of male and female reproductive organs on different strains of the fungus.

If it's meaningful to make generalizations, I think it's probably true that, in the following order, algae, mosses, liverworts, clubmosses, horsetails, ferns, conifers and flowering plants, there's increasing overall susceptibility to pests and diseases; possibly coincidentally, this may reflect the order of evolutionary advancement, too. So, within these broad categories, the more advanced the plant, the more likely it is to be attacked by a wide range of problems.

Pinophyta
(conifers and relations), such as *Pinus sylvestris*

Magnoliophyta
(flowering plants), such as *Geranium* x *oxonianum* 'Claridge Druce'

3 Life forms

"There's a very different way of looking at plants that is both interesting and instructive in understanding the relationship between plants and their native environments, and between plant problems and their hosts. This concept is called the plant life form."

Clearly, all plants are different. There are the differences between species and varieties, and there are the differences between individuals of the same species. Nonetheless, there are differences that transcend all of these categories and that are apparent to anyone, even those with absolutely no knowledge of plants. If you show a young child a group of plants and ask for a description of them, you will be presented with such terms as big, small, flat, twisted, tufted, soft, hard, stiff, bendy, prickly, smooth. If you ask someone a little older and more experienced, you might be offered such words as rosette, bulb, tree or shrub. These terms are all used to describe manifestations of the adaptation of plant species to particular environmental circumstances; they are governed by the forms and structures displayed by the flowers, stems, leaves and roots. When these terms are defined more precisely, through a knowledge of plants' life histories, they can be used to describe examples of plant life forms.

The plant life form description system that is most widely used by modern botanists is based on the position, on the plant, of the buds that are the means of survival during periods of dormancy. The system has four main groups of perennial plants, each further subdivided, along with a group representing annual plants, which survive in seed form and have no perennial buds. The groups range from tall trees, with their buds well above ground level, through plants having the buds increasingly closer to the ground, to those whose dormant buds are buried in soil, mud or the floor of some aquatic habitat. The various life-form categories are listed in the chart on page 35.

The native vegetation of different parts of the world contains different proportions of these life forms, and this inevitably influences the types of pest and disease that occur. In a desert, for example, very few plants survive above ground for very long. Annuals are predominant, capitalizing on the short, occasional rains to complete their life cycle from seed to seed in a matter of only a few weeks. Their natural enemies are pests and diseases that also become active and develop quickly during the short rainy season. These, too, must have some means of survival during the long, inhospitable periods of the year or they must be capable of seasonal migration (locusts are a classic example of a migrating pest).

At the other end of the scale, a tropical rain-forest flora is dominated by trees, with a sprinkling of epiphytic and stem-succulent plants, such as orchids. In this warm, moist environment, growing conditions are optimal and, with few climatic difficulties to overcome, vegetation can become luxuriant. Pests and diseases have

Deciduous woodland

little or no need to develop survival mechanisms and those that are highly dependent on moisture to survive are especially widespread. Insects predominate, and those that are of lesser significance in temperate climates, such as beetles and whiteflies, assume great importance. Bacterial diseases also tend to be more serious than they are in cooler regions.

In mountainous areas, it is mainly bushy, flopping, creeping and cushion-type vegetation that is found. Arctic flora is dominated by plants that are fairly low growing, with buds that are only just above the soil; they thrive in these conditions because the deep winter snow affords protection to the buds, and in the short summer, the air close to ground level warms soonest, allowing leaf and flower development to take place rapidly. Like those of the desert, pests and diseases in mountain habitats must also be able to capitalize on the short season and have a means of survival through extreme cold. The ability of some fungi to continue growing at extraordinarily low temperatures (see page 52) underlines the remarkable adaptability of disease-causing organisms.

The natural vegetation of most of modern Britain is dominated by basal-bud and rosette plants. The advantage to a plant of having its buds at ground level is obvious in an environment where grazing animals abound and where anything taller is likely to be browsed off. There's a fairly long growing season, but the fact that the bulk of the potential food dies down in autumn means either that pests and diseases must function at low temperatures or, more commonly, that they too must develop a means of survival through moderately hard winters. In these conditions, fungi are more important than bacteria, while insects are the primary pests, with aphids, which are less dominant in the tropics, being especially significant. Mites, too, tend to be fairly common.

garden challenges

It can be deduced that the plants from alien environments that we grow in our gardens may be ill-adapted to the wide set of conditions that prevail there. It's clear that anything other than a rosette plant will be at the mercy of browsing animals like deer and rabbits. Climatic problems are also self-evident: the typical tropical plants – small trees and epiphytes – won't survive anywhere with freezing winter temperatures, although the relatively atypical tropical forms, such as earth plants with buds below soil level, just might.

Creeping plants from cold climates are generally very well adapted to survive winter cold but may be prone to damage in hot, dry summers. And, although also well able to cope with winter cold, cushion plants are very vulnerable to problems associated with moisture. They act like sponges and, while moisture in their natural habitat is combined with cold, moisture in our gardens is often accompanied by temperatures that are ideal for fungal growth – hence the susceptibility of so many alpines to winter mould development.

Many half-hardy annuals are from climates much hotter and drier than ours. They tend, therefore, to be especially vulnerable at the beginning and end of their lives when grown in our gardens because they are unaccustomed to growing in the slightly cooler and damper conditions that prevail then. They exemplify well the features of plants growing under what are called marginal conditions: in normal, or average seasons, they will survive and may flourish well; in seasons that are hotter, colder, wetter or drier for longer or shorter than normal, they may be in difficulty.

TABLE OF LIFE FORMS

Life form	Examples
1 Survival buds well above ground level	
a Trees and shrubs (evergreen or deciduous)	
Large trees (30m/100ft tall)	Silver fir, hemlock, horse chestnut
Medium trees (8-30m/25-100ft tall)	Service tree, magnolia, willow
Small trees (2-8m/6-25ft tall)	Apple, medlar, juniper
Shrubs (2m/6ft tall)	Rose, potentilla, weigela
b Epiphytes (plants growing on other plants, especially on trees)	Some orchids, bromeliads and ferns
c Stem-succulents (plants with large, fleshy stems)	Cacti, some senecios and euphorbias
2 Survival buds very close to ground level	
a Bushy plants (aerial shoots die away to leave buds at stem base)	Michaelmas daisy, border phlox, solidago
b Flopping plants (aerial shoots flop over so that buds are protected close to the ground)	Some clematis, stellarias and labiates
c Creeping plants (aerial shoots creep and root at ground level)	Many thymes and campanulas, creeping jenny
d Cushion plants (very compact creeping plants, confined to a cushion form)	Thrift, many saxifrages, some artemisias
3 Survival buds at ground level, all aerial parts die away	
a Basal-bud plants (survival buds arise at ground level)	Raspberry, ceratostigma, gypsophila
b Partial rosette plants (most leaves are in a basal rosette, but a few form on the aerial stem)	Chamomile, bugle, carnation
c True rosette plants (all leaves are present in a rosette at the base of the aerial stem)	Some saxifrages, dandelion, daisy
4 Survival buds form below ground level or under water	
a Earth plants (survival buds present on a rhizome, bulb, corm or tuber)	Iris, crocus, dahlia
b Mud plants (survival buds submerged in aquatic mud but aerial shoots extend above water level)	Water plantain, reedmace, arrowhead
c Water plants (survival buds borne below water and aerial shoots do not extend above water level)	Water lily, Canadian pondweed, hornwort
5 No survival buds; survival as seeds	
a Annuals	Shepherd's purse, lunaria, nigella

4 The merits of mongrels

"Hybrids are supremely important, not only in modern gardening generally, but also in relation to the incidence of pests and diseases."

Hybridizing is a means of combining some of the features of two separate plants in one individual. For example, suppose you have specimens of two similar species, one species has some individuals with large flowers and the other has some individuals with many flowers, and you want to obtain individuals with many large flowers. Cross the two species artificially and weed out the resulting individuals that don't match up to your criteria, collect seed from those that do and, in time, you should arrive at a population with flowers both many and large. Unlike F1 hybrids (see page 39) once you have produced this new hybrid, it's maintained in a pure form by open pollination: a group of individuals is allowed to grow together and pollinate each other. Provided these characteristics remain relatively constant in your new population when its individuals are allowed to cross freely among themselves, you can congratulate yourself on having produced a new cultivar, and name it accordingly.

However, by making the crossings and selections for particular characteristics, you may well unwittingly eliminate some other feature that enabled the species to survive. When plants are bred for larger flowers, especially double flowers, some of the floral parts intended to aid seed production are modified to the extent that they become visually colourful and appealing but functionally useless. Your new cultivar may produce few seeds, therefore, and present you with a continuing difficulty in perpetuating it.

All this applies strictly to plants that are cross-pollinated: pollen from one plant must be transferred to flowers of another to effect fertilization. However, some species or varieties are self-pollinating and only one individual is needed to produce seed. If this is the case, a plant breeder can maintain a collection of the cultivar by bulking together the seed produced by many individual plants, carefully chosen for their similarity.

Rosa canina, a wild rose species, is very different from the hugely distorted garden forms

breeding for resistance

Before breeding for resistance can occur there are a few hurdles to overcome. The biggest is the most important and yet, perhaps, the most commonly overlooked: there must be a source of resistance genes. Resistance to aphids or mildew or any other problem doesn't materialize from thin air: if no related plant has the desired characteristic, then all the hybridizing in the world can do nothing about it. Where genuine resistance is unavailable, however, tolerance is a good second best. This is the ability of a plant cultivar to withstand attack by a pest or disease without being seriously affected.

If resistance does exist, it will probably be found in a related wild species; a recent striking success story is a graphic example. For almost as long as gardeners have grown carrots, the carrot fly (*Psila rosae*) has been their biggest problem, its larvae burrowing into the growing roots. Even if an insecticidal control was available and

"Resistance to an important problem can be just as desirable a characteristic as big flowers or many flowers, and provided it's an inherited feature and the way it's inherited can be identified, it too might be selectively bred into a new cultivar."

easy to apply, it might not be desirable because carrots notoriously accumulate chemical taints, and in any case, some otherwise rather effective insecticides are broken down in the soil by microbial action – in short, chemical control of carrot fly has never been a realistic option for gardeners and isn't much more appealing for commercial growers. Hence the impetus to study all and every wild relative of the domestic carrot, *Daucus carota*, to see if resistance could be found. A number of wild *Daucus* species, most notably *Daucus capillifolius* from North Africa, were found to have resistance. Furthermore, and very importantly, *D. capillifolius* could easily be hybridized with cultivated carrots and most especially with the cultivar 'Sytan', the form that already displayed the highest level of resistance. The result has been a number of new cultivars with very high levels of carrot fly resistance, among which 'Fly Away' has been the most widely marketed, although others are likely to be released in the coming years.

The researchers who produced the carrot fly-resistant carrots were fortunate in that they weren't hamstrung by one of the more frustrating genetic characteristics, one that has defeated many another pest- or disease-resistance breeding programmes: the phenomenon called linkage. Linkage refers to genes that are physically so close together on a chromosome that they are virtually inseparable and are always inherited together. Had the carrot fly resistance in wild carrots been linked to one that produced thin, spindly, white roots, then a horticulturally acceptable carrot with plump orange roots and carrot fly resistance would have been impossible to breed. In some of my own research, I came to the conclusion that linkage had a part to play in the difficulties of developing clubroot-resistant vegetables. It appeared to be impossible, for instance, to produce hybrid cauliflowers that combined disease resistance with a good, properly formed head. Modern genetic engineering can provide a way around these difficulties by the manipulation of single genes, but it has very limited relevance to garden plants (see page 41).

The carrot fly story throws up a number of other important issues. The fact that carrot fly has been a continuing problem for commercial growers as well as for gardeners provided the real impetus for a research programme. The costs of such research simply couldn't have been borne by the relatively tiny value of the market for garden seed. Indeed, by the standards of professional horticulture and agriculture, even the commercial carrot crop is small beer. It's no coincidence that some of the biggest benefits to gardeners have come as spin-offs from really huge commercial markets. For instance, the advent of selective lawn weedkillers was a result of the development of weedkillers for vast cereal acreages.

Another chance factor was that the cultivar 'Sytan' already had some carrot fly resistance. 'Sytan' isn't an old cultivar but it could easily have been, and if it had been, then, until very recently, its survival would probably have been an accident. Countless old cultivars of countless garden plants have been lost forever, rejected because their most obvious attribute was superseded by that of another cultivar. Who knows what other features, relevant to pest or disease resistance, were either overlooked or considered unimportant in these lost plants? A hypothetical example will prove my point.

Suppose that a particular plant species was selectively bred for larger and more shapely flowers, and that those individuals selected for propagation had slightly less hairy leaves than the plants with poor blooms. Who would have taken note of this, or considered it important? Of course, no-one would, and so eventually the hairy old types would disappear at the expense of their more floriferous and balder companions. Years pass and the newer cultivars have become very prone to virus problems. Someone investigates the problem and realizes that the new plants are usually also attacked by aphids, that hairless leaves are very much more attractive to the aphids' feeding activities, and that the aphids carry the virus. The researchers immediately request some plants that are hairy, so that the aphid/virus resistance may be bred back in again. But the request comes too late: the hairy old types have gone forever and taken their irreplaceable genes with them. Fortunately, such things have now been appreciated and gene banks, in which old cultivars are deliberately saved and perpetuated, are now present for important crop species in

CROSS PROTECTION

An additional and interesting technique for the protection of plants against problems is called cross protection, and it is of particular value in combating viruses. The principle of cross protection is that by artificially introducing a weak strain of a virus into a plant, the plant then develops resistance to pathogenic forms of the same virus. It is essentially similar to the use of attenuated strains of virus to inoculate humans and so endow them with resistance to diseases. There are, however, relatively few instances of its real value in horticulture and it certainly is not yet a technique that gardeners can do themselves.

many parts of the world. Although that isn't to say that countless invaluable strains haven't already disappeared.

F1 hybrids

Cultivars produced in the ways described above are still very variable within themselves, even though certain desirable features have been incorporated into them. With the development of large-scale commercial growing, especially of vegetables, came the demand for plants with greater uniformity, in both yield and maturing time. It became increasingly inefficient and very costly to harvest a crop in several visits, spread over several weeks as fresh batches of plants reached maturity. This trend became even more marked with the introduction of automated harvesting systems, which required entire fields of plants to be at identical stages of development. The result of this demand, over the past few decades, has been the F1, or first generation, hybrid.

The method of producing an F1 hybrid cultivar is highly labour-intensive, hence the seeds are relatively more costly. The process must be performed anew for each fresh batch of seeds as the seeds produced by an F1 hybrid itself are a genetic hotchpotch and quite useless for planting to grow on as garden plants. Not all types of vegetable, let alone ornamentals, are available as F1 hybrids. This may be because of genetic difficulties in their production or because the open-pollinated types already display acceptable uniformity; for example, strongly self-pollinating plants, such as lettuces and French beans, are exceedingly difficult to hybridize and the

F1 HYBRID PRODUCTION VERSUS OPEN-POLLINATION

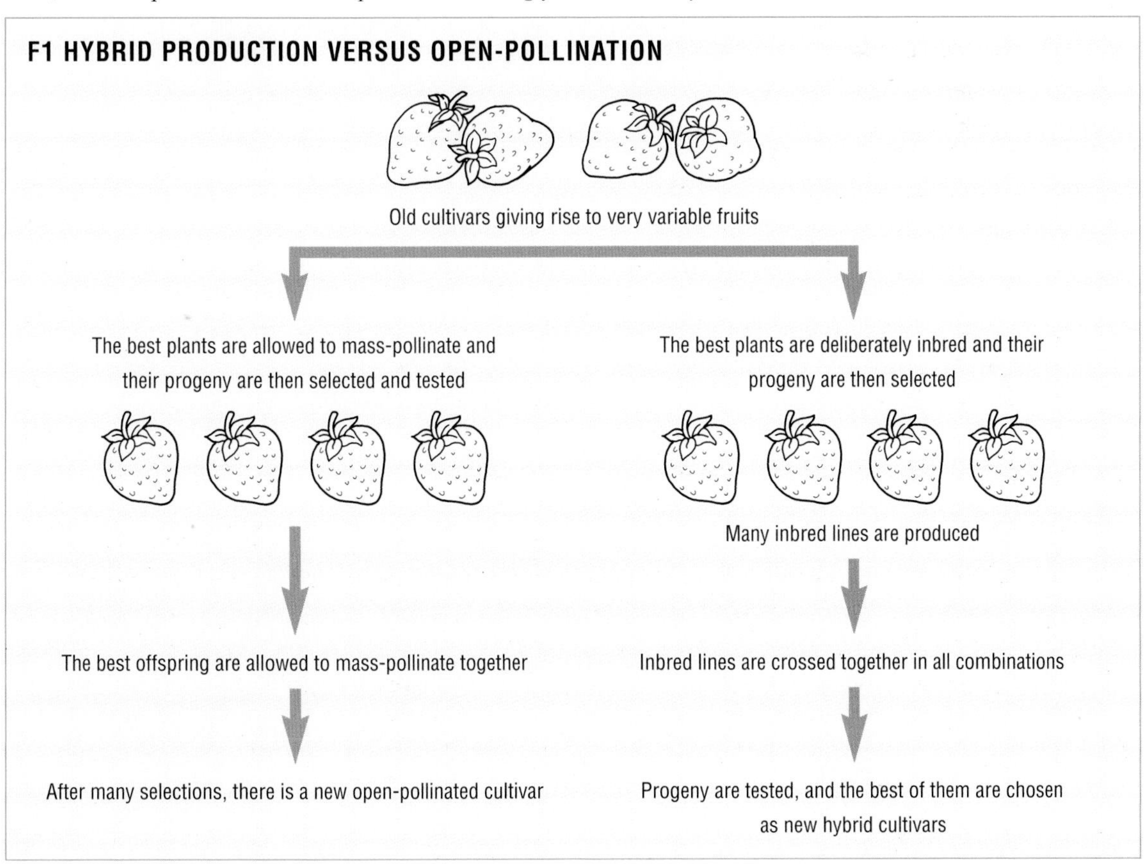

returns probably wouldn't repay the effort involved.

Generally, hybrid plants, as with cross-breeds or mongrel animals, perform very successfully in comparison to the pure species or the open-pollinated cultivar, a phenomenon popularly called hybrid vigour. Although vigour is, in itself, a fairly vague term, it's useful in conjuring up the image of a plant well able to 'take care of itself', although the precise manner in which this is manifested could range from a deeper reaching root system or a greater leaf area to a more robust stem. Certainly F1 hybrids possess the uniformity of size and maturity so beloved of the commercial grower, and this, combined with hybrid vigour, very often gives them excellent competitiveness; the more efficient weed suppression for instance, of some hybrid cultivars is very marked. Uniformity can be a mixed blessing – if uniform maturity and size is combined with uniform susceptibility to a pest or disease, for instance, there can be devastating consequences. Even uniform resistance to such problems is often of little merit, because the pest or disease species, which will have a genetic constitution broader than that of the highly selected crop, is much better equipped to find within its population, or by mutation, individuals able to overcome this resistance (see pages 48–49).

So should gardeners grow F1 hybrids for their generally good competitiveness with weeds, larger yields and more showy flowers, or avoid them for their corresponding disadvantages? There's no overall answer, but it should be remembered that hybrid cultivars were produced originally because of the dictates of commercial growing; pest and disease considerations aside, having all your Brussels sprouts maturing at the same time might not be as desirable in a garden as it is in a commercial field.

clones

A clone is one of a group of individuals derived by vegetative or non-sexual reproduction from a single individual. They are all alike genetically and don't even show the variation that naturally occurs within the individuals of a species. The plants themselves may differ by virtue of being grown in different soils or in different ways, but genetically they are identical.

Clones have a particular significance in plant pathology and in horticulture. Horticulturally, clones are very important because many of the most significant garden plants aren't and/or can't be routinely propagated by using sexual reproduction and seed. Roses, potatoes, dahlias and carnations are all examples: the best garden forms either don't produce seed, or do so feebly and erratically. They are genetically uniform but while this may guarantee similar flowers and fruit, as with F1 hybrids, it can be a mixed blessing, also guaranteeing similar susceptibility to disease. Vegetative reproduction also guarantees that any virus contamination in the tissues is passed on from one individual to the next.

physiologic races

One of the most frustrating problems that the plant breeder faces when attempting to develop cultivars that are resistant to diseases lies in the phenomenon of physiologic races. And it is the existence of physiologic races that commonly explains the equally frustrating phenomenon gardeners experience when plants which began life as resistant to a particular disease subsequently succumb to it a few years later.

At its simplest, a physiologic race is a strain of a plant pathogenic fungus that is identical to all others in its species, except in its ability to attack only certain varieties

Genetically modified oil seed rape crops are among those being grown experimentally in Britain

or cultivars of the host plant. The explanation for this lies in that some genes in the plant offer resistance to certain races of the pathogen. Depending on the races of pathogen present in a certain region, therefore, individual cultivars may or may not display resistance to a particular disease. Sadly, the seemingly obvious solution – choosing appropriate cultivars for each locality (or even hybridizing cultivars so that the existing resistance genes may be added to) – does not provide an answer because the pathogen is likely to respond by mutating (by rearranging its own genetic make-up). This type of mutation is a major reason why gardeners find that plants that were resistant to mildew, rust or other diseases when first grown, succumb a few years later.

genetically modified plants

Inevitably, I must say something about genetic engineering and GM (genetically modified) plants. So much publicity has now been given to this subject that I think most people have a passing acquaintance with it. Genetic engineering offers a way of combining genes (and hence the characteristics for which they are responsible) from more than one organism. Thus far, it's no different from conventional plant breeding and hybrid production. However, hybrids can only be produced between organisms that are fairly closely related. Usually, hybridization is only successful between closely related species, rather rarely between genera and extremely rarely between families. It quite commonly occurs in nature as well as in plant nurseries. In nature, however, geographical as well as genetic barriers operate, too. For example, *Larix* × *marschlinsii* (hybrid larch) could never occur naturally because although its parents are two closely related species, one occurs in Europe and the other in Japan. But long ago, that problem was circumvented by people collecting plants from all corners of the globe and bringing them together.

What genetic engineering has done is to remove almost all existing barriers between organisms. Genera, families, even kingdoms are no longer unbridgeable. Genes from bacteria can be placed in mammals, genes from fish or sea urchins in plants. I don't propose to discuss the inevitable moral or ethical considerations of genetic modification, but shall highlight a few of the practical ones that are relevant to this book.

On the evidence so far, it seems unlikely that genetically modified crops are harmful in the sense that eating one would poison you. But there are environmental considerations that mean their use should be considered extremely carefully. Once grown, a genetically modified crop will be available to hybridize naturally with closely related wild species growing nearby, hence its modified characteristic could be passed on. Crops such as potatoes and tomatoes have no close wild relatives in Europe and so, for them, this threat doesn't exist. Oil seed rape, however, does have relatives among our wild plants. Rape crops have been modified to be tolerant of weedkillers so that closely related weeds growing among them will be killed by herbicides, while the crop itself is unharmed. If that tolerance is passed on to the wild plants by hybridizing, it could result in weeds that would themselves be difficult to control. And once released into the environment, the process is irreversible – a gene simply cannot be recalled. It's also possible that weedkiller-resistant crops will tempt farmers into using additional weedkiller knowing that their crops are resistant to it.

It's often the totally unexpected consequences that prove the most thorny. It was demonstrated in one study that crops engineered to be more pest-resistant were twenty times more likely than normal crops to pollinate other plants and so pass on the resistance. A population of insect-resistant wild plants would have extremely serious environmental consequences as a large number of insect species could be eliminated through the lack of host plants on which to feed. The wild plants that were endowed with the enhanced resistance could also become much more effective competitors, so upsetting the delicate natural 'balance' (see page 80).

To some extent, like F1 hybrids before them, genetically modified plants are being developed first in those areas that most repay the cost of the effort, although most major crops have now been modified in some way. It's only when a high value commercial crop also happens to be grown in gardens (and that legislation has been passed to permit its use) that gardeners in Britain will find themselves being offered the chance to grow a genetically modified variety. On the evidence of current public opinion, that day seems a long way off.

integrated pest management

Integrated pest management is a term with which many gardeners may be unfamiliar, although it is something that they probably already practise albeit in a relatively crude form. Some years ago commercial practice recognized that there are many instances where any single approach is inadequate to combat a particular problem. Perhaps a chemical control is only partially successful because the pest or pathogen is partially resistant to it. Perhaps there are straightforward application difficulties: the chemical cannot be delivered precisely to the site of the problem. Perhaps the plant has some resistance to the problem, but it is not totally protected because of, say, the existence of mixtures of physiologic races of a pathogen. Perhaps a later-sown crop escapes serious attack because the pest is then in a relatively inactive phase of its lifecycle. There are numerous possibilities, meaning that any individual approach falls short of a satisfactory answer, but combine two or more techniques and even if the whole was only as great as the sum of its parts, the effort would be well worthwhile.

This approach is sometimes called integrated control or, more recently, integrated pest management ('pest' referrring to disease, too), inevitably with an acronym, IPM. In commercial crops the technique has become highly sophisticated and research is directed at finding precisely how to optimize the benefits from each part of the process. In gardening, you can generally substitute commonsense. Based on experience and trial and error, you will discover if one approach alone is sufficient to keep a particular problem in check. If not, try another. For instance, if regular winter cultivations and crop rotation are not enough to keep pea moth in check, and adjusting the sowing time still does not effect complete control (see page 75), try a range of different pea varieties and then, if there is still room for improvement, consider the careful application of an appropriate chemical control, too.

It should never be forgotten, however, that if, for whatever reason, you eschew any particular method (such as a chemical spray), you may have to accept less than complete control. And nor should you ever forget that if, having tried every available method of control in every possible combination, the problem still remains significant, there is no shame in admitting defeat and growing something else instead. We all have to do this sometimes.

RESISTANT VARIETIES

Even adding resistant and tolerant cultivars together, the total number that offer real benefit to gardeners is relatively modest. However, there are some garden plants in which resistance to a pest or disease problem may be a major factor governing the choice of cultivar. Seed and nursery catalogues will usually mention if a particular cultivar is resistant to any problems.

Plants	Pest/pathogen for which resistant varieties are available
Antirrhinum	Antirrhinum rust (*Puccinia antirrhini*)
Apple	Apple and pear canker (*Nectria galligena*) Sawfly (*Hoplocampa testudinea*) Scab (*Venturia inaequalis*) Several viruses
Carnation	Carnation rust (*Uromyces dianthi*)
Chrysanthemum	Chrysanthemum eelworm (*Aphelenchoides ritzemabosi*) Chrysanthemum leaf miner (*Phytomyza syngenesiae*) Chrysanthemum rust (*Puccinia chrysanthemi*) Chrysanthemum stool miner (*Psila nigricornis*)
Clematis	Wilt/dieback (*Ascochyta* spp. and other factors)
Cucumber	Leaf blotch (*Corynespora cassiicola*)
Currants	Leaf spot (*Pseudopeziza ribis*)
Grapevine	Vine phylloxera (*Daktulosphaira vitifoliae*)
Hollyhock	Hollyhock rust (*Puccinia malvacearum*)
Lettuce	Downy mildew (*Bremia lactucae*) Lettuce mosaic virus Root aphid (*Pemphigus bursarius*)
Mint	Mint rust (*Puccinia menthae*)
Narcissus	Several viruses
Potato	Blight (*Phytophthora infestans*) Common scab (*Streptomyces* spp.) Dry rot (*Fusarium* spp.) Keeled slugs (*Milax* spp.) Skin spot (*Polyscytalum pustulans*) Several viruses Yellow cyst eelworm (*Globodera rostochiensis*) Wart (*Synchytrium endobioticum*)
Prunus spp.	Cherry blackfly (*Myzus cerasi*)
Raspberry	Cane and leaf spot (*Elsinoe veneta*) Cane blight (*Leptosphaeria coniothyrium*) Raspberry mosaic and other viruses
Rhododendron	Rhododendron bug (*Stephanitis rhododendri*) Rhododendron whitefly (*Dialeurodes chittendeni*)
Rose	Black spot (*Diplocarpon rosae*) Leaf-rolling sawfly (*Blennocampa pusilla*) Rose rust (*Phragmidium tuberculatum*) Rose powdery mildew (*Sphaerotheca pannosa*)
Strawberry	Strawberry powdery mildew (*Sphaerotheca macularis*)
Swede	Clubroot (*Plasmodiophora brassicae*)
Tomato	Tomato mosaic virus Leaf mould (*Fulvia fulva*)

5 Pathogens – organisms that cause disease

If you visit your doctor with an ailment, you may well be prescribed an antibiotic (although perhaps rather less frequently than was once true because of the possibility of disease-causing organisms gaining resistance to them). An antibiotic or bactericide is a chemical that has some suppressing effect on bacterial activity. If you have a viral infection, on the other hand, your doctor will probably say he cannot prescribe anything for it: along with most other types of medicine, antibiotics have almost no effect on virus activity. However, with viral infections, the doctor may be able to prescribe an antibiotic to treat the secondary bacterial infection that is causing you the discomfort (quite commonly, one disease-causing organism follows on the initial infection of another). It's pretty unlikely that your doctor will have need to prescribe a fungicide or a pesticide. If you take your pet to a vet, it would be a somewhat similar story, although pest problems might loom slightly larger.

From this it's clear that, just like plants, animals can suffer from problems. However, the causes are rather different. While fungal infections and pest attacks are relatively unusual in clinical and veterinary medicine, they are pre-eminent in plant pathology, in which bacteria and viruses are numerically of rather lesser importance (although individual bacterial or viral problems can be of great significance).

fungi

The fungal kingdom is a very diverse one, embracing groups of organisms that are rather different from each other, and is very evidently polyphyletic (representative of several different evolutionary origins). Nonetheless, almost all fungi (certainly all 'typical' fungi) have a combination of features that renders them uniquely different from any other organism, living or, as far as is known, extinct.

types of fungi

Fungi are classified largely on the basis of the types of spores they produce; and spores may be produced by sexual and asexual reproduction (see box). Fungi only known to produce asexual spores (usually called conidia), and to have no known sexual reproductive process, are placed in a group called the Deuteromycotina; they are generally referred to as deuteromycetes (in older books, they are called imperfect fungi) and a huge number of plant disease-causing species belong here. Most look like a mould; in most instances all you see is a mass of mycelium, more or less like cottonwool and usually ranging from white through grey and brown to jet black. Familiar garden examples include the wilt disease fungi *Fusarium* and *Verticillium*, the grey moulds *Botrytis* and the leaf-spot forming *Colletotrichum*.

Numerically the largest group of fungi consists of those that produce spores called ascospores, by sexual reproduction inside microscopic, enclosed stocking-like structures. The group is called the Ascomycotina, and they are usually referred to as ascomycetes. The species appear in a wide variety of shapes and forms. Important disease-causing types range from the minute cup-shaped, spore-bearing bodies

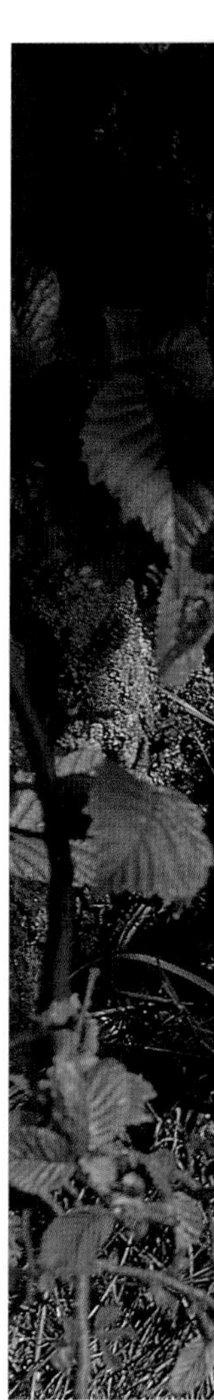

"Fungi are ubiquitous, extraordinarily fascinating, hugely important organisms, grouped in a distinct kingdom that is of equivalent taxonomic status to plants and animals."

Polyporus squamosus, a wood-decaying bracket fungus

of the canker-causing *Lachnellula*, through the tiny, knob-like *Nectria cinnabarina*, the cause of coral spot dieback, to the white velvety moulds of the innumerable powdery mildews.

Many fungi can reproduce both asexually and sexually, and thus have two different forms, depending on which state they are in. Detailed research quite commonly reveals that a fungus which has been classified and named as a deuteromycete is, in reality, simply the asexually-reproducing state of another fungus, named or classified in another group – generally the Ascomycotina. So the same organism has two names. According to agreed rules, the name of the sexually-reproducing state takes priority and so the deuteromycete name becomes redundant.

Fungi that produce their sexual spores on exposed surfaces, not in little bags, are placed in the group Basidiomycotina, and are generally referred to as basidiomycetes; their spores are called basidiospores. This group is generally thought to be evolutionarily the most advanced among the fungi and it also displays the widest range in overall appearance. Among disease-causing forms, basidiomycetes range from all of the familiar mushrooms and toadstools (only a few of which cause plant diseases), and the often enormous bracket fungi seen growing on trees, to the hugely important but microscopic species of rust and smuts. Some basidiomycetes, most notably the rusts, produce several types of spores, but the presence of basidiospores remains the important classificatory feature. (I should add that specialists are increasingly tending to place the rusts in a rather distinct group, away from the remainder of the basidiomycetes.)

The remaining species of fungi are placed in a number of smaller groups, among which the most important in plant diseases are the Oomycetes; their characteristic sexually-produced spores are called oospores. Oomycetes are unique among fungi in containing the chemical cellulose (possibly betraying an ancestral relationship to algae). Among the many plant pathogens in this group are *Phytophthora*

The effects of soil-inhabiting damping off fungi in a tray of begonia seedlings

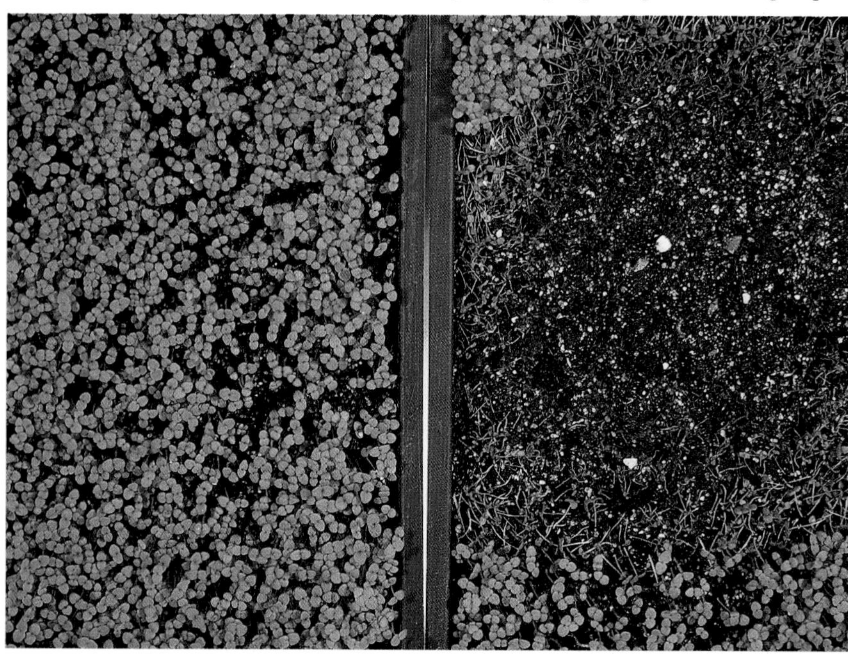

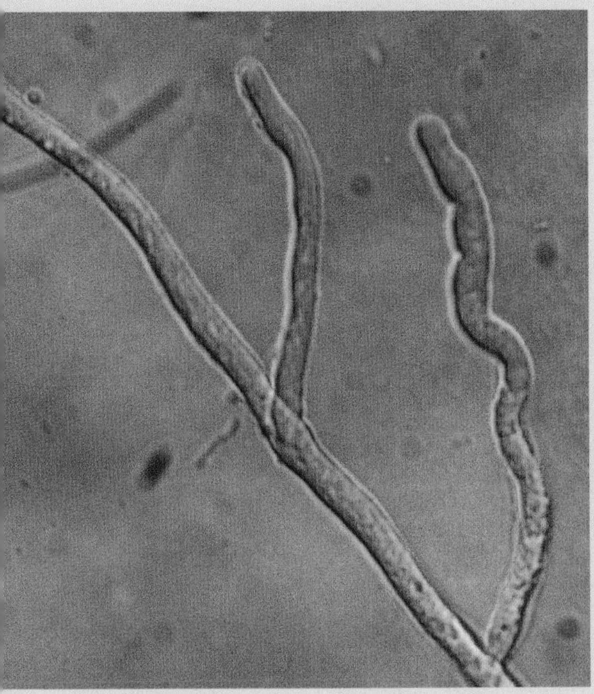

A fungal hypha, magnified 1000 times

DEFINITION OF A FUNGUS

A fungus is a parasitic or non-parasitic organism, feeding heterotrophically, reproducing by sexual or asexual spores and usually forming hyphae.

Parasitic or non-parasitic is fairly self-explanatory, although the important overlap between the two categories is one that I shall be exploring shortly.

Feeding heterotrophically sounds terribly technical, but all it means is that fungi cannot manufacture their own food, as plants do, by photosynthesis. They have to feed on existing organic chemicals, that are already part of the structure of other organisms, alive or dead.

Reproducing by sexual or asexual spores Spores are the means by which fungi reproduce and progeny are dispersed from the parent. Unlike seeds, which fulfil a similar role in flowering plants, spores occur in a wide range of forms which are characteristic of the different groups of fungi. And, unlike seeds, which are always the result of the fusion of male and female cells during sexual reproduction, spores are formed in a variety of ways, some following sexual reproduction, some not. Also, unlike seeds, they are made up of, at most, a few cells and are therefore always microscopic. Spores, often blown by the wind, are the mechanism by which plant diseases can spread with such astonishing rapidity; their microscopic size and invisibility is the reason why disease symptoms appear on garden plants as if by magic, and without warning.

Usually forming hyphae introduces the essential structural unit of almost all fungi. Apart from very obvious fungal bodies, like mushrooms and toadstools, the word fungus most readily conjures up visions of a mould (a growth on damp things in damp places). Moulds are most commonly described as fluffy, like cottonwool. Both fluffiness and similarity to cotton wool are due to the hyphae (singular hypha) of which the mould is composed. And it's this essentially thread-like body that, in varying degrees of aggregation and modification, gives rise to the enormous range of sizes and shapes (including mushrooms and toadstools) among the fungi. The fungal hypha has no close parallels among other living organisms (although it has some similarities and possible relationships to the basic unit, usually called a filament, of some algae of the type familiar as blanket weed in garden ponds). It differs in many respects from a cell (the basic unit of plants, animals and most other living things) in being a thin-walled, transparent tube, filled or lined with a layer of watery liquid cytoplasm. It's commonly around 5μm in diameter (1μm or micrometre is a millionth of a metre), and its length is potentially almost infinite. Hyphae are typically branched in many and often complex ways; a collective mass of hyphae, some of which may be joined together through the fusion of their branches, is called a mycelium.

Hybrid tea rose 'Super Star' was once disease-resistant but now succumbs to mildew

infestans, which causes potato blight, the downy mildew fungi and several species responsible for damping-off and similar decay. All those that are visible to the naked eye appear mould-like.

Among other important plant pathogens belonging to even smaller groups are those fungi responsible for clubroot and potato wart. These smaller groups (which used to be lumped together under the now obsolete name Phycomycetes) have no particular spore type in common although many of the important pathogenic forms produce free-swimming swarm spores or zoospores, which move in films of water in the soil or on plant surfaces. Many of these organisms are atypical fungi in producing no hyphae and no mycelium. There are good arguments for considering them to be the survivors of ancestral types.

As with all other living things, there's some variation even within individual species of fungi, and in one particular respect, this is crucial for their role in causing diseases. It's fairly common for particular fungal species to have strains or races that are only able to affect a proportion of the individuals of a given host plant. Some of the best examples of this are found among the cereal-infecting rust fungi, but there are instances among garden plant pathogens, too, including *Plasmodiophora*, the cause of clubroot. Each strain attacks a range of host-plant varieties, but not all. Sadly, however, especially in garden plants, the situation is seldom clear cut enough for gardeners to avoid problems by choosing those varieties that aren't attacked by the pathogen strains present in their area. And, in addition, the strains aren't fixed entities but can mutate or experience selection to overcome the resistance in their host plants.

A graphic garden example of strains overcoming resistance is illustrated by powdery mildew of roses. I have the 1961 edition of *The Rose Annual*, published by the Royal National Rose Society. It describes a new variety called 'Super Star', introduced the previous year and illustrated on a coloured frontispiece. This variety won the President's International Trophy, for the best new seedling rose of the year, and a gold medal. It was awarded an astonishing 18 points out of 20 for freedom from disease; ten years later, in the Royal National Rose Society's 'Selected List of Varieties', it was suggested that it 'may need protection from mildew'; today, it's little more than a curiosity and is severely affected by mildew wherever it's grown. Its resistance has gone, probably because new strains of the mildew fungus have arisen (although I shall have more to say about the relative durability of plant resistance to problems on page 61).

bacteria

Bacteria are placed in a kingdom called Prokaryotes, separate from fungi, plants and animals, and they are the most ancient forms of known life. They are present everywhere, in every environment on earth from the hottest volcanic spring to the coldest polar ice, and they exist on and in every other living organism. A single drop of bacterial slime contains many millions of individual bacteria and it has been estimated that three-quarters of all living organisms are bacteria.

Structurally, bacteria are much simpler than fungi. Each bacterium normally comprises a single microscopic cell, which may be rod-shaped, spherical or more or less thread-like, but which is typically only about 1μm in diameter and bounded by a cell wall. All plant pathogenic forms are rod-shaped. Characteristically, they have no cell nucleus or any of the microscopic features found in more advanced organisms. Some bacterial cells are capable of movement and a few (although no plant pathogens) can produce very durable spores. Bacteria reproduce by simple binary fission (by dividing themselves in two), and can multiply with incredible rapidity, especially under warm conditions. Most bacteria, like fungi, are heterotrophic (they need to obtain their organic carbon compounds from some outside source).

The classification of bacteria is based almost entirely on rather complex chemical criteria and is of no significance in respect of their role as plant pathogens. Bacterial species, however, are named using binomials, just like fungi and more advanced forms of life. And rather like the races or strains of fungi, strains of bacteria exist within individual species, each strain only able to infect certain host plants but the strains being alike in all other respects. Bacterial strains are called pathovars, abbreviated to pv.

Two other groups of organisms that are related to bacteria in the Prokaryote kingdom also have among their numbers a few important garden plant pathogens. One is the cause of common scab, one of the most common of potato diseases. It belongs to the group actinomycetes. These are best described as mycelial bacteria; like fungi, they produce mycelia but in other respects are clearly related to bacteria. Rather more important are phytoplasmas, formerly called mycoplasmas or mycoplasma-like organisms (MLOs). Whereas typical bacteria have a cell wall, phytoplasmas do not. They are extremely difficult to study, and for many years the diseases they cause were thought to be due to viruses. Among the highly characteristic problems caused by phytoplasmas are 'yellows' disease, in which there's often a striking yellow coloration of the foliage, and the even stranger green flower conditions.

"Bacteria-like organisms existed on earth for some two thousand million years before anything else appeared. They are smaller than fungi and there are many fewer species – perhaps 2,000 – but in numbers of individuals, they exist in quantities that beggar belief."

6 How pathogens grow and feed

"To understand how fungi and bacteria cause plant diseases, it's important to appreciate how they live and what they need from the environment. Fungi are rather more sophisticated and diverse in this respect than bacteria."

fungal growth

Moisture is almost always necessary for a fungal spore to germinate and, like all other growth processes in living things, it requires an optimum temperature. Very often, a chemical stimulus is needed, too – some plant pathogenic fungi seem to be stimulated to germinate in the presence of exudations from their host plants, while, conversely, some plant exudations inhibit germination and act as part of the plant's defence mechanism against infection (see page 61).

In almost all fungi, spore germination takes the form of the emergence from the spore of a special hypha known as the germ tube; sometimes this also responds to external stimuli: the germ tubes of some leaf-infecting fungi, for instance, are stimulated to grow towards stomatal pores (page 14), through which they immediately gain access to the tissues within.

Concentric rings of growth of the fruit-rotting fungus *Sclerotinia fructigena* on 'Conference' pears

Provided conditions are suitably moist and warm, once germination has occurred fungal growth takes places rapidly and the hyphae soon form a mycelium. Unlike plants, which possess clearly defined meristems, where new growth takes place and new cells form, fungal mycelia don't normally have any clearly differentiated growth regions; each hypha elongates through growth in a region immediately behind the apex, where the wall is appreciably more plastic.

Given a uniform nutritional environment in which to develop, fungi typically produce circular colonies as they spread out radially from a germinating spore. This pattern is familiar in the colonies of brown-rot fungi (right) on rotting fruit, in the 'fairy rings' of many toadstools, which emerge above ground close to the periphery of the extent of their subterranean mycelium, and in the very obvious concentric rings revealing the growth of such pathogens as *Septoria* (page 52) in producing spots on the leaf of a host plant.

The hypha is the basic structural unit of all fungi. When toadstools and similar large fungal fruitbodies are torn gently apart and examined under a microscope, it can be seen that they are made up of masses of hyphae. The purpose of these fruitbodies is to produce spores in an environment where they can readily be dispersed by the wind or other means. Hyphae mass together to form other structures that are of considerable importance in plant disease biology. These structures are called mycelial strands, rhizomorphs and sclerotia; they aren't associated with the production of fungal spores, but they do enable the fungus to grow or survive through relatively hostile conditions.

The rhizomorphs of the honey fungus, *Armillaria mellea*, and related species, can spread through the soil from a diseased tree stump to attack living roots some

metres away. These rhizomorphs are often likened to black bootlaces and, although bland and innocent-looking, they are hugely significant in gardens. They also show some of the highest levels of sophistication found among fungal bodies, for within them are regions very similar to the growing points, cells and conducting tissues that occur in plants.

Mycelial strands are structurally less complex than rhizomorphs and are looser in texture. One of the best known manifestations is that of *Serpula lacrymans*, the dry rot fungus, which has almost cobweb-like growths.

Sclerotia (singular sclerotium) are survival bodies that enable a fungus to live through unfavourable times. Most sclerotia are black as, like many survival spores, they contain accumulations of dark pigments called melanins. Most are also only about 1mm in diameter, but they are very important in enabling many plant pathogenic fungi to survive over winter in the absence of their host plants and to germinate to produce hyphae again in the spring. In some instances, however, survival can be for very much longer; for example, the onion white rot fungus *Sclerotium cepivorum* produces sclerotia that appear to be able to endure in a viable state in the soil for up to thirty years. This fact, of course, renders normal crop rotations (see page 132) of three or four years irrelevant.

growing conditions

Like all other living things, fungi grow in response to the relative abundance of

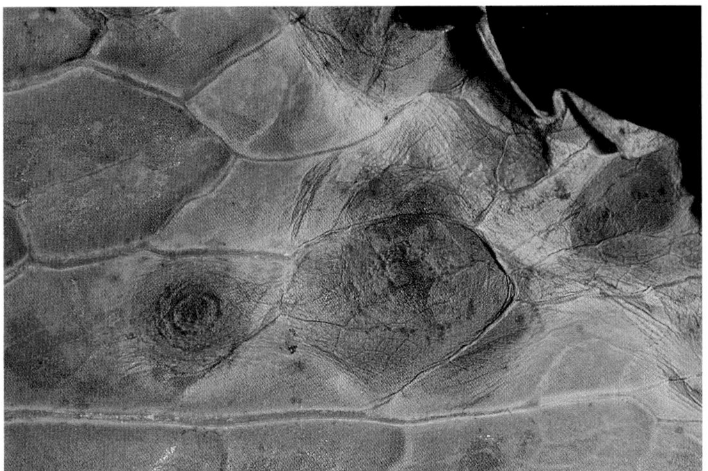

Brassica ring spot caused by *Mycosphaerella brassicicola*

particular foods. They also grow in response to additional well-defined environmental influences: temperature, moisture, concentrations of oxygen and other gases, pH (acidity or alkalinity) and other chemical or physical factors. Knowledge of these factors can sometimes aid disease control, or at least help to predict disease outbreaks.

Fungal growth depends on biochemical processes essentially similar to those occurring in other organisms, and their optimum growth takes place in a similar temperature range – mostly between about 15°C (59°F) and about 30°C (86°F), with a maximum tolerable temperature of below 45°C (115°F) and a minimum above 0°C (32°F). Nonetheless, there are exceptions, some occurring in most gardens. For

Sclerotia of *Botrytis tulipae* on a tulip bulb

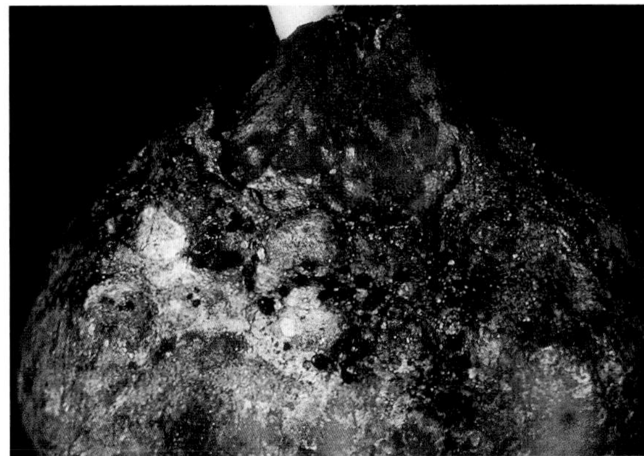

example, fungi play a very important role in the breakdown of organic matter in a compost heap, where they must be able to tolerate very high temperatures indeed; species that occur there have maximum and minimum growth temperatures of 60°C (140°F) and 30°C (86°F) respectively. By contrast, a pathogenic species that infects conifer needles has been recorded growing in Swedish forests in temperatures as low as –21°C (–6°F).

Moisture is highly significant for all fungi. Foods are digested and absorbed in aqueous solution and the moisture content of the surroundings influences the availability of oxygen and carbon dioxide. The fact that hyphae are made up largely of water means that periods of dryness present one of the sternest tests of fungal endurance. In reality, it's only when hyphae are modified to form sclerotia that they can be considered robust enough to tolerate a prolonged drought. Relatively

Honey fungus, *Armillaria mellea*

few plant disease-causing fungi, therefore, are active during very hot summers, a notable exception being the powdery mildew fungi, which, for reasons that aren't fully understood, prefer to grow in dry conditions.

Light has an effect on the growth of some fungi; this is surprising because they have no light requirement for photosynthesis. But a response to the alternating light and dark of day and night can clearly be seen on rotting apples by the concentric rings of spore-bearing tufts of *Sclerotinia fructigena* (page 51).

feeding habits

To say that fungi (and bacteria) derive their foods from other organisms, either living or dead (see page 54), is a simplification, and a better understanding of the way that pathogens achieve their ends will, I hope, come from a little closer analysis. Again, fungi are more complex than bacteria.

In practice, fungi may obtain their foods from four sources: dead organisms, living organisms, the non-living products of living organisms or from the non-living parts of living organisms. By organisms, I mean green plants, animals of all kinds or other fungi. Those fungi that depend on other living organisms adopt one of two feeding systems: either they ensure that the host remains alive while they are feeding on it or they kill the host as part of the feeding process. However, the boundaries between these categories are often blurred.

There are three terms used to describe the feeding habits of fungi and other organisms. A saprotroph uses dead organic matter as a food source. A biotroph uses living cells as a food source. A necrotroph kills the living tissues of an organism and then uses the dead tissues as food. The terms aren't mutually exclusive: a fungus like grey mould (*Botrytis cinerea*) may live biotrophically on the leaves of a tomato plant, necrotrophically on the leaf cells that have died as a result, and saprotrophically on the remains of tomato plants that have been killed by frost and thrown onto the compost heap.

While a biotrophic fungus has a continuing supply of foods as long as its host plant or animal remains alive and is itself growing, a saprotrophic species, in theory, has no such assurance for it is dependent on a finite body of tissue. The practical significance of this will vary greatly from species to species. Imagine one colony of a saprotrophic fungus, grown from a single spore, restricted in its food requirements to the dead leaves of one species of host plant. If the fungus is growing on a single host leaf, it will very soon need to move on to a fresh food source – generally by producing spores for dispersal. But if that same fungus is growing on one leaf among countless others on the soil of a shrubbery, it will be able to spread from leaf to leaf and to continue in vegetative growth almost indefinitely, without ever needing to resort to dispersal or survival structures.

It's useful to refine the terms saprotroph and biotroph using the expressions obligate and non-obligate as this will help to explain how garden diseases operate and which types of fungi are significant in particular ways. An obligate biotroph is confined to living organic matter as a food source and can exist apart from its host only in a dormant state. There are many examples of obligate biotrophs among garden diseases, but fungi of this type are restricted to particular groups – rusts and the different kinds of mildew are among the most familiar. Conversely, an obligate saprotroph is restricted entirely to dead matter; the many species of fungus that bring about the breakdown of compost are good examples, and clearly no obligate saprotroph will cause plant diseases. There is, however, one group of obligate saprotrophs that lives only on dead tissues, cannot attack living tissues and yet still causes major plant problems. These are the fungi that attack the inner parts of trees and bring about decay of the heartwood. Heartwood is dead tissue but it plays an essential role in conferring stability on the tree. Remove it and the tree may well die due to physical insecurity.

Non-obligate biotrophs and non-obligate saprotrophs can exist with greater or lesser facility on both living and dead material. These are extremely common and important fungi: they can persist in active growth on all manner of dead plant remains and then transfer their attentions to living plants when the opportunity arises. The grey mould fungus (*Botrytis cinerea*), which is mentioned a great many times in this book, is the best known example.

The wood-decaying bracket fungus *Ganoderma applanatum*

fungus foods

Fungi, like all organisms, are made up largely of organic substances and, by a widely accepted definition, an organic substance is one that contains carbon. So a source of the element carbon is, quite literally, the most vital of all foods; however, carbon is combined with other chemical elements within the bodies of other organisms in a vast number of ways, and not all fungi have the necessary enzymes to tap them all. It's a simplified generalization to say that, compared to saprotrophs, most biotrophs, certainly most obligate biotrophs, can use relatively few and chemically simple sources of carbon: amino acids and various sugars for instance. Nonetheless, among the fungi at large, there are species that have enzymes able to degrade, to a greater or lesser extent, all of the carbon compounds that occur in other organisms, including chitin, pectin, starch and, most importantly, cellulose and lignin.

As the fungi degrade these different compounds, the symptoms of disease that are produced vary. Chitin, a carbohydrate polysaccharide, doesn't occur in plants, although fungi that attack insects (and, therefore, play a part in the natural regulation of pests) degrade the chitin of their outer skeletons. Pectin is an important substance in 'gluing' plant cells together (it's what makes jam set), and so fungi that can break it down produce soft rot and decay in plant tissues. Starch is a very common plant food storage material (potato tubers and wheat grains, for instance); if it's broken down, the structure of the storage organ is seriously affected. Cellulose is present in the walls of all plant cells and so an organism able to degrade it will disintegrate tissues very rapidly. Lignin, a feature of the walls of plant conducting tissue and in the composition of wood, is a complex and durable chemical. The ability to degrade lignin is limited to a few fungi but among the most important are those, referred to on page 54, which cause decay in the heart of tree trunks. Interestingly, not all wood-destroying fungi degrade lignin: some can bring about extensive damage solely by breaking down cellulose. You can see which system is being used by the colour of the wood in a decayed tree trunk. If cellulose alone is degraded, the lignin remains intact and gives the appearance of a brown rot; if lignin alone is degraded, the cellulose remains and the tissue displays a white or pale-coloured rot.

Some fungi (and bacteria) can use oils and fats as carbon sources. And, although this is outside the realm of plant diseases, it's worth noting that there are species capable of degrading petroleum-based substances. Most synthetic organic compounds are fairly resistant to attack by micro-organisms, but some plastics, such as polyurethane, can be degraded by certain species, presumably through mutant forms with novel enzymes arising.

The various enzymic abilities aren't mutually exclusive. Very frequently, for instance, a single species of fungus possesses cellulose-degrading enzymes to 'open up' plant cells and other enzymes that are then able to attack the starch or other materials inside. And very commonly, too, a single fungal species doesn't work alone. Just as with plant communities, so communities of micro-organisms exist, one species affecting the host plant tissue and changing it in a way that then permits another species to invade. For instance, a cellulose-destroying species which breaks down plant cells immediately creates an environment on which starch-, oil- or other chemical-attacking species can capitalize.

bacterial feeding habits

Most bacteria are obligate saprobes, living only on dead organic matter; they are far and away the most important organisms for bringing about decomposition and recycling. Like fungi, they use enzymes to break down raw materials and so provide them with a food source; they also work in communities so that damage caused by one type of bacteria allows another to invade. The relatively few bacteria that do feed on living tissues and cause plant diseases have one significant disadvantage: because they don't produce spores, sclerotia or other bodies to help them survive, they are vulnerable to extremes of heat, cold and dryness. Many plant pathogenic bacteria are, in effect, obligate parasites and are unable to survive when the host plant dies. Those that cause disease on annual plants or the above-ground parts of herbaceous perennials commonly die out in the autumn. Some may survive in an underground perennial body, such as a bulb or a tuber, while some of those that infect woody host plants persist in lesions such as cankers. A few survive, at least for a short period, in the soil but most soon become desiccated or killed by winter cold. For all of these reasons, it isn't surprising that bacteria are more significant as plant pathogens in warm, moist climates such as those found in the humid tropics.

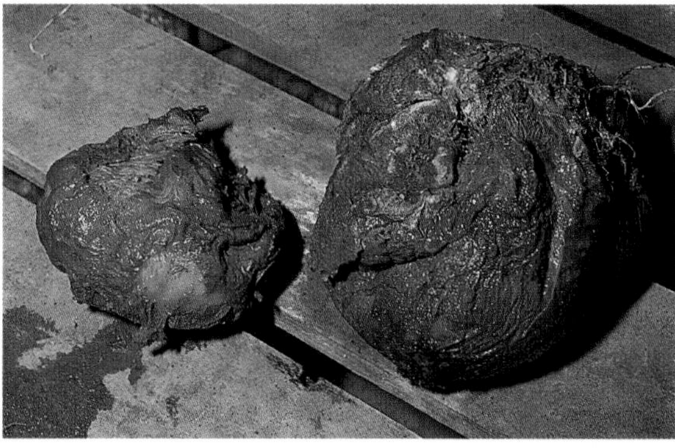

The effects of bacterial soft rot on stored swedes

7 Attack and defence

attack

Many fungi grow and feed on the external surfaces of their host, with hyphae that may penetrate very slightly below the surface; others can only grow on organs, tissues or cells that are buried inside. However they feed, they must be able to enter the host; in both plants and animals, there are three main ways in which this may be done: they may invade via natural openings or via wounds, or they can penetrate the intact outer surfaces.

natural openings and accidental wounds

Natural openings through which plant-infecting species gain access are commonly the stomatal pores on leaf surfaces. Incidental or accidental wounds are the second means of entry. An incidental wound, such as the scar remaining after leaf fall in deciduous plants, differs from what I call a natural opening in that it's transient: the leaf scar permits access to the conducting and other tissues of the plant stem for only a short time before it heals. To make use of this type of wound demands some measure of opportunism on the part of the invading organism, and the same is true with the accidental wounds that also arise from time to time on all plants.

Some of the commonest and best-known examples of fungi and bacteria invading plant tissues through leaf scars are those that cause cankers. The apple canker fungus, *Nectria galligena*, and the forms of the bacterium *Pseudomonas syringae* that brings about canker on cherries and plums are good examples. The ubiquitous grey mould fungus, *Botrytis cinerea*, is also a common leaf-scar invader and its familiar symptoms on tomato and hydrangea stems usually result from this type of invasion. With *Nectria galligena* and other canker-causing fungi, the generally damp weather conditions at the time of autumn leaf fall are also those under which the spores are most effectively released.

Accidental wounds on both plants and animals are many and varied. They also occur unpredictably and if organisms are to make the best use of the opportunities that these wounds offer, they must have spores (or in the case of bacteria, cells) more or less permanently available in the environment. It isn't surprising, therefore, that those groups of fungi (like most toadstools) which have markedly seasonal spore production and release (most arise in the autumn) include relatively few wound-invading species. The really effective wound colonizers, such as *Botrytis cinerea* and the large, bracket-forming fungi, generally produce and liberate their spores over periods of many months.

The increasing trend towards mechanical harvesting and handling of crops in commercial growing has increased the incidence of wounds on plants and plant products. For instance, until stricter quality standards were introduced fairly recently, many cooks would have noticed one consequence of the mechanical sorting and grading of potatoes: there was an increased incidence of the coloured mycelium of species of the fungus *Fusarium* in small pockets of decay within the flesh –

"In every instance of a fungus or bacterium causing disease, it must first have breached some host defence mechanism."

Characteristic foliage yellowing of a wilt disease on English elm: the early stage of Dutch elm disease caused by *Ceratocystis* spp. (see page 60) these being among the species that can only attack the tissues through wounds and bruises such as those caused by mechanical graders.

penetration of intact surfaces

The third means of entry is effected by those pathogens that can penetrate the fully intact outer surfaces of plants. Although many examples of these are known, the relative importance of chemical (and presumably, enzymic) digestion of the surface and purely mechanical disruption aren't fully understood; the same species can sometimes also use more than one approach. The germ tubes of the germinating spores of the rust fungus, *Puccinia graminis*, for example, invade grass leaves through their stomata, but enter directly through the leaf cuticle when the fungus invades the barberry, its other host.

right: Canker caused by *Nectria galligena* on a Ballerina apple

The spore-bearing lesions of pelargonium rust, *Puccinia pelargonii-zonalis*

disease development

Mere entry into a plant or animal by a fungus or bacterium doesn't mean that a disease has been caused. Many types of fungi are capable of penetrating the tissue of particular species within which they then die out, evidently incapable of tapping the food resources. Nonetheless, a biotrophic species inside the correct host, and able to combat the host's continued defences, then undergoes a wide variety of further development. Sometimes the growth of the pathogen is fairly obvious externally. The visible growth of a typical powdery mildew fungus, such as *Podosphaera leucotricha* on apple leaves, gives a fair indication of its lateral spread, at least, within the plant. Immediately below the visible surface mycelium, hyphae will be growing between the outer cells of the leaf and there will be penetrations by specialized feeding hyphae, called haustoria, into the still-living cells themselves. However, there will be little more than this occurring within the plant.

The same limited development is true of many rust fungi, such as *Puccinia pelargonii-zonalis* on pelargonium leaves, but within fungal groups, or even genera, there are differences. For example *Puccinia menthae*, the cause of mint rust, has a mycelium that permeates virtually the entire body of the host. This is called a systemic infection and is the reason why every year a diseased mint plant will produce new shoots that are already infected; the pelargoniums, on the other hand, must be invaded anew. Thus, it can be seen that cuttings taken from a diseased mint plant will themselves be diseased, while those taken carefully from rust-free shoots of infected pelargoniums should be healthy.

Systemic infections are extremely rare among the less specialized, non-obligate biotrophs, for such widespread permeation of the tissues requires very special fungal feeding adaptations if the host isn't to be killed. However, as most biotrophic fungi *are* non-obligate, gardeners have a better than even chance at controlling them with surface-acting sprays, although systemic fungicidal chemicals do provide an opportunity to track down the fungus, no matter where in the host it hides (see page 154).

Systemic colonization of an annual host's tissues may coincide with the growth of the host itself, and some of the smut-disease fungi demonstrate this particularly well. There are species among grass-infecting smuts whose spores are carried on the seed of the plant and germinate as the seed germinates to infect the young seedling. Mycelium then grows

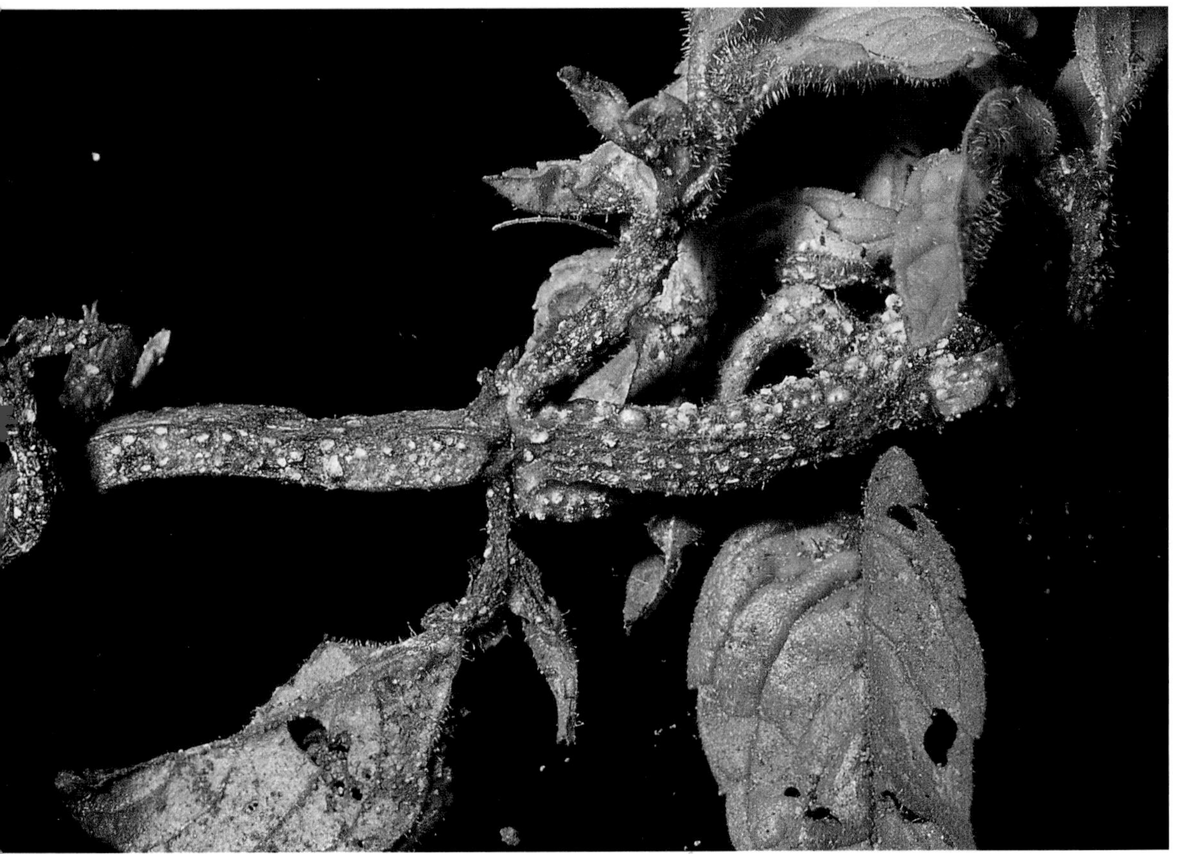

These spore-bearing lesions betray systemic infection by mint rust, *Puccinia menthae*

within the plant's tissues to arrive eventually in the ovaries, where sporulation occurs and so another generation of contaminated seeds is formed. No species that affects garden plants has quite this system, but the fungus *Ustilago vaillantii*, which causes the disfiguring anther smut of scillas and related ornamentals, passes from parent to progeny in the young bulbs. So, here too, the new plant is doomed from the outset. (This type of transfer of a pathogen from one generation to the next is also extremely important with viruses, see page 66.)

"No matter how a particular organism attacks them, plants don't give up without a fight; all have in-built defence mechanisms."

I've cited apple mildew as an example in which external appearance gives a fair indication of the internal spread of a fungal pathogen. This isn't always the case, however, and there are no better examples of this than among the fungi that attack trees. The appearance of the brackets of species like *Rigidiporus ulmarius* or the toadstools of *Pleurotus ostreatus* on branches and tree trunks is almost invariably associated with very extensive fungal development within the tree, and consequently with decay of the timber and probably structural instability of the branch or whole tree. If fungal fruitbodies appear on the main trunk at some distance from the ground, the long-term prospects for the tree are pretty poor, particularly if they are those of a known root-infecting species (rather than one that invades through stem wounds), as this offers proof that the fungus has already colonized an extensive area of tissue from the original point of infection.

Many fungi and bacteria can be easily categorized as infecting root, leaf, stem or flower in that they invade through and remain in only one part of a plant. Quite commonly, moreover, they penetrate below the surface of the host but are then restricted to particular tissues or regions. Canker-causing fungi like *Nectria galligena*, on apple trees, or the bacterium *Xanthomonas populi*, on poplars, penetrate the bark as far as the cambium tissue. There they grow slowly and radially outwards, killing slightly more of the cambium each year with the result that an ever-enlarging circular or oval lesion, where no new bark forms, arises on the stem or branch. Ultimately, if pathogen growth and cambium death extend around the circumference of the branch, the distal part suffers dieback beyond the lesion.

Fungi that cause wilt disease, such as *Ceratocystis ulmi* and *Ceratocystis novo-ulmi*, which are responsible for Dutch elm disease, or the species of *Fusarium* or *Verticillium*, which attack a wide range of hosts, display a number of interesting features both of attack and plant defence. Many are associated with pest activities that may or may not cause damage on their own. As might be expected, many wilt-causing fungi infect through the roots, where minute damage caused by eelworms breaches the outer tissues. Dutch elm disease fungi are very intimately associated with the bark-feeding beetles *Scolytus scolytus* and *Scolytus multistriatus*. These beetles, carrying fungal spores, feed on tree branches, eating out small channels in the crotches of twigs. This enables the fungus to enter the water-conducting tissues, where it produces yeast-like cells. The bark beetles then tunnel under the bark of the weakened trees and lay their eggs. The hatched larvae burrow further and make the characteristic fan-shaped galleries within which the spore-forming bodies of the fungus are produced. In warm summer weather, the mature beetles emerge from the galleries bearing fungal spores, collected either by eating or by mere physical contact. These beetles then fly on to healthy trees and the cycle is repeated.

Once killed, the tree can remain a reservoir of infective beetles for about two years. Considerable disease is also spread between closely growing trees, such as those in hedgerows, through common (linked) root systems; the beetles aren't involved in this process.

The other interesting feature of wilt diseases is that they can also cause damage almost without any tissue breakdown or enzymic action. The foliage wilting caused by wilt disease results from the blockage of the water-conducting elements of the stem. This is partly brought about by purely physical means as the growth of fungus in the tubes acts like a blockage in a drainpipe, but it's also caused through the fungus producing chemicals that are toxic to the plant. This latter feature seems to be characteristic of this group of diseases, even though they are caused by a wide range of types of fungi and bacteria.

defence

Just as we have our defences against infection (white blood cells and wound-healing tissues for example), so do plants. The ease and rapidity with which their defences can be broken down, dictates how swiftly and severely any damage takes place. By understanding the defence mechanisms, we can often make better judgements about how to provide protection by capitalizing on a natural process and finding some means of enhancing it, or perhaps by totally avoiding a particular problem.

There are two main ways in which plants can combat attack by pest or

A caterpillar of the buff tip moth, *Phalera bucephala*, on elm

Angular leaf lesions on melon caused by *Corynespora cassiicola*

pathogen: by a defence mechanism that prevents initial penetration, and/or by responding to any penetration that does occur.

prevention of invasion

The surface tissues of leaf, stem, root or other organ may physically be too thick or too tough for penetration to take place. An aphid with a stylet 0.5mm long, for instance, will never suck sap through a layer of bark 1cm thick. And the mandibles of a caterpillar that can cope with the tissue of the flower petals on a rose may not be able to bite through the angular tissues of the same plant's stem, where increased strength is provided by cells whose walls are toughened with additional cellulose and lignin. Sometimes, it's the physical nature of the surface, rather than its thickness that is the critical factor. Many plants have hairy surfaces whose purpose may be in part to limit water loss (page 16) but which serve an essential additional protective function. The inability of aphids to penetrate the hairy surface of the leaves of some types of potato is a well-known example.

Fungal penetration may be frustrated by the presence of chemicals in the tissue that the fungus has no enzymic capability to destroy. The fatty substance cutin, for example, is deposited on the cell surfaces to prevent penetration and to limit water loss. Therefore, fungi without cutinases (enzymes that degrade cutin) cannot invade intact epidermal tissue on leaves or other organs; their only means of penetration is through natural wounds (an opportunistic response) or by behaving as secondary invaders, following an initial breach in the tissue caused by a fungus or bacterium that does possess cutinase. In some instances, the necessary enzyme may be present but the thickness of the tissue is just too great for the pathogen to gain entry before its energy resources are exhausted.

Even if a pest or pathogen has the chemical or physical capability to penetrate the tissues of a plant, it may then be faced with further chemical obstacles. Some tissues produce chemicals with insecticidal properties. The presence of derris in species of *Derris* and *Lonchocarpus*, two tropical members of the plant family Papilionaceae, and pyrethrum in the ornamental daisy *Tanacetum cinerariifolium* are well known because they are artificially extracted to produce insecticides for our use. Many other plants produce substances that may not occur in quantities or in a form that is suitable for us to utilize but which perfectly adequately provide protection for the plant itself. In addition to *Tanacetum*, the family Asteraceae contains numerous examples: insecticidal chemicals have been identified in species of *Chrysanthemum, Echinacea, Heliopsis, Artemisia* and *Anacyclus* among others. Similarly, fungal penetration may be prevented or delayed by the presence of toxic chemicals on the surface of the tissue. Such substances may work by being sporostatic (prevent spore germination), sporicidal (kill spores) or by killing the hyphal

Angular leaf lesions caused by lettuce downy mildew, *Bremia lactucae*

germ tube before it can penetrate.

The inner tissues may, like the outer layers, have toughened parts that cannot be breached. Very commonly, pest activity results in surface scarring with little penetration into deeper tissue, evidence of an inability to breach some deeper barrier. This is also very common with pathogen attack. The markedly angular lesions characteristic of so many diseases (lettuce downy mildew caused by *Bremia lactucae* and currant angular leaf spot caused by *Mycosphaerella ribis* are familiar garden examples) are evidence of the lack of any enzymes in the fungus able to penetrate the thickened wall of the 'veins' of conducting tissue.

response to penetration

In addition to its normal, ever-present defences, a plant may mobilize special resources when attacked. Quite commonly, toxic chemicals or materials such as gums or resins are produced only in response to tissue damage, and these can form a layer that either kills or isolates an invading organism. The production of resins by species of *Prunus* as a result of almost any form of damage is a very familiar garden example: the resin oozes from the bark as evidence of problems within. Due to the nature of plants, however, this response isn't instant. With tissue-biting pests, it's almost invariably too slow to prevent further damage while the pest itself is present, but once an individual pest moves away, the surface healing may be sufficient at least to partly repair the existing defence. By examining the damage on leaves and stems and judging how much the eroded surface has turned brown and dry, it's possible to gauge how recently the pest attack occurred. Very frequently I am shown damaged plants by owners wondering how they should respond. If tissue healing is well advanced, I can tell them that no chemical spray or similar treatment will have any effect because the pest itself has moved on some days or weeks previously.

This so-called wound response can be very effective against fungal or, to some degree, bacterial attack, where these develop more slowly than pest activity. On the shortest timescale, individual cells containing fungal hyphae may secrete substances that isolate the pathogen and prevent its further spread. This cannot be seen by the naked eye, although when small groups of cells respond in this way, the effect may be apparent as a small spot, blotch or other lesion.

WOUND RESPONSES IN TREES

left:
The slow healing of pruning cuts occasioned by ill-advised use of bitumen 'paint'

left:
The fruit bodies of the canker-causing fungus *Lachnellula willkommii* around short-shoot or leaf scars on a larch

Perhaps the most obvious and dramatic examples of wound responses, partly because they are big and fairly slow to appear, arise on trees. Anything chemical that happens in woody tissue is inevitably fairly gradual: the enzymic breakdown by fungi of masses of cellulose or lignin takes months if not years, and so the tree itself has time to respond. It has been known for a long time that the characteristic dark-coloured zone-lines that appear in wood attacked by decay fungi are some form of response to infection. Only relatively recently, however, has the full and sophisticated nature of the response by trees to attack been fully appreciated. Careful examination of the wood of a tree, sawn through at the point of some external wound, reveals zones of different colours and textures. These lines reflect attempts by the tree to use toxins, resins and other substances to poison the advancing fungus or to produce impervious substances that limit its further spread by isolating it in compartments. The process has been named compartmentalization (the basic studies were performed in the United States, hence the transatlantic nature of the terminology).

An understanding of compartmentalization has changed the approach to the treatment of decay in trees. For instance, it's now known that it's important to leave intact the 'collar' at the base of the branch when the rest of the branch is removed. The old procedure, which removed a branch flush with the trunk, meant that the tree was unable to compartmentalize any invading fungi within the branch stub and that these fungi had immediate access to the main trunk. Painting pruning cuts with bitumen or similar products is now

Healing overgrowth around a large basal stem wound on *Pinus nigra*

recognized to be detrimental, in most cases, to the natural compartmentalization process. That it's still done by many local authorities seems astonishing, particularly if the reasoning behind it that I was given by one municipal tree worker is a generally held view: when I asked why he was painting pruning cuts, he replied that *he* knew and *I* knew that it was of no value, and possibly harmful, but that it was still done because if the wounds were left unpainted, 'the public' would object that the job hadn't been done properly.

One particular aspect of wound healing on trees has interested me greatly over the years. The development of canker lesions reveals just how sophisticated is the interaction, not only between the tree and the pathogen, but also between a number of different organisms that exist in the canker tissues.

A canker lesion extends annually as the fungal or bacterial pathogen kills a little more of the cambium tissue each season. There's usually a see-saw action with some overgrowth of wound tissue at the edge of the lesion as the tree attempts to heal the wound each summer, while it's growing actively, and a corresponding extension by the pathogen in the dormant season, when the tree is unable to produce wound tissue. The pathogen isn't alone for long within the canker, however: in a sequence that has close parallels in higher plant ecology, a succession of other species of fungi and bacteria invade the moribund tissues in the centre of the canker. These are generally 'weak' (that is, wound-invading) parasites or mere saprotrophs with no parasitic ability of their own.

In many instances, among these invading species are some that produce substances toxic to the primary canker pathogen. Its growth is thus slowed or inhibited, and not only does its ability to extend the canker become impaired, but it may, in time, be replaced entirely within the lesion. As the canker can no longer extend, the healing overgrowth by the tree isn't set back each dormant season and, within a few years, the lesion will heal entirely: it will still be visible externally, but will pose no threat to the tree. So the tree has been 'aided' by other organisms in its battle against the pathogen. Interestingly, canker lesions, unlike mechanical wounds and abrasions, seldom seem to be the route by which decay fungi enter a tree. Presumably they require fully exposed wood tissue to gain a foothold.

8 Viruses and plant diseases

"Viruses are so unlike any other living things that to understand what they are, how they achieve their ends and how the problems they cause might be combated, it's necessary to suspend belief and forget much of what you know about fungi and bacteria."

A healthy apple tree of the variety 'Catshead'

Sadly, it's impossible to discuss viruses without reference to some biochemistry because a virus is little more than a self-replicating collection of molecules. Most viruses, certainly most plant-infecting viruses, comprise a nucleic acid (not usually the now familiar DNA, but its relative RNA), surrounded by a protective envelope of protein. Quite evidently, therefore, you cannot see a virus – not even with the most powerful microscope. Only since the advent, during the twentieth century, of electron microscopy have viruses been 'visualized' (a bit of semantics to describe a process by which they can be made apparent to the human eye, even though it can only 'see' visible light and not the beam of electrons that the electron microscope employs).

Although viruses have been visualized, studied and understood relatively recently, the characteristic symptoms they cause have been known for centuries. In the nineteenth century, methods for the isolation and examination of fungi and bacteria from plant tissues were developed, but viruses proved elusive. What was apparent, and simply enhanced the mystery, was that, in many instances, the effects could be transmitted from one plant to another by grafting. (Even today, if no specific virus has been identified, there are diseases whose cause is simply put down to a 'graft-transmissible agent'.) It was clear that 'something' in the sap was transferred from one plant to another, caused disease and yet was too small to be trapped on a filter that would remove bacteria. This 'something' also passed from the parent plant to its offspring through vegetative multiplication (bulbs, corms, tubers and all other processes that don't entail sexual reproduction), and in a few cases, it could be carried in the seed. The 'something' was clearly a living entity because as long as a hundred years ago, it was shown to multiply (or replicate) in infectious sap. A period of time was necessary (while the pathogen replicated) before the sap in a healthy plant, injected with sap from a diseased individual, itself became infectious. Modern biochemistry finally identified the cause.

Viruses are 'total' parasites; they cannot survive permanently away from the living cells of their hosts. A simple explanation of their action on a cell is that, while in it, they usurp some of its functions. Because of this unique action, it isn't surprising that the symptoms of virus diseases are generally pretty distinct and are unlikely to be confused with the effects of fungi, bacteria or pests (any confusion that does arise is more likely to be with some nutritional deficiencies, see page 103). The overall effect of many virus diseases isn't a discrete symptom of any sort, but rather a slow and general debilitation, apparent to gardeners

by an inexorable decline in plant performance. Viruses spread through the sap as it moves from one part of a plant to another. By this means a herbaceous plant may have virus present throughout its tissues (a systemic contamination) within about a month of an initial infection; it may take longer in a large tree. In trees viruses don't move (as many bacteria and a few fungi do) within the water-conducting woody xylem tissues, which are dead, but in the living food-conducting phloem.

Classified by criteria that reflect their size, shape and chemistry, viruses are generally also given a name that relates to the plant within which they were first identified. These names can be misleading if, subsequently, the particular virus is found to have a wide plant range which embraces some hosts that are more important or common than the original. Arabis mosaic virus is a good example. It was first identified in England in 1944 in the native hairy rock cress *Arabis hirsuta*, but has since been found to cause serious diseases in one hundred species spread across 35 families, some of them very important cultivated plants.

how viruses spread

Viruses are unable to exist for long periods outside host cells; they are also unable to move or to penetrate plant cells. So, how do they manage to gain entry to the tissues, how do they manage to pass naturally from one plant to another that is some distance away, and, more significantly still, how can it be that they are such important pathogens? There are three methods.

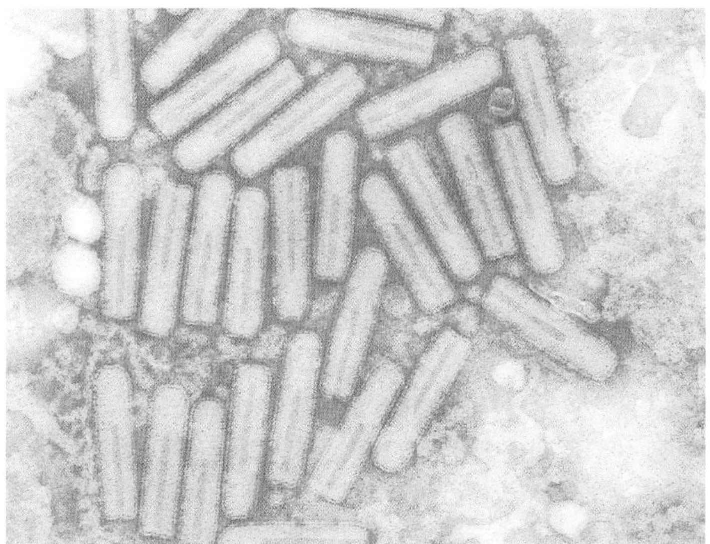

top:
Virus particles visualized by an electron microscope and magnified 1,000,000 times

above:
Potato 'Rocket'

First, the systemic contamination of the host's tissues and the frequent passage of the contamination from parent to offspring means that the virus doesn't necessarily need to travel anywhere. If the parent is contaminated, the virus will probably already be present inside every plant 'from birth' and so any species or variety that is propagated by vegetative means will be a serious candidate for virus problems. It's no coincidence that among garden plants most significantly affected are potatoes, fruit plants, dahlias and carnations, all of which are frequently vegetatively propagated.

But viruses cause problems in plants that aren't propagated vegetatively (and evidently arrive *de novo* to infect plants, such as potatoes, that may have been artificially raised free from contamination. Where do they come from? The answer lies with the second method of viral spread. This can occur with some fungi and bacteria (see pages 58–60), but here assumes much more massive importance: transmission by vectors.

Any creature that naturally comes into contact with infected plant sap will automatically collect virus. If it then moves to a healthy plant, it will take the virus with it, and can be called a virus vector. It doesn't need much imagination to realize that sap-feeding insects are the most likely candidates. In temperate climates, aphids outweigh all other things in importance. Flying or being wind-blown, and being generally present in large numbers, means they can very effectively and very rapidly spread a viral disease. In tropical climates, whiteflies and other insects tend to be of greater importance in spreading viruses. At the other end of the scale, rather slow and short-range spread through the soil comes from eelworms feeding on the contaminated sap of roots or even the zoospores of some types of fungi moving through the soil in films of water.

But viruses are specific to their hosts and can only live permanently within the hosts' tissues, so how can they survive outside the host and inside another creature? Surely a plant virus doesn't infect aphids? No, it doesn't (and to put your mind further at rest, nor do plant viruses have any effect on people; eating a plant affected with virus will cause you no harm whatever). The answer is that, despite their sophisticated lifestyle, some viruses *can* survive for periods outside their hosts and some can even multiply there.

Viruses fall into two important groups in respect of aphid transmission. Non-persistent viruses are picked up very rapidly by the feeding activities of an aphid (in less than thirty seconds), but remain infectious for a short period only, just sufficient to enable a few plants to be infected when the aphid moves on. Persistent viruses, however, are only picked up by the aphid after a fairly long period of feeding (generally more than ten minutes): it's then at least twelve hours before they can be transmitted to another plant, but after this, the aphid can continue to infect plants for at least a week and sometimes several months. Clearly, persistent transmission is much more important than non-persistent in the spread of virus diseases.

Finally, in the artificial environment of the garden (or the commercial crop), there's a third method by which viruses can be transmitted, a method that doesn't exist naturally. Handling or use of tools on virus-infected plants means that contaminated sap will unavoidably be picked up on fingers, secateurs or other implements. If these are brought into contact with the sap of healthy plants, in many instances, transmission is unavoidable. Not every type of virus is susceptible to this method of spread but some very important ones are, including tobacco mosaic virus, the cause of serious mosaic disease in both tobacco and tomato plants. This virus can survive in an infectious state in dead plant material; a study in Germany found that it was in every commercial brand of cigarettes, and it seems that smokers who then handle plants would be able to infect them with the disease. Viruses, like many fungi and bacteria, exist in different strains, not all of which are equally able to infect every host plant: the tobacco mosaic virus strain in tobacco isn't necessarily the one causing severe disease in tomatoes. The need for cleanliness and hygiene (and not smoking) is clear, however.

A healthy dahlia flower

SYMPTOMLESS VIRUSES

Perhaps the most frustrating aspect about viruses is that some can exist in some plants in a symptomless form. They are present, contaminating the tissues but there are no effects, apparent or inapparent, on the plant itself. This may seem to be of little interest and of no relevance in a book of plant problems, but, sadly, such situations do become relevant if a vector feeds on the symptomless plants, collects virus and transmits it to another plant on which the effects are all too evident. Of course, without scientific study, there's no way of knowing if a virus is present and causing contamination in a symptomless manner but, if nothing else, the possibility should be a sound reason (among the many others) for keeping garden plots free from weeds. For weeds, whether symptomless or clearly diseased, provide the source of viruses that infect many garden plants (see page 112).

9 Pests and plant damage

"Although they seem to be a much more diverse group than fungi, bacteria or viruses, the number of ways that pests cause damage to plants is in reality rather limited."

Pests are animals; an animal is an organism capable of voluntary movement – and generally of movement from one place to another, has cell walls containing no cellulose, and is possessed of sensory organs enabling fairly rapid responses to stimuli.

Movement isn't exclusive to animals; most protists and many bacteria can also move and, indeed, many plants have limited powers of movement (the sunflower whose head always faces the sun clearly moves to a limited extent) but lack the ability for directed self-sustaining movement from one location to another, or, more accurately, locomotion. Even within the animal kingdom most of us can think of creatures that are apparently sedentary: limpets on the seashore or, among garden pests, scale insects, for instance. Nonetheless, even these seemingly immobile creatures do move freely at certain stages of their life, and where an animal does seem genuinely fixed to the spot, the situation can be explained as a response to a particular environmental pressure.

By and large, animals move because of their mode of obtaining nutrition. Unlike plants, whose food requirements can usually be satisfied without their needing to look for it or hunt it, most animals would very soon exhaust the food reserves that can be reached from a sedentary position. There are exceptions, but generally, where an animal is at least partially stationary, it's because, like the scale insect, it is almost literally glued to its dining table.

The significance of animal nutrition is even greater than its relationship to motility, however. All animals, exactly like fungi and bacteria but unlike plants, feed heterotrophically: they need an existing source of organic carbon-containing chemicals as they cannot manufacture their own. This fact is as true of the largest British 'pest' (and the largest British land animal), *Cervus elaphus*, the red deer, which weighs over 120kg (265lb) and stands almost 1.5m (5ft) high at the shoulder, as it is of one of the smallest, *Globodera rostochiensis*, a soil-inhabiting cyst eelworm, barely 1mm in length. Whereas disease-causing organisms do their heterotrophic feeding by secreting enzymes into the external environment and then absorbing the digested contents, animals do it the other way round. An animal's enzymes remain inside its body, so to get its nutrient source in contact with its enzymes, it has to do something that no other organism does: it eats. The technical term for this is holozoic nutrition and, if you are a gardener, it's pests eating that causes the trouble.

I've explained how a plant requires a large surface area to function effectively (page 13) and how the rigidity afforded by the substance lignin enables an organism the size of a tree to arise (page 17). At a more fundamental level, however, almost every basic structural cell of a plant has a rigid outer wall, lignified or not. Individual

Scale insects on *Chlorophytum*

animal cells may contribute towards structural strength (skeletal cells, for instance), but they are the exceptions: the typical animal cell is essentially a floppy little bag full of watery protoplasm. The blue whale, the largest animal that has ever lived, can weigh over 100 tonnes, but is nowhere near as heavy as the redwood tree (*Sequoiadendron giganteum*), which has been estimated to be 20 times this weight. Lacking rigid cell walls, however, the whale requires the buoyancy of sea water merely to exist.

The animal kingdom contains many more species than any other kingdom of organisms. There are, perhaps, 10 million species in the world although only about 1.4 million have been described scientifically. Some will have become extinct since you began reading this book, and a few more will have been discovered in the time since I wrote it. This vast multitude is fairly readily broken down, however, into several large groups, primarily by the way that the body is supported or held together.

The principal division is into the vertebrates (fish, amphibians, reptiles, birds and mammals), which have an internal skeleton, and the much more numerous invertebrates, with no such internal structure. Although there are birds and mammals among garden pests, there are no fish, reptiles or amphibians (frogs and toads make an appearance in this book through their role in helping to keep down pest numbers). It's invertebrates, however, that loom especially large in any consideration of garden problems.

invertebrate pests

The invertebrate pests in our gardens mostly belong to the huge group Arthropoda, members of which have jointed legs and other appendages, such as antennae, and a hard, horny, segmented outer skeleton, composed of chitin. The most important groups of arthropods are insects, arachnids (spiders and their relatives), myriapods (centipedes and millepedes) and crustaceans (crabs, lobsters and woodlice, among others). A few other important invertebrate garden pests belong to soft-bodied groups with no rigid skeleton of any sort; these include molluscs (slugs and snails), certain groups of worms and eelworms (nematodes).

right: The garden spider, *Aranea diadema*, has trapped a fly

Most animals reproduce sexually, the union of male and female cells arising after a mating. Even in some of the more highly developed animals, there are exceptions, or apparent exceptions, to this rule, while in some of the lower groups, such as molluscs and earthworms, there exist modifications of the sexual theme that may have a significant bearing on the animals' role as pests. Slugs and snails (molluscs), for example, are hermaphrodite and can function as males or females; a union between any two individuals, therefore, can result in the production of offspring. More significant still is the system that prevails in a few insect groups, including aphids, where most individuals are parthenogenetic females, capable of producing offspring without mating. Even in groups like the beetles, where sexual mating is usual, parthenogenesis exists; the vine weevil (*Otiorhynchus sulcatus*), one of the most successful of all pests in gardens, is a graphic example of this. Almost all vine weevils are female and, interestingly, this very efficient reproduction system seems to more than compensate for the apparent disadvantage of not being able to fly.

Common frog, *Rana temporaria*

life cyles

Animal groups have differing life cycles, and these, too, can have a very important bearing on their role as pests. Mammals, of course, give rise directly to living young that are identical to their parents and more or less independent at birth. Within about three weeks, baby rabbits and voles, for instance, can be eating as voraciously as their parents. Birds lay eggs, which must be hatched, and so the time to independence is slightly prolonged, although here, the fact that the parents must feed the young offspring can mean that any damage to plants resulting from feeding activity is increased. However, the collection of insects and other pest creatures by insectivorous and omnivorous birds in order to feed their young more than offsets this.

Aphids and some allied insects give birth to living young and as this is combined with parthenogenesis, it should come as no surprise to discover that they can be very serious pests. Both these features are combined with the fact that the young are produced in very large numbers and reach maturity very quickly, thus the reproductive potential becomes prodigious. It has been calculated, for example, that a single aphid *could* give rise to about

left:
Black slug,
Arion ater

below left:
Common brown centipede,
Lithobius forficatus

Black millepede,
Tachypodiulus niger

"Beetles comprise the largest group of insects and, indeed, the largest group of all animals, with well over a quarter of a million known species and almost certainly a vast number yet to be described."

ten million tonnes of offspring within a hundred days. In due course, I shall explain how this is, fortunately, never realised.

Other than almost all mammals and a few exceptions like aphids, most groups of animal lay eggs, although in some, such as woodlice, these eggs are retained within a pouch so it seems as if the female is giving birth to living young. In some instances (birds, millepedes, earthworms, for example), the eggs hatch directly into miniature versions of the adults and usually feed in the same way as their parents, but in many others, at least one additional life-cycle stage is involved: most significantly, the majority of insects produce a larval form that in turn passes through a pupal state before the adult emerges. Butterflies with their caterpillars and chrysalises are the most familiar examples of this, but the same system prevails in other important groups like beetles. Quite commonly, different stages in the life cycle feed in different ways and this governs the overall importance of the creatures as pests. Butterfly and moth caterpillars, for example, feed on plants and may be important pests if the plant happens to be a crop species, but the adults feed only (if at all) on nectar and so are never pests (in fact some are important and beneficial pollinators). Cranefly adults don't feed – they live an ephemeral existence with procreation as their sole purpose – but their larvae, called leatherjackets, feed voraciously on roots and cause much damage to grass, potatoes and other plants.

There are more species of beetle in the world than most other groups of animals put together (although, interestingly, they are outnumbered in Britain and other temperate countries by the group that includes bees, wasps and ants, and also by true flies). Not surprisingly, they have a range of feeding activities. A few types of beetle larvae feed on plants and may be important pests, while their adults are carnivorous: the larvae of vine weevils (*Otiorhynchus sulcatus*) cause great damage to roots, corms and tubers in the soil, while the adults cause quite different and rather less significant damage by feeding on the leaves of evergreen shrubs. By contrast, in many other beetle types (for example, the Colorado beetle, *Leptinotarsa decemlineata*), both larvae and adults feed on similar types of plant and their combined effects can be enormous.

Leatherjacket larvae, *Tipula* sp.

time to maturity

The time taken for their young to mature, the generation time, has considerable bearing on the relative importance of different animal species as pests. During summer an aphid can reach maturity in about one week. This is probably the shortest period for any garden pest and it means that there are a great many generations each year. Deer and bullfinches have a generation time of twelve months and so produce offspring only once a year. Aphids, of course, are small and bullfinches and deer relatively big, but size isn't relevant to the time it takes to reach adulthood: eelworms are minute, considerably smaller than aphids, but a baby eelworm doesn't reach maturity for two or three weeks.

Where pests don't have the more or less continuous breeding cycle that exists in aphids and where the pest activity is caused by only one stage in the life cycle, there will be marked month-to-month variations in the damage caused to crops. Butterfly and moth species, for example, vary greatly in their pest potential. The leek moth (*Acrolepiopsis assectella*) produces two or three generations in most parts of northern Europe and up to six in warmer places. Although not a major pest in Britain, its caterpillars are likely to be seen at almost any time from early spring to late autumn in southern Europe, where it's a much more serious problem. The large white butterfly (*Pieris brassicae*) produces two or three generations a year, and caterpillars are most likely to be seen in early and late summer. The pea moth (*Cydia nigricans*), by contrast, has only one generation per year. It lays its eggs during June and July and the caterpillars that hatch penetrate the young pods: therefore, only peas that are in flower during June or early July are likely to be attacked. This situation is comparable with the seasonal fluctuations in the release of some fungal spores and the opportunities for infection to occur, and, as we shall see later, understanding of these factors can have major importance for the adoption of control measures.

the significance of temperature

The activity of all living things is governed by temperature because, ultimately, we are all dependent on chemical reactions which themselves are temperature controlled. The activity of disease-causing microorganisms slows down as temperature falls and, in temperate climates, the winter is an especially vulnerable period for them (see page 55). Comparable problems exist for almost all animals. Metabolism slows down as winter approaches and food becomes scarce, either because the food is another species of animal or because it's an annual plant that has died off or a perennial that has died down.

Two groups of animals seem to have found an ideal answer to the problem. Instead of fluctuating with that of the environment (popularly called cold-blooded), the body temperatures of birds and mammals remain more or less constant. In reality, this doesn't always help

Adult crane fly, *Tipula* sp.

Hedgehog, *Erinaceus europaeus*

because the energy (and food) input needed to maintain this elevated temperature is relatively much greater and so the temperate winter still presents a problem because food is harder to find. Different species and groups of animals have adopted different ways to overcome this and these approaches have a bearing on their role as garden pests. Warm-blooded animals that remain active during the winter tend to become very much more obvious in gardens because natural sources of food become scarce. Stored garden produce, for instance, becomes vulnerable to such creatures as mice, voles and squirrels, buds on fruit and other garden plants become targets for emboldened finches, overwintering seeds and bulbs may be uprooted by badgers and foxes, while bark is browsed by deer and rabbits, which may steer clear of gardens in other seasons.

For other warm-blooded animals, there are two options: emigrate or go to sleep – there are winter days when gardeners would welcome the same choices! Birds, of course, are well equipped to move to warmer environments, and it's significant that almost no migratory summer visitor birds are of importance as garden pests; pest species tend to be residents or winter visitors. No British birds hibernate and the only British mammals that genuinely do so are bats, dormice and hedgehogs (which may become active in mild winter weather). None are garden pests and, indeed, bats and hedgehogs play a significant beneficial role in controlling insect and other invertebrate pests.

A few cold-blooded animals migrate and, among garden creatures, some butterflies and moths are the most obvious. Of course, not all are pests, and the most conspicuous are the nymphalid butterflies, such as the painted lady (*Cynthia cardui*) and the red admiral (*Vanessa atalanta*), which migrate to Britain from southern Europe and North Africa in spring. Among pest species, the silver Y moth (*Autographa gamma*) similarly migrates north in the spring, the next generation moving south in the autumn as they are unable to survive northern winters. This long-range movement seems to be of little disadvantage to them, other than that the impact of this pest occurs perhaps a little later in the summer.

Some cold-blooded animals remain active in the winter but are killed in large

"All pests, no matter what their biology, size or other attributes, can be divided into two groups, the suckers and the biters."

Locust, *Locusta migratoria*

numbers if the temperature remains below freezing for long periods. Some hibernate as adults in sheltered places – under stones and logs, in crevices in bark or underground, for example. Those that are pests are then vulnerable to physical or chemical control measures. Many others spend the winter in an immature form; eggs are one possibility, although with insects, the non-feeding pupal state is ideal for overwinter survival (direct analogies can be made between it and the winter-survival spores, or sclerotia, of fungi). Here again, the sedentary nature of this type of existence offers an opportunity for gardeners to break the life cycle.

suckers and biters

As is obvious from what has already been said, almost all of the damage that animal pests cause to plants is through that characteristic animal habit of eating. There are odd exceptions, such as the disturbance that is brought about incidentally by the tunnelling activities of moles or ants, but although locally very annoying, they are of minor importance in the overall scheme. In essence the distinction between suckers and biters is between creatures that feed on liquid or semi-solid matter and those that require something more substantial. Sucking pests remove sap from living plants. Analogies can be drawn with those creatures that suck blood from other animals and those fungi, such as rusts and mildews, that are obligate biotrophs: in all cases it's important that the host remains alive.

The most important sap-sucking pests are found among the insects. Aphids, whiteflies, scale insects and mealy bugs are usually the most prevalent in British gardens, but adelgids, froghoppers, capsid bugs, lace bugs, leafhoppers, psyllids (popularly called 'suckers') and thrips can also be troublesome, and in other parts of the world may assume major significance. An individual sap-sucking pest will cause a plant no harm; however, a large infestation can cause serious damage, and among the sap-suckers are many species with highly fecund reproductive systems. Few sap-sucking pests, even *en masse*, kill their hosts, but they very seriously weaken and disfigure them through sheer force of numbers. In addition, sap-feeding creatures provide an ideal method for the transmission of viruses from the living sap of one plant to that of another (see page 69). This has a bearing on the effectiveness of insect control as a virus control.

Biting pests comprise the remainder and embrace groups ranging from molluscs to mammals. The act of biting suggests teeth, which are self-evident in mammal pests like mice and voles. Birds don't have teeth but the beak is a very effective and destructive substitute, while insects have horny, chitinous mandibles which are astonishingly efficient in demolishing plant tissues – the destructive power of beetle mandibles on hard timber almost beggars

Blackbird, *Turdus merula*, at nest

belief. The rasping radula of soft-bodied slugs and snails might be limited to affecting only soft plant materials but is, nonetheless, capable of reducing an apparently robust plant like a hosta to a mere network of lignified veins.

The damage caused by biting pests is more extensive, quicker and more obvious than that caused by sucking creatures. And many fewer biters are required to produce a pretty dramatic result. The damage is also very readily quantifiable in relation to pest numbers: it's very apparent that ten rabbits or ten caterpillars will do ten times as much damage as one. And *à propos* caterpillars and similar larval creatures, it will also be apparent that they very often seem to 'hunt in packs': the result of insect eggs commonly being laid in batches. Two closely related garden pest species make interesting contrasts here. The large white butterfly (*Pieris brassicae*) lays its eggs in groups of up to one hundred. It's a major problem species and sometimes entire brassica plants can seem to be alive with caterpillar activity. By contrast, its close relative the small white butterfly (*Pieris rapae*), lays its eggs singly; the odd caterpillar feeding in the heart of a cabbage makes it a far less important problem. There are exceptions where size and quality replace quantity: the elephant hawk moth (*Deilephila elpenor*) usually lays its eggs singly but they hatch to produce one of the largest caterpillars in Britain and if the egg happens to have been laid on one of your fuchsia plants, you will very soon know all about the relationship between size and appetite!

Adult brimstone butterfly, *Gonepteryx rhamni*

10 The nature of ecology

An ancient beech hedge is a complex ecological habitat

"Pests and diseases didn't materialize from nowhere when man began to garden, and nor, in most cases, are they mutations of non-pest species. Every pest and every disease-causing organism that creates a problem by feeding on plants in our gardens exists on a pretty similar diet elsewhere."

Something that frustrates gardeners no end is the fact that their gardens play host to innumerable pests and diseases, yet the plants in woods, fields and meadows beyond the garden wall seem to be immune. No one anguishes over the need to spray wild plants with fungicide or insecticide and yet they survive, and have done so for millennia. While all this is true, the explanation isn't straightforward. It's partly to do with biology (and more specifically with a branch of biology called ecology), and partly to do with human nature.

Firstly, the human nature part: we don't own the plants in the fields and hedgerows, we didn't buy them, we don't pay for fertilizer to feed them and nor do we know them intimately through seeing them every day. They simply don't matter as much to us as our garden plants do, and so we just don't notice if they are less than perfect. For, make no mistake, less than perfect they surely are: look closely at the leaves of a meadow cranesbill (*Geranium pratense*) and you may well see geranium rust (*Uromyces geranii*); examine the young shoots on the oak tree and you will very probably find oak mildew *(Microsphaera alphitoides)*; and turn over the leaves of beech trees and you will very soon see colonies of the same aphid, *Phyllaphis fagi*, that occurs on your garden hedge. I do agree, however, that you seldom see wild plants devastated to the extent, for instance, that garden nasturtiums or Brussels sprouts can be devastated by the caterpillars of the large white butterfly *(Pieris brassicae)*. But this has to do with the nature of the nasturtium and the Brussels sprout and the way that we grow them.

the balance of nature

One of the most freely used and yet rarely defined phrases in natural history is 'the balance of nature' (otherwise known as ecology). I am sure it means different things to different people but to me, it means the multitude of complex interactions and inter-relationships that exist between every living thing in a habitat, especially a mature habitat, and which result in the habitat appearing to us to be constant, unchanging. For example, year on year an old hedgerow or a mature woodland seems to remain more or less the same. The odd tree will fall, the odd clump of wild flowers spread a little but generally, what goes out is balanced by something else coming in.

Now let us consider the effect of pests. A large white butterfly arrives in the hedgerow, lays it eggs on the leaves of the wild brassica hedge mustard (*Alliaria petiolata*) and then flies on to lady's smock (*Cardamine pratensis*), where it lays a few more. Living in or near the hedgerow is a

natural enemy of the butterfly caterpillars. This could be an obvious one, such as a blue tit, or something more insidious, such as the braconid wasp, *Apantales glomeratus*; this lays its eggs on some of the caterpillars, which are then parasitized by the resulting larvae. Some of the caterpillars will survive and some of the foliage of the hedge mustard and the lady's smock will be eaten or disfigured but aesthetically it doesn't matter and the damaged parts will soon be replaced by others that grow up to take their place. The blue tit and the braconid wasp will move on to feed on other insects, just as the large white itself has moved on to lay eggs on a different host plant. No single living organism in the habitat has been really adversely affected by the sequence of events. This is an example of what makes up the 'balance'.

selective breeding and foreigners

Gardens aren't like the hedgerow or the mature wood. Even the most stable parts of a garden – the shrubberies and perennial borders – change as we prune, take out, move around, re-arrange and re-stock. And some parts – most obviously the vegetable plot or an annual flower bed – change beyond recognition from one season to the next. There isn't much balance of nature there. Now let us reconsider the nasturtiums and Brussels sprouts and discover specifically why they have been laid low. Almost all of it's due to the hands of human intervention.

Even before they were planted, the nasturtium and Brussels sprout had been interfered with. The nasturtium, *Tropaeolum majus*, isn't a native British plant. It was introduced into European gardens from South America in 1684, and in the three hundred years since, it has been crossed, selected and altered by plant breeders. The Brussels sprout, *Brassica oleracea* 'Gemmifera', is almost a native. Its ancestor is the wild cabbage *Brassica oleracea*, which occurs on British sea cliffs, and it's the most recently developed of the many cultivated forms (cauliflower, kohlrabi, broccoli and kale being among the others), probably originating in the Low Countries in the seventeenth century. It bears precious little resemblance to a wild cabbage, again as the result of breeding and selection.

below: Oak powdery mildew, *Microsphaera alphitoides*

bottom: Beech aphid, *Phyllaphis fagi*

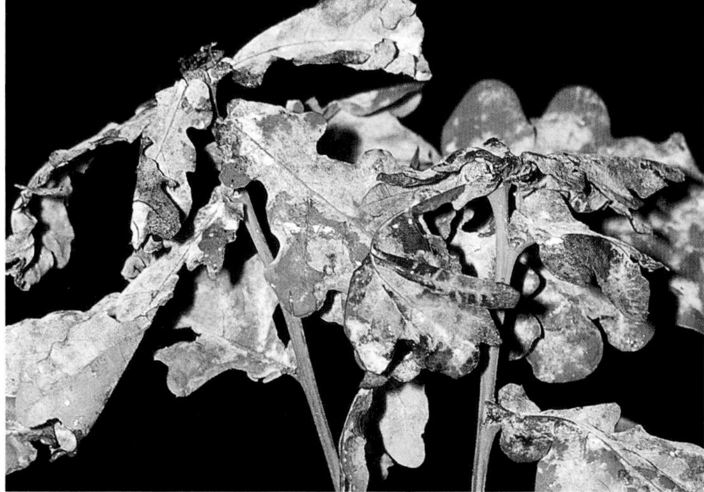

One of the effects this type of breeding can have on pest or disease resistance was explained earlier (see page 36); in short, by selecting for some other horticultural character, resistance may be lost. There are other considerations, too. Breeding may not only remove resistance: it might even enhance a characteristic that a pest or disease finds appealing. Just as they are attractive to us, the soft, fleshy tissues of the Brussels sprout may be more attractive to a caterpillar than are those of the wild cabbage.

The nasturtium raises another very important point. It comes from a country where the large white butterfly doesn't occur. To put it crudely, before 1684, no *Tropaeolum majus* had ever encountered a large white and vice versa. So there had never been any opportunity for the development of a population of nasturtiums that had resistance to, or tolerance of, large white caterpillars. And this goes for most of our other garden plants: they are exotics and they too are encountering our pests and diseases for the first time. A particularly familiar disease reveals another side to this situation.

The groundsel (*Senecio vulgaris*) is a very common native British plant. It doesn't occur in Australia. Other related plants in the family Asteraceae are native to Australia, however, and they are affected there by a rust disease fungus called *Puccinia lagenophorae*. The effects on these plants aren't particularly devastating (there's a

Wild cabbage, *Brassica oleracea*

Cineraria, *Pericallis* x *hybrida*

balance of nature in Australian habitats, too) and neither the rust fungus nor the native host plants are seriously threatened. It happens, however, that the rust fungus is also able to attack a plant called *Pericallis* × *hybrida*, a cultivated hybrid between two Canary Island species of Asteraceae called *Pericallis lanata* and *Pericallis cruenta*. We all know this hybrid as the familiar florists' cineraria. The rust attacks *Pericallis* pretty freely for just the same reason as I have outlined above – *Puccinia lagenophorae* doesn't occur naturally in the Canary Islands so *Pericallis* has never had an opportunity to select a population resistant to it.

That isn't the end of the story because cineraria plants imported from Australia brought the disease to Britain and Europe, where the rust met groundsel, another plant with no resistance to it. It's now almost impossible to find a population of groundsel in Britain that isn't affected by the rust. Groundsel is a wild plant, but this doesn't negate my argument about wild plants not being devastated by diseases or pests, because, in this case, human intervention bears the responsibility. Incidentally, there's yet another message from this story: it's only because groundsel is such a remarkably effective competitor (and, therefore, an important weed) as I explain on page 131, that its own survival hasn't been seriously threatened by the rust.

SELECTION

"The plant breeder's practice of selecting for resistance or tolerance demonstrates the essence of the Darwinian theory of evolution through natural selection."

All populations are more or less variable. You need only look at a room full of people to realise that. Not only do they differ physically; they also differ in behaviour and, most important for present purposes, in their susceptibility to diseases. The same applies to plants. And the less inbred plants are (the less they mate or hybridize with their close relatives), the greater is this variation. Suppose a particular disease (like the Australian rust) has the effect of weakening a plant in some way (that it *will* weaken is almost a part of the definition of a disease or a pest). The plants that are attacked may then be smaller than their companions or slower to flower and set seed, or set fewer seeds, or set seeds with lower viability. Any plant with the slightest natural resistance to the disease will, therefore, be at an advantage. (Some of the ways that resistance might be manifested and the difference between resistance and tolerance are discussed on page 36.) Being at an advantage means that it will grow better and be better able to flower and set seed or produce more seeds. Provided that whatever conferred the resistance is a heritable character, its offspring, in turn, will possess a little resistance to the disease. And so it continues, from generation to generation, until a population arises that has a significant ability to resist the disease. In Darwinian terms, the 'fittest' have survived; this isn't those fittest in the popular modern sense of spending time in the gym or being strikingly attractive, but those best fitted, or best able, to survive – a balance has been struck.

monoculture

There's one other aspect of gardening that makes garden plants significantly different from wild ones, and that relates to their likelihood of being seriously attacked by pests and diseases. In gardens, just as on farms, many types of plants are grown as monocultures (large numbers of individuals of one type of plant are massed together). The most extreme garden examples of this are annual flower beds and the vegetable plots, where row after row of one type of plant (very often one variety of one type of plant) are grown to the exclusion of everything else. This is relatively unusual in the wild: hedgerows, cliff-tops, stream-sides, woodland edges are all fairly obviously mixtures of species, and so, very often, are natural woods and areas of natural grassland. There are few surviving natural woods in Britain and no natural grasslands, but there are some that have been free of human interference for a long time and so provide acceptable replicas. If you look closely at these habitats, you will see that individuals or individual groups of one species tend to be dispersed among other species. Usually, there's not very extensive physical continuity.

The significance of this for the incidence of problems is that a pest or disease arriving or landing on a suitable plant in the row or bed in a garden has an easy passage onto others that also suit it. In the wild, its way is less direct: a pest or disease on a grass stalk can't hop directly onto the next grass stalk because there are unappetising sorrels, clovers and other plants in the way. I realise that in many instances, growing mixtures can be unacceptably tricky and impractical (vegetables growing to different sizes and at different rates, for example), but nonetheless, the risks that monoculture creates might make specialist growers of roses, chrysanthemums, dahlias and other 'hobby' plants think carefully about how they plant them.

A rose hedge underplanted with a monoculture of geranium

11 The influence of climate

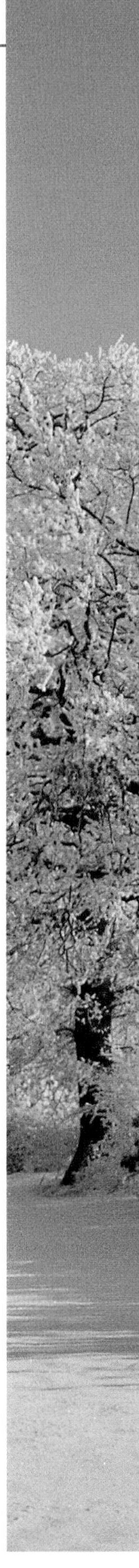

"There's almost no aspect of gardening anywhere that isn't influenced by the climate to some degree. Plant problems are no exception."

Weather is short; climate is long. Such was the definition made by an old schoolmaster I knew. And I suppose he was right: weather is the day-to-day changes in meteorological conditions experienced at a particular place; climate is the long-term pattern of weather. There are both direct and indirect ways in which climate and problems are inter-related. The most straighforward way to look at these is to consider, in turn, the different components of weather (temperature, precipitation, light and daylength, and wind). And it must always be remembered that they interact: there's no snow without freezing temperatures and no drought without high levels of sunlight.

temperature

The climatic temperatures experienced in any area depend mainly on the angle at which the sun's rays strike the earth: the greater the angle, the hotter will it be. The warming effect is greatest at the equator, where the sun is at its largest angle to the land (90 degrees), and lowest in the polar regions, where the sun is at its shallowest angle. Even within an area as small as the British Isles, there are considerable north-south differences in temperature. It's almost solely to enhance the heat of the sun that gardeners use greenhouses, cloches and coldframes.

All life on earth depends on solar radiation. However, less than half of it finally reaches the earth's surface: the majority is lost, principally by reflection back into space. Solar radiation may be subdivided into many different wavelengths; the most significant for plants are the shorter wavelengths of visible light and the warming, longer wavelengths tending towards infra-red. Neither penetrates into the soil but the surface-warming effect of the sun's heat is conducted into the top few centimetres and the re-radiation of this into the air is a very important factor in governing the temperatures that plants experience.

During the night-time cooling period, most of the long-wave radiation leaving the earth's surface is retained through the absorbing properties of atmospheric water-vapour and carbon dioxide. If skies are clear, especially in winter when daytime warming by the sun isn't great, the heat loss from the earth can be sufficient to cause temperatures at ground level to drop below freezing. This is called a radiation frost and it has considerable bearing on plant health. There are two types of radiation frost: ground frost and air frost.

ground frosts

If the heat loss is such that the temperature at or slightly above soil level falls to −1°C (30°F), it's called a ground frost. Bearing in mind my earlier comments about overwintering and plant life forms (pages 32–34), it will be apparent that the typical plants of our climate are dormant when ground frosts are likely to occur. Their tender parts are fairly well protected at or below soil

Severe frost and snow on birch trees

level and are unlikely to suffer directly from freezing damage. Those that retain an above-ground structure (trees and shrubs) have retreated into a dormant state and are comparably fairly well protected. Non-native plants, which are naturally adapted to milder climates, however, including a good many garden ornamentals, may need additional insulation for their buds and growing points. They are sufficiently hardy to survive outdoors but only if a mulch of organic matter or other protective material is laid over the crowns in autumn.

air frosts

If the heat loss from the soil is such that the temperature at 120cm (4ft) above ground level falls to 0°C (32°F) or less, this is called an air frost, and damage from it can be much more serious. The likelihood of winter air frosts means that those parts of tender plants above soil level need protecting, too. In many British gardens, it's necessary to tie together the leaves of evergreen perennials, such as kniphofias, or to tie the dead foliage of plants such as gunnera around the crowns to provide the necessary added insulation. In some parts of the world, where winters are colder, even ornamental trees are routinely wrapped with artificial protection (and very unsightly they look, too).

Winter air frosts are reasonably predictable and protection can be applied accordingly. Spring air frosts, however, are much more insidious – no matter how hardy a plant and how well protected it is against winter frost, once growth has

Damage caused by late frost on young shoots of box

begun in the spring, its young leafy shoots and especially any early season blossom will be vulnerable. If spring frosts occur immediately before bud burst, the buds may be killed. Leaves may be merely scorched at the edges or killed and although they may droop, they don't usually drop. Shoots may be scorched at the tips or die back to the old wood and flowers are usually killed outright. Repeated spring-frost damage to some trees can render them permanently dwarfed, with an appearance reminiscent of browsing injuries, and sometimes, although relatively unusually, stem and branch cankers or splitting can arise.

"Cold air is denser than warm air. Consequently, it will roll down slopes and collect in hollows. The concept of the 'frost hollow' or 'frost pocket' is a familiar one and can be as small as part of your garden or as large as a valley floor."

There's a limit to the measures that can be taken to protect plants against spring frosts. They can be a very serious problem in commercial fruit orchards where damage to the blossom will have huge financial implications. Commercial growers mitigate risks by such methods as large-scale orchard heaters or constant water sprinklers, which keep plants warm by making use of the latent heat released by water as it freezes. These techniques aren't very practical in gardens, so, before choosing early-blossoming shrubs, it's worth bearing several things in mind. There are some shrubs that bloom naturally in the winter (*Cornus mas*, *Prunus subhirtella* 'Autumnalis' and *Hamamelis*, for instance) and their blossoms will withstand several degrees of frost. Among fruit plants, you could select slightly later-flowering varieties; one of the main trends in blackcurrant breeding in recent years has been to develop varieties that both flower later and fruit earlier. Remember, too, that features of the site itself will have a bearing on the likelihood of damage: a dry, free-draining soil is a poorer conductor of heat than a wet one and there's less transfer of heat from reserves in the ground. Dry soils are, therefore, more likely to give rise to radiation frosts. A good cover of vegetation, such as grass, can also limit the amount of heat loss, and shrubs growing in lawns are less liable to spring frost damage than are those in bare soil. Overhanging trees can also limit the loss of heat upwards and serve to protect plants beneath them.

frost hollows

Quite commonly, frost in winter has nothing to do with heat loss from your garden soil but is the result of cold air being carried long distances as a part of the air movements that contribute to our overall weather. This type of frost, which causes pockets or hollows of freezing conditions, can be important in its long-term limiting and damaging effects on garden plants. The practical effect of being in a frost pocket is that your garden will be colder than the surrounding region (or at least, it will have lower minimum temperatures, which is the important thing) and so you will be unable to grow plants that you might otherwise expect to. If the garden is in a genuine hollow, there's little that can be done other than to choose plants with special care. If, however, your garden is on a slope or at the foot of it, then very often matters can be greatly improved by the

SIBERIAN LARCH

One of the biggest problems associated with gardening in Britain is the fact that spring frosts can occur almost into early summer, because our geographical position means that cold polar air can suddenly swoop southwards well after we thought winter had ended. Both plants and gardeners can be caught out. A plant that illustrates this problem very graphically is one on which I did some research several years ago. Although not a garden plant, the Siberian larch (*Larix sibirica*) should, by most people's reckoning, be able to tolerate the very worst that any British weather can produce, coming as it does from one of the coldest regions on earth. But it's a complete failure in Britain because it comes into leaf with the first warm weather of the year, which generally occurs on a few days in February. Its young shoots are then invariably damaged by a return to freezing temperatures: in Siberia, when spring starts, it tends to stay.

Winter cold damage to evergreen cotoneaster

simple expedient of strategically siting some bushes, or opening a gap in a hedge or fence to divert the flow and allow the cold air to roll on down and away.

It tends to be winter cold that gives rise to a characteristic type of frost injury called frost lift or frost heaving (the forcible ejection of plants from frozen soil). This commonly occurs with small or seedling plants and may be a problem in nurseries where young woody plants are being raised. It can also sometimes be a problem, especially on highly organic soils, with overwintered vegetable crops, which can suffer severe damage through the roots being broken. Low temperatures, generally those just above freezing, can give rise to another type of damage called chilling injury. It's particularly common on stored potato tubers where it appears in the form of small diffuse, blackish patches in the flesh.

left: Siberian larch, *Larix sibirica*, damaged by repeated spring frosts

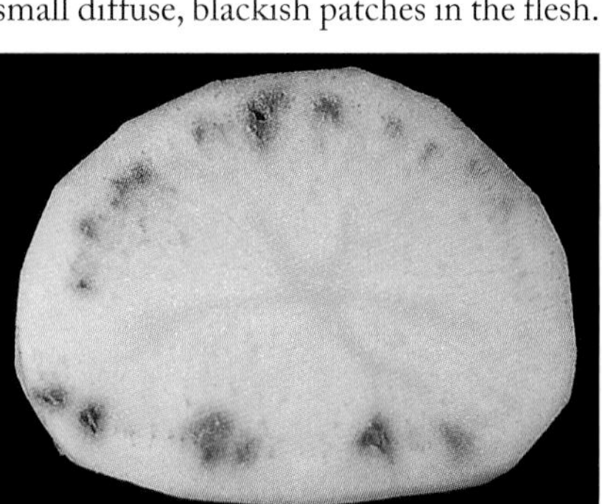

Chilling injury in potato tubers

frost damage

The mechanisms of frost damage to plants are complex and not very well understood. They are important, nonetheless, for they contain the key to hardiness, which seems to be related to the ease with which water can be withdrawn from plant cells and frozen in the inter-cellular spaces, and to the rapidity with which subsequent thawing takes place. A slow thaw, allowing the cells to rehydrate gently, is much less damaging than a rapid one. For this reason, plants growing in east-facing situations, where they are struck by the early morning sun after a cold night, are much more likely to be damaged than those in north-facing ones.

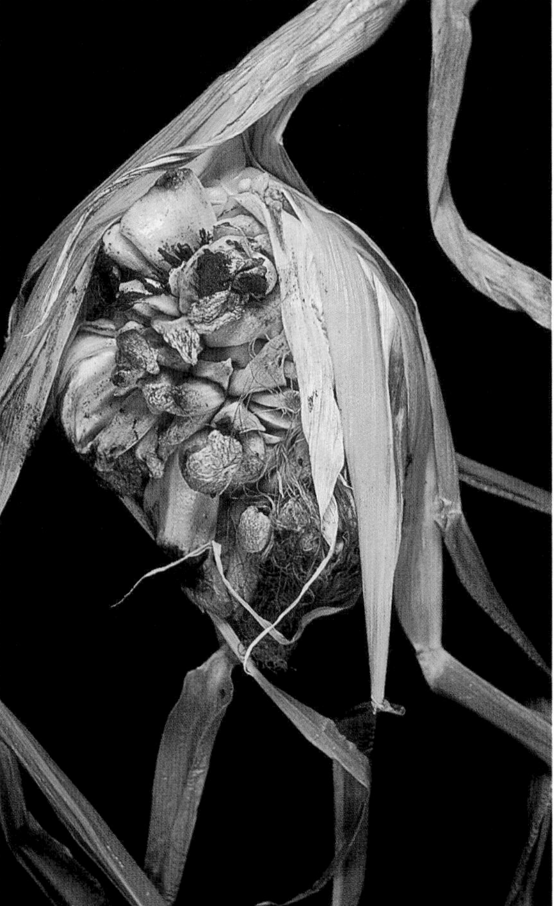

Symptoms of sweetcorn smut caused by *Ustilago maydis*

high temperatures

Although plant problems are much more commonly caused by low temperatures than by high ones, there are occasions when high temperatures can cause damage directly. The two most common conditions are both known as sun scald. One form arises when hot sun strikes thin-barked trees, such as beech, cherries, maples or poplars, and results in the death of the bark, either in patches or down the entire south or south-west face of the trunk. The other form of sun scald occurs when fruit are similarly struck by hot sun: apples, gooseberries, grapes, pears and tomatoes are most frequently affected. On tomatoes, there's commonly a rather specific and very annoying related symptom, usually known, descriptively, as greenback: the fruit develop a hard green or sometimes yellow area on the side where it's struck by high levels of sunlight. Greenback incidence can be lessened by not stripping away the foliage and so exposing the fruit to too much sunlight. Interestingly, greenback susceptibility is an inherited characteristic and many modern cultivars, including most F1 hybrids, have fairly good resistance to it. Occasionally the leaves of indoor plants can be scorched in a similar way, and if flower bulbs are exposed to hot sun after lifting they may be damaged and fail to flower as a result. Most commonly, the scorch symptoms result in papery, pale brownish patches on the affected parts. The problem can be minimized on greenhouse plants by adequate ventilation and particularly by applying summer shading.

A second type of high-temperature injury is caused to the stem bases of plants by hot soil. On woody plants the symptom is usually known as heat canker and commonly heals satisfactorily. On other plants, especially on root vegetables, the effect can be very damaging and is then called strangles.

temperature extremes

Extremes of temperature can contribute indirectly to plant problems by their effect on pests and pathogens, although I think the practical importance of this is often overstated. I've grown a bit weary of gardeners telling me that 'what we need is a hard winter' in order to kill off garden pests. In reality, I've never found that very cold winters make much difference to pest or disease incidence in the following season: mainly because most are extremely well insulated in their overwinter quarters. And it shouldn't be forgotten that, if temperatures are low enough for long enough to cause significant depletion of pest populations, they are equally likely to cause similar depletion of parasites and predators. Those pests that do survive may reasonably expect, therefore, to have a better chance of making their presence felt.

Some pests and diseases will be more apparent during or following a period of low temperature, but this is because the host plants have been weakened. However, among pests, thrips and red spider and related mites are certainly commonest in hot (and dry) conditions, as are powdery mildew diseases. The smut disease of sweet corn (*Ustilago maydis)* and sooty bark disease of sycamore (*Cryptostroma corticale*) are also seen almost invariably during or following hot weather. Sometimes, the reason for this relationship is as simple as the fungal spores requiring very high temperatures in order to germinate; in other cases, it's more obscure.

precipitation

Water is essential for all living organisms – plants, diseases and pests alike – but can directly or indirectly contribute to problems. In our climate, most water falls as rain, although drizzle, dew and fog also contribute small amounts of liquid water, while hail, snow, sleet and hoar frost add greater or lesser volumes of more or less solid water. The volume of water falling as snow is about one-tenth that falling as an equivalent depth of rain.

Most forms of precipitation can cause direct damage to plants, although it's only occasionally serious: heavy rainfall, especially that associated with thunderstorms (convectional rain), will beat down veg etation of all kinds, especially flowers, but rarely causes long-term harm. Rain is a very powerful force, however, in the dispersal and localized spread of many diseases and some pests. Heavy rainfall, beating on the soil, will splash soil particles containing bacteria and spores of pathogenic fungi onto low-hanging fruits of all kinds and is a very common predisposing factor to the rotting of marrows, melons, strawberries, cucumbers and other crops. A layer of clean mulching material such as straw will help minimize this transfer.

Rain will also transport spores from an initial point of infection (usually called the infection 'focus'), to other parts of a plant. The frequent appearance of one large lesion, surrounded by several smaller ones, as in apple scab disease or rose black spot, is often a manifestation of this, although this type of lesion pattern can also be the result of a saturated atmosphere, as occurs with fog, mist or even dew. Different mechanisms exist within the main groups of fungi for the detachment of their spores and their dispersal from the parent fungal colony, but almost all require a locally saturated atmosphere. Moisture is also needed for spore germination (see page 50), so a high relative humidity is the pre-requisite

"I cannot think of any important garden pests or diseases that are intrinsically favoured by low temperatures, but there are a few instances of abnormally high temperatures favouring certain problem species."

to both the beginning and end of the disease spread process.

The consequences of a moisture-laden atmosphere can be very much greater than the spread of apple scab across a single fruit or of blackspot within a rose bush, however. It could be said, with some truth, that the present world dominance of the United States of America is due in no small part to the same phenomenon! There's little doubt that persons of Irish ancestry have played a role in the inexorable rise of the power and authority of the USA. And the very reason that so many Irish men and women migrated to the USA was the appalling conditions in Ireland in the 1840s, brought about by the outbreaks of potato blight and the food famine it created. Potato blight is caused by the Oomycete fungus *Phytophthora infestans*, which, like other fungi, requires dampness for its spores both to be liberated and to germinate. A succession of damp, cool summers (and, of course, the absence of any control measures) meant that the disease was able to build up over a few seasons to epidemic dimensions. An interesting development from the potato famine story is that, by very precise understanding of the conditions needed for spore release and germination, it's now possible to predict outbreaks of some diseases, including potato blight, with some certainty and so use control measures more effectively. (For more information about predicting plant problems, see page 124.)

The pyramidal shape of many conifers facilitates snow sliding off

rainfall and soil problems

Very heavy rainfall for a short period, or even moderate rainfall throughout a summer, will result in compaction of the soil surface. This is made worse in a garden, especially a vegetable garden, by the soil being walked on. The long-term (once a year) answer is to dig to break up the compacted layer, but this won't solve the short-term effect, which can be detrimental to plants: the compaction prevents the free penetration, not only of water itself but also of nutrients, applied as fertilizer and, most importantly, of air. Consequently, root function is impaired and plants weakened and possibly rendered more prone to pests, especially root diseases.

Another consequence of heavy precipitation of any kind can be waterlogging of the soil, which means that water is unable to drain away. In its worst form, waterlogging causes flooding, with water lying to some depth over the soil surface. Floods can uproot and wash away plants or, less drastically but still importantly, they can cause a significant loss of worms (through drowning) and create a fairly long-term problem of poor soil aeration and plant growth. Transport of weed seeds and spores of pathogens also commonly takes place in flood water. Temporary waterlogging, such as is found in naturally heavy soils with a high clay content (see page 98), can have serious consequences, particularly for those plants that are intolerant of the poor air-water balance; these will never be very successful, while others suffer through root decay.

In waterlogged conditions a different soil micro-flora, especially of bacterial types, develops. Instead of species that use oxygen and bring about aerobic decomposition of organic matter, bacteria that act anaerobically proliferate. Whereas the end-products of aerobic decomposition (decay in the presence of oxygen) are the organic constituents of humus, which is beneficial to plant growth, the end-products of anaerobic decomposition (in the absence of oxygen) include methane, which is positively harmful. (Anaerobic decomposition is characterized by the almost black appearance of the decayed matter and an unpleasant smell.) As with almost all types of root damage (see page 19), the effects are first seen above-ground as wilting shoot tips, yellowing of the foliage and general debilitation.

hail, snow and glazed frost

Hailstorms occur every year. Although they generally cause little harm in winter, in summer they bring about characteristic white flecking on any fleshy plant material. Large-leaved plants with fairly soft foliage, such as tulips and onions, are very commonly affected. The damage usually arises on the side facing the prevailing wind, which helps to distinguish hail damage from the symptoms of some otherwise similar fungal leaf spots or attack by insects like leafhoppers. Hail damage is generally unsightly rather than intrinsically harmful, but the lesions can allow the entry of pathogenic organisms or pests, especially if the plant is stressed for some other reason.

Any damaging effect of snow must be set against its role in providing an insulation to the soil and to any dormant plant parts (as well as overwintering pests and diseases) against penetrating frost. The weight of snow can cause serious damage, especially when it lies on the branches of evergreen trees and shrubs, which break under the strain. The pyramidal ('Christmas tree') shape of many evergreen coniferous trees is believed to be an adaptation to facilitate snow sliding off the branches – a large number of conifers occur naturally in areas with high snowfall. Unfortunately, many of the ornamental variants of conifer selected and bred for gardens lack this practical shape: in fact, many cultivated forms of the most popular of all ornamental conifers, the Lawson cypress, *Chamaecyparis lawsoniana,* have quite the reverse shape, with the branches pointing upwards; if not carefully and discretely wired together, these will open like a peeled banana under the weight of a heavy snowfall.

Glazed frost is the name given to the layer of ice that forms after periods of freezing rain. It isn't common but, largely because of its unexpectedness, it can cause serious physical damage to garden plants as it soon builds up on branches to a weight much greater than that of a corresponding thickness of snow. Few trees and shrubs have branches either sufficiently rigid or sufficiently pliable to tolerate it.

lack of rain

Lack of precipitation can cause problems at least as serious as an excess, and lack of rain for prolonged periods constitutes a drought. Formerly, a period of fifteen days without rain was defined as a drought, but the appreciation that the impact of such a period varies greatly depending on the time of year means that this, supposedly precise, definition is no longer used.

The consequence of lack of water in the soil is desiccation in the plant because it loses more water through its leaves than it's able to replace through the roots. A related phenomenon is called physiological drought. This arises when there's plenty of water in the soil but the plant is unable to extract and transport it sufficiently fast to prevent damage occurring to the above-ground parts. These conditions can arise when strong or warm, drying winds are prevalent, or there's low humidity or high temperatures; it also commonly occurs when the soil is frozen.

The symptoms of water shortage are an overall dullness to the foliage followed by wilting. Immature fruits and flowers may drop. If the shortage of water becomes more prolonged, both the leaves and roots become toughened and the leaves gradu-

"It's important to realize that, even if it has rained, plants may still be short of water because the particular soil type doesn't retain water well."

ally turn brownish. Under severe conditions leaves may drop and the plants die. A very common effect of water shortage, as with other forms of severe stress, is that plants run to seed, or 'bolt'. (For other causes of bolting see page 110.)

Dry air can produce specific and individual symptoms, different from those of general water shortage. Flowers and buds may drop or flowers become imperfectly fertilized (a situation often compounded by the death of pollen grains brought about by the high temperatures that usually accompany dry air). On tomatoes and other plants this results in a condition called 'dry set': the fruits fail to develop beyond a few millimetres in diameter.

Commonly, the secondary effects of water shortage, even of slight water shortage, are more important. Much the most familiar example of this arises on tomatoes, peppers and a few other types of plant as the incorrectly named blossom-end rot. Here the dark, but undecayed, lesions at the blossom end of the fruit are caused by a deficiency of calcium (see page 103); the movement of calcium in the plant has been impaired due to water shortage. Irregularity of water supply – an alternation of dry periods with adequate moisture – causes splitting of any plant parts that have a high moisture content. Soft watery fruits with thin skins, like tomatoes and plums, are especially prone to this.

"All green plants need light in order to grow, and one of the skills of the gardener is an understanding that different species require or tolerate different light levels."

light

Plants that have adapted to life on the shaded floor of a woodland will grow inadequately in full sun, while species requiring high light levels will display yellowing and general debilitation when overshadowed by larger plants. A good many instances of garden plant problems can be attributed to incorrect siting.

Inadequate light early in the season is a common explanation for unsatisfactory development of young seedlings in greenhouses or on window sills. There's adequate warmth for germination and growth, but the plants become elongated, yellow and spindly: the horticultural term is 'drawn', the botanical one 'etiolated'. To avoid this in British greenhouses, the solution is to sow the seeds later. I've never experienced the problem in my own garden greenhouse where, unlike my research greenhouses, I don't use artificial supplementary lighting: I've simply delayed sowing until the time when experience has shown me that the problem doesn't arise.

Light can have also have a bearing on problems associated with germination itself. In many seeds, germination is suppressed in the presence of light and these should be buried slightly below the surface of the soil or compost, but in a few species, such as primulas, light is required (generally to inactivate some germination inhibitor), and they must be surface-sown. It's important to check sowing instructions when growing any species with which you are unfamiliar.

There are occasions when high light levels can have specific and damaging effects, although, in a great many of these instances, such as greenback development in tomatoes, it is, in reality, the high temperature that accompanies the high light that really causes the problem. The development of green chlorophyll in potatoes when they're not stored in the dark is, however, exclusively light-induced. (Potato tubers consist of stem, not root, tissues and so are potentially photosynthetic.) Green potatoes are inedible and poisonous due to the development of the alkaloid solanin, at the same time as the chlorophyll. A curious and unique effect, associated with high light intensity (and some warmth), occurs when cold water is splashed onto the leaves of saintpaulias and other related plants in the family Gesneriaceae. They develop ringspot and line pattern symptoms that are indistinguishable from those induced on many plants by viruses.

daylength

Some of gardening's biggest frustrations and mysterious problems come from the phenomenon of daylength. No matter what gardeners do by way of feeding and other care, some plants just fail to flower at certain times, while others may unexpectedly burst into flower or leaf in particular situations (the production of flowers and retention of foliage by otherwise deciduous plants growing close to street lighting is a common example of the latter). An explanation comes from appreciating the geographical origin of the species concerned.

Mainly to coincide with the time of year when the insects or other creatures that bring about their pollination are active, some plants flower naturally when days are long in the summer, some when days are short in the winter and some almost all year round. They are called long-day, short-day and neutral respectively and, not surprisingly, these differences generally reflect the latitude of their native homes. Long-day plants, such as spinach, tend to come from the higher latitudes close to the poles and short-day plants, such as salvias, from the lower latitudes nearer the equator.

To make these factors operative, the plants have a mechanism by which the differences in daylength can be detected and so provide a stimulus for the tissues at the stem apex to develop into petals and stamens instead of leaves. Why long-day plants continue to flower in conditions of continuous light, and the way in which the light affects the hormonal activity governing petal and stamen formation, is very imperfectly understood. Very much more

A garden exposed to full sun

is known of the system in short-day plants, however, and it's clear that it's the long night rather than the short day itself that is the critical factor. If short-day plants are grown in short-day conditions but then artificially exposed to bright light (more specifically to bright red light) for a short duration during the night, flower initiation is retarded. This phenomenon is used commercially to retard flower formation in short-day plants, such as chrysanthemums, so they can be produced in bloom at any time of the year, but isn't something that can be replicated in a garden or even very easily in a garden greenhouse.

The chemical receptor of the light stimulus is a protein called phytochrome and it exists in two forms, changing from one to the other with light of different wavelengths. One of these forms seems to stimulate hormonal or other changes to take place at the shoot apex and so initiate the development of flowers. Once a plant has received a flowering stimulus by being exposed to conditions of the appropriate daylength, if one of its leaves is then grafted onto another plant that has received no such stimulus, it can bring about flower development in the second plant.

Wind pruning of coastal pine trees

The retention of foliage by plants grown under long-day conditions (or accidentally subjected to them by street lighting) is the result of a comparable mechanism to that of flower development. Chemical receptors prevent the development of substances that bring about the separation of leaf-stalk tissues from the parent plant, so the foliage is retained. The plant (or part of it) is 'tricked' into disregarding the natural shortening of days that occurs with the onset of autumn.

lightning

Some of the most mysterious of all plant problems can be attributed to lightning. Although gardeners will generally be all too aware of lightning strikes that take place in their gardens while they are present, strikes that have occurred in their absence can result in apparently inexplicable large patches of dead plants in beds, large scorched areas on lawns or tree trunks shattered vertically.

wind

Wind, the movement of air, is an ever-present phenomenon. The fact that the air does move is the key to the successful uptake by plants of water and nutrients from the soil, as these are drawn up the conducting xylem tissues of the stem largely through the effect of moisture evaporation at the leaf surface. But excessive wind can result in excessive moisture uptake and loss, mimicking the effect of drought (see page 93).

As with the other environmental phenomena, some plants are naturally adapted to conditions of high and prolonged wind. In Britain these are species that grow in high or exposed westerly areas, subject to oceanic winds across the Atlantic. Most garden plants, however, aren't adapted to these conditions and, particularly in exposed gardens, will experience problems.

More or less continuous strong, drying winds will result in the two related phenomena of wind-scorching and wind-pruning: on very exposed sites trees often appear to be permanently leaning over, as if blown by the wind. This effect is the result of the death of buds on the windward side of the trees: they are killed by induced localized drought. On other exposed sites, brown scorching or wind-blast damage, caused by similar dry and/or cold wind effects, can affect foliage and, hence, tree growth and is the major factor in limiting the growth of forests at high altitude in Britain. On the sea coast it's commonly accompanied by the damaging effect of windborne salt spray. The symptom may appear as an overall browning of the foliage on the side of the plant facing the wind, while on individual leaves the margins may be very markedly more browned than the centres. Even in relatively sheltered gardens and orchards, cold wind is probably the commonest cause of roughening or russetting on apples and other fruit.

The damage caused by wind can take various forms, ranging in severity and given specific names.

The most mild form is windrock. The plants are moved to and fro in the ground but aren't uprooted. The consequence can be that the stem base is chaffed and pathogenic organisms invade. If rainwater fills the soil hollow produced at the stem base and then freezes, further serious damage or death can occur. Windrock is very common on young trees, shrubs and herbaceous plants that have a large top in relation to their root system but can generally be avoided by careful attention to staking.

Windbreak is the snapping of tree trunks or branches or stems of other plants at some distance from the ground and is very common after autumn and winter gales. It cannot be prevented but the resulting broken stub should be sawn off close to the basal collar (see page 64). (Exactly the same phenomenon will arise when trees are very heavily laden with fruit. Plums are particularly prone to this because of their brittle wood.)

The most serious type of wind damage is called windthrow, in which trees are uprooted. Although this effect is obviously beyond anyone's control and no stake will prevent it, it's very often possible to predict in advance which trees are most likely to be affected. Tall trees with large crowns, especially when overgrown with ivy and/or standing on shallow soils and/or with defective or small root systems, are very prone to windthrow. Trees that have always grown isolated from others will generally be inherently more stable than those either in plantations or from around which neighbouring trees have been removed.

Wind may also induce damage in a number of indirect ways, for example by transporting chemical pollutants and by its influence on temperature and humidity (see page 91).

"The physical strength of the wind, as manifested in gales, is among the most depressing of the problems that can befall a gardener: I know it well, having returned to my own garden on one occasion to find every single tree damaged."

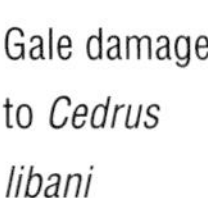

Gale damage to *Cedrus libani*

12 Understanding soil

Almost all plants grow naturally in soil. If you look closely, you will find that even plants growing on top of stone walls or on house roofs are really rooted in small pockets of accumulated and blown soil. (There are a few exceptions – epiphytes, clinging to the bark of trees, sometimes with their roots dangling in the air; plants floating unanchored in water; parasitic or semi-parasitic plants with feeding structures buried in the tissues of another plant – but these contribute little to gardens.) Not surprisingly, therefore, soil can also be the medium through which many problems manifest themselves. I have discussed soil as the source of harmful organisms, but there can also be problems that arise from the soil itself.

One of the most important ways in which the soil's normal functions can be disrupted to the detriment of plants growing in it is by waterlogging or drought (see pages 91–94). The likelihood of waterlogging or of soil drought, and indeed the likelihood of other soil-mediated problems, can to some degree be predicted by the nature of the soil itself.

soil physics

Soils are extremely variable: anyone who has gardened in more than one place will have realized that. Some soils dry out very quickly, some become very sticky when wet, perhaps to the extent of being unworkable in winter, others very soon develop a hard crust, or cap, after heavy rain or being walked on. Nonetheless, they aren't so variable as to defy classification. This classification is based on words with which gardeners will be familiar, even if they are unaware that they can have a very precise meaning. The basis of the physical classification of soils is the relative percentages of sand, silt and clay that they contain. The demarcation between these three types of particle is clearly defined by the following size limits:

Particle type	*Particle diameter range (mm)*
Sand	0.06–2.0
Silt	0.002–0.06
Clay	<0.002

Two words are often used – often incorrectly – to describe the physical attributes of soil: texture and structure. The *texture* of a soil is an expression of the relative proportions of sand, silt and clay particles that it contains, and from an analysis of these relative proportions, the soil can be named accurately as a sand, clay or loam. Sandy soils are often described as light, while clay soils are said to be heavy. The *structure* of the soil, by contrast, describes the way and extent to which the mineral particles are aggregated into what are usually called crumbs. Between the individual mineral particles within the crumbs are holes or pores that contain the soil air and/or water. In a clay soil, these are much smaller than in a sandy soil. There are also pores between the crumbs, and it's a healthy blend of large and small pores that makes what gardeners call a well-structured soil; by contrast, beach sand or a very heavy clay is virtually structureless.

It's already apparent that a clay soil will be most prone to waterlogging and a sandy soil most subject to drought. But there's another factor, the third major soil compo-

Geranium robertianum established in paving cracks

"Soil, or potting compost, is indispensable to plants. It's the medium in which they are anchored and from which, through their roots, they obtain almost all of their water and mineral nutrients."

nent to consider: the once living but now dead organic matter, or humus. This, too, contributes significantly to soil texture. Soil scientists classify soils on the basis of the percentage of organic matter they contain, but it's sufficient for gardening purposes to appreciate that most soils contain between one and five per cent organic matter; in a peaty soil, this percentage will be very much higher. Humus is naturally spongy and naturally sticky as it contains organic glues. The relative amount of humus in a soil, therefore, will affect drainage, or, more precisely, water retentiveness. Paradoxically, both heavy clay soils and light sandy soils can be 'improved' by the addition of organic matter.

PLANTS AND SOIL

Because plants grow naturally in all types of soil, choosing appropriate species for your garden soil should, in theory, minimize the likelihood of the plants being placed under stress, and hence being more likely to pathogen attack or other problem. In practice, this situation seldom arises for it's in the nature of gardening that we choose plants we like aesthetically or that will fulfil a particular role for us, almost irrespective of the site and soil in which they grow naturally. But this underlines the importance of appreciating the conditions in which your plants do occur in the wild and then amending or ameliorating your soil to suit them. The greater the difference between the plants' natural growing conditions and those that your garden can offer, the more likely it is that you will have to use an appropriate artificial compost, generally in a container, for them to succeed.

RAISING pH USING GROUND LIMESTONE

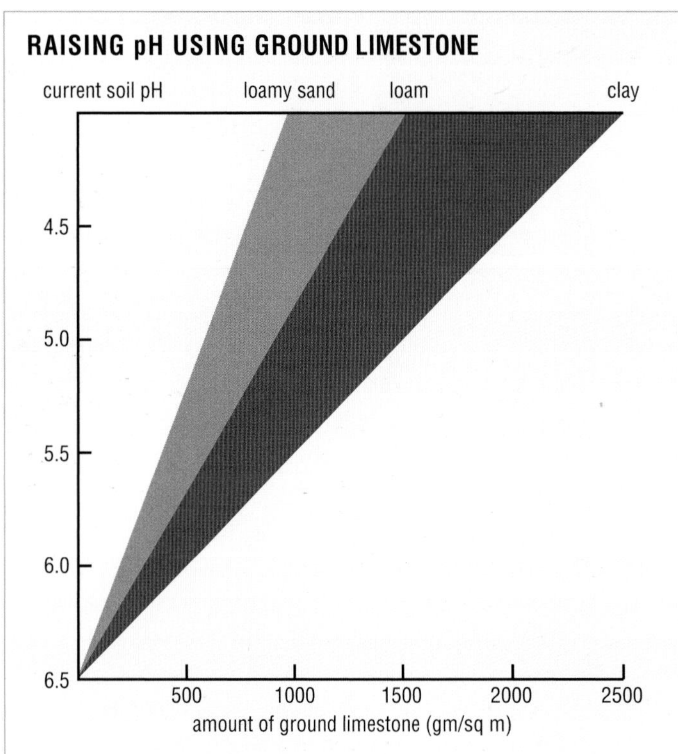

The quantities of ground limestone needed to raise various garden soils to pH 6.5 (the value of most general use)

soil chemistry

The soil features described so far can be called soil physics. While they can have a considerable bearing on the appearance of plant problems, the problems themselves are generally mediated through some other agency: heavy, wet soils will render plants likely to attack by pathogens, for instance. In terms of a direct effect on plant growth, soil physics usually takes second place to soil chemistry.

As the soil is the source of plant mineral nutrients, it's evident that the chemical make-up of the sand, silt and clay particles very largely dictates which nutrients are present. Soil humus contributes relatively small amounts of some elements, nitrogen especially, but seldom all, and seldom supplies minor nutrients. I shall return later to the inadequacy of organic matter in general as a source of plant nutrient.

soil pH

Before considering the nature of the mineral nutrients and their bearing on plant problems, there's another aspect of soil chemistry that needs consideration: its relative acidity or alkalinity, usually defined as its pH. This is a rather complex unit of chemical measurement but, for present purposes, it's sufficient to know that it's measured on a scale ranging from 0 (very acid) to 14 (very alkaline), the mid-point of 7 being known as neutral. It's worth knowing, too, that pH is a logarithmic scale. In other words, a pH of 4 represents ten times more 'acidity' than a pH of 5 and one hundred times more than a pH of 6. (This is why, when gardeners try to alter soil pH, it becomes increasingly difficult, the greater the change being attempted.) In practice, all British soils fall approximately between the pH 3.5 of a very acid, peaty soil and the pH 8 of a thin soil overlying chalk rock.

Overall, differences in soil pH are probably the most important individual factors in accounting for the natural presence of certain plants on some sites and their absence from others with otherwise similar environmental features. The pH of the soil has a number of effects on plants, but of greatest importance is that most elemental plant nutrients are taken up less readily from an alkaline soil: although the nutrients may be present in adequate quantities, the high pH renders them unavailable. Plants, such as clematis and some gentians, which can tolerate these conditions and grow satisfactorily in alkaline soils, are known as calcicoles; those, such as many vegetables, and indeed other species of gentian, that cannot, are called calcifuges; while a group that includes rhododendrons and many heathers are intolerant of all except the most acid soils.

Changing soil pH might seem to be the way to avoid some of the problems associated with nutrient deficiency. Unfortunately, altering pH either over a large area or a long time is very difficult. In general, however, it's easier to raise than to lower – an acidic soil can be made alkaline much more readily than the other way round. The pH of soil can be raised by adding one of a group of alkaline substances usually referred to as lime. They include calcium oxide (burnt lime or quicklime), calcium hydroxide (slaked lime), calcium carbonate (ground limestone or ground chalk; the latter is simply a chemically purer form), and the mixture of calcium and magnesium carbonates known as magnesian limestone. Calcium carbonate is the cheapest and calcium oxide the most expensive form of lime and they are, respectively, the least and most efficient at neutralizing (or raising the pH of) an acid soil. The amount to be applied to the soil to achieve a particular change in pH value depends on a number of factors, the most important being the texture of the soil itself. The graph (left) shows the amount of ground limestone that needs to be added to different types of soil to raise the pH from various starting values to pH 6.5, the level most generally useful for garden plants. If you add the lime as calcium oxide or calcium hydroxide, you should add half of these amounts.

It shouldn't be forgotten that lime also adds calcium, one of the essential plant nutrients, to the soil. If, by chance, plants show symptoms of calcium deficiency but you don't wish to raise the pH, the problem may be alleviated by adding calcium in the form of calcium sulphate (gypsum). If, moreover, plants show signs of manganese deficiency, as they often do on alkaline soils, then magnesian limestone should be used as a source of both elements.

Lime-induced chlorosis on a raspberry plant

Logic suggests that if adding an alkali will raise the pH of an acid soil, so adding an acid should neutralize an alkaline one. Indeed it will, but the main problem arises because appropriate mineral acids, such as sulphuric acid, are extremely dangerous to handle. By adding sulphur chips to

Symptoms of potassium deficiency on grapevine leaves

your soil, you will achieve some lowering of the pH because the sulphur combines with the soil water to form weak sulphuric acid, but the effect won't be as great or as long-lived as the opposite results obtained from liming.

nutrients

The soil chemical elements most essential to plants are the 'big three' – nitrogen, phosphorus and potassium (all required in large amounts and commonly abbreviated to N, P and K, their chemical symbols) – together with calcium, magnesium and sulphur (which are required in lesser amounts). Collectively these six are called major nutrients. In addition, plants require smaller amounts of the minor, or trace, elements, iron, manganese, boron, copper, molybdenum, zinc and sometimes sodium and chlorine.

If any of these elements are deficient, the plants will display characteristic symptoms. Nonetheless, all isn't necessarily easy: lack of the same element can give rise to different symptoms on different types of plant; some elements give puzzlingly similar deficiency symptoms; different elements can interact with each other to produce a confusing picture; and some symptoms of nutrient deficiency can be remarkably similar to effects produced by viruses, weather, pollution or other causes. (I have tried to separate out these possibilities in the keys later in the book.)

With soil-nutrient deficiencies, as with pests and diseases, the same question arises: why are they important in gardens but not on plants growing in the wild? The answer is two-fold. Nutrient deficiencies can and do occur on wild plants (wild blackberries, for instance, almost invariably show some signs of iron deficiency), but they are often overlooked and seldom have a major *noticeable* effect on the plant's cropping. And nutrient deficiencies are much commoner and much more evident on garden plants because we are making very heavy demands on these plants and on the soil in which they grow. By repeated, intensive cropping, by expecting higher yields than would occur naturally, by removing dead plant matter before it rots down, we are ensuring that the natural reserves in the soil are depleted faster than they are being replenished.

To what extent can deficiency symptoms be predicted and their effects avoided? For the reasons indicated above, the three major nutrients will almost inevitably become deficient in gardens, above all in vegetable gardens, unless routine applications of balanced fertilizer are made (see pages 104–105). And, with the exception of molybdenum, almost all trace elements will be unavailable to plants (not deficient, merely unavailable) on alkaline sites. Knowledge of the local climate and geology can sometimes help to predict basic soil deficiencies, irrespective of cropping. The geology may well dictate which minerals are present locally (although it should also be borne in mind that mineral

NUTRIENT DEFICIENCIES

Deficiencies of sulphur are almost unknown in British soils while chlorine, sodium and zinc deficiencies are also uncommon and restricted to very few crops. The others need to be considered individually.

Nitrogen can be deficient in almost all soils, especially if they are heavily cropped and where rainfall is high. Very leafy plants, such as many types of vegetable, are especially prone to the effects of nitrogen deficiency.

Phosphorus, like nitrogen, is also often deficient in regions with high rainfall as it's readily leached from the soil. It's also commonly deficient in very acidic or very alkaline soils and in many clay soils. Most types of plant can be affected; a deficiency of potassium often gives rise to poor flower and fruit production.

Potassium is often deficient in light sandy soils and also on chalky and peaty soils that have a low proportion of clay particles. Vegetable and fruit crops are particularly prone to the effects of low potassium levels.

Calcium deficiency symptoms occur most commonly on acidic peaty soils and on those acid soils that originate from rocks with a low calcium content, such as siliceous sandstones and igneous rocks, such as granite. Deficiency symptoms may also be seen on light, free-draining sandy soils but are uncommon on heavy clays or alkaline soils derived from limestone or chalk. Symptoms are most common on fruits and on non-leafy vegetable crops (those that are grown for some quality other than their leaves).

Magnesium deficiency often accompanies calcium deficiency on sites such as those with light, acid, sandy soils. It's readily leached from soil so is commonly deficient in regions with a high rainfall. Excessive use of potassium-containing fertilizers can also result in symptoms of magnesium deficiency.

Iron is very rarely deficient in soil but its deficiency symptoms are among those most commonly seen. The paradox arises because iron is the element whose availability is most affected by alkalinity. Plants growing in soils overlying chalk or limestone are most likely to exhibit deficiency symptoms. Fruit plants, roses, skimmias, rhododendrons and camellias are among the types most severely affected.

Manganese may be deficient in a wide range of soil types but the effects are especially severe on highly organic soils (such as peats), wet, marshy soils and on poorly draining sands. Many different types of plant may be affected but some of the classic symptoms occur on peas and beans.

Boron is sometimes deficient in soils derived from parent rocks such as granites, which are low in boron content, or in freely draining sands from which it's readily leached. More commonly, boron is present but unavailable, either because the soil is highly alkaline or sometimes because it's present in minerals such as tourmaline, which plants are unable to utilize. Deficiency symptoms can, therefore, arise after liming or in dry summers following wet winters or springs. The effects are most commonly seen on fruits and on many vegetable crops.

Copper deficiency is usually seen in highly organic soils, such as peats, and is rare on mineral soils. Fruit plants are most likely to display the symptoms.

Molybdenum is hardly ever deficient in soils but is sometimes rendered unavailable to plants on *acidic* sites. The effects are almost confined to cauliflowers and broccoli.

particles can be transported considerable distances by wind and rivers so the soil in your garden doesn't necessarily reflect the nature of the rocks beneath it). The local climate may have a bearing on how readily the minerals are eroded from the rocks or leached (washed out) from the soil. Finally, it should always be remembered that some plants are far more susceptible than others to deficiencies of specific minerals. For example, your soil may have a deficiency of molybdenum, but until you grow cauliflowers, you will never know.

Centranthus ruber established on a wall

FERTILIZERS

Fertilizers are the means by which appreciable amounts of mineral nutrient can be added to soil, either to prevent or to correct nutrient deficiencies. Most gardening needs can be supplied and most deficiencies prevented by the use of a small number of fertilizers. A rather different range, including some specialized products, may be needed, however, to correct any deficiencies that do arise.

General-purpose solid fertilizer

The commonest artificial compound fertilizer available in Britain is the granular mixture called Growmore, which contains 7% of each of the major nutrients nitrogen (N), phosphate (P) and potash (K); it is commonly expressed as a 7:7:7 fertilizer.

The commonest organically based compound fertilizer is blood, fish and bone, a blend of dried blood, finely ground bonemeal and sulphate of potash (not, of course, organic). Like all organically based fertilizers, it is of more variable composition but is approximately 5.1:5:6.5. The nitrogen from the dried blood tends to be slightly more slowly available than that from the ammonium sulphate in artificial mixtures and the phosphorus is released more slowly from the bonemeal component.

General-purpose liquid fertilizer

Relatively high in potassium, liquid feed is very useful during rapid summer growth, the potassium being valuable in flower and fruit development. Therefore, it should be the main fertilizer for most gardeners during the height of the season. There are several branded liquid products. They vary in their relative nutrient contents and most contain additional minor and trace elements, which is an advantage since they tend to be used extensively for plants growing in soil-less composts as well as for those in the ground. The concentrated liquid tomato fertilizers are of this type and generally have a composition of around 5:5:9 derived from inorganic components. Most of those purchased in the form of soluble powders or crystals also fall into this category, having nutrient ratios of about 15:5:20.

Bonemeal (organic) or superphosphate (artificial)

I believe there's little difference between these alternatives for the slow release of phosphorus to aid the establishment of perennials. They should be used routinely at the rate of about 175g per square metre in the planting of trees, shrubs, herbaceous perennials and bulbs.

Lawn fertilizers

Lawns should generally be fed twice a year – in spring and in autumn – but the plants' nutrient requirements are different at these times. I recommend a fertilizer with a relatively high nitrogen content for spring and summer, and one relatively lower in nitrogen for autumn and winter.

Rose fertilizers

Several proprietary fertilizers have been formulated specifically for feeding roses. These contain a blend of the major nutrients but with special emphasis on potassium to encourage flower development. Most branded products also contain additional magnesium because roses are prone to deficiency of this element. I generally apply rose fertilizers at the rate of about 35g per square metre following the spring pruning and again after the first flush of summer flowers in late June. Although formulated specifically for roses, these fertilizers also provide an ideal balanced feed for other flowering shrubs so I feed them all at the same time.

Sequestered iron

This is iron in an organic form that can be absorbed readily by plants even from fairly alkaline conditions.

Fertilizers for specific and less common deficiencies

Sulphate of potash may be used where potassium deficiency alone is a problem.

Manganese sulphate, sprayed on plants at the rate of about 1.5g per litre for every two square metres will give temporary relief from the effects of manganese deficiency.

Pelargoniums, like all garden plants, will only thrive well with adequate fertilizer

Borax will correct boron deficiency if it's raked into the soil at the rate of about 3g per square metre at planting time. Although the effects are quick to appear, the chemical doesn't persist for long in the soil and repeated applications may be necessary from year to year. The relatively rare symptoms of copper deficiency can be corrected by spraying growing plants with 5 litres of 0.05% copper oxychloride solution per ten square metres.

Molybdenum deficiency, which occurs almost exclusively in cauliflowers, can be circumvented by watering the very young plants with a solution of ammonium or sodium molybdate at the rate of 2.5g per half litre for every square metre.

13 Other problems

Among the trickiest of plant problems to diagnose are those that don't originate from any of the most obvious causes: neither pest nor pathogen, neither climate nor soil. By definition they are all disorders, but they are difficult to identify because they may display symptoms confusingly similar to those caused by other things. They may also require experience in order to know where to look for clues and how to analyze them. But a good many of them can also be problematic simply because they are 'one-offs': there is nothing else like them, there are no clues and if you have never seen them before, you will be stumped. This chapter gives a little of their background and explains how they originate (I have subdivided them on the basis of their causes although this doesn't necessarily reflect their appearance), and I hope that the keys on pages 187–213 will enable you to identify even the most mysterious.

"Plants suffer from accidents just as readily as you or I. My concern is with some of the more common causes of plant wounds: in almost every case, human intervention is involved."

accidental damage

Given time, accidental wounds will heal although they may allow a pest or pathogen to enter (see page 56) and, as discussed elsewhere, the plant will develop symptoms that can be recognized. The important thing to recognize is that it's very rare for mechanical wounds to arise naturally: a tree falling in a storm may strike another tree and remove some bark but this event is an exception. The majority of mechanical wounds must, therefore, be avoidable.

What might be called authentic accidents (and, therefore, perhaps excusable) range from ramming a tree with a lawnmower or wheelbarrow to treading on a box of bedding plants. Into the category of carelessness come leaving a tying wire in place for far too long on an expanding stem, nailing a fence rail to a convenient tree trunk, laying concrete around the base of a tree or shrub (so asphyxiating the roots) or clumsy handling of vegetables and fruit, especially those intended for storage. Inexperience or lack of expertise will result in the problems that arise from incorrect planting and pruning. For example, failing to spread the roots carefully when planting will give rise to poor anchorage, instability, feeble growth and even a girdling form of dieback as the stem base is strangled. Leaving a hollow at the base of a stem in which water can collect may result in injury if the water freezes. And leaving branch stubs when pruning will almost inevitably provide entry points for decay fungi or bacteria, while inadequate pruning can result in a mass of twigs and congested growth which leads to general debilitation. We are already, therefore, into that grey area where the specific care needed to avoid problems merges imperceptibly into the basic commonsense and importance of good gardening practice.

"Chemical damage can be divided into chronic, where tissue is injured but not killed, usually by exposure to low levels of pollutants for long periods, and acute, where tissues are killed, often by a brief exposure to a high level of pollutant. The commonest symptoms are flecks or spots of bleached tissue on the leaves and areas of marginal browning."

chemical damage

No one gardens for very long before discovering that plants are susceptible to damage from chemicals. The packaging of a number of garden pesticides bears a warning that the product isn't to be used on some types of plant (ferns and fuchsias are commonly cited). The reason is that the products are blessed with a characteristic called phytotoxicity: they are poisonous to certain types of vegetation. Complete phytotoxicity is provided by garden chemicals that are called weedkillers.

Widespread air pollution from chemicals is, fortunately, much less significant in Britain and other developed countries since the passing of clean air legislation and the control of emissions. Nonetheless, it still exists and among the most significant airborne pollutants are carbon monoxide, sulphur dioxide, nitrogen oxides, chlorides (including common salt, sodium chloride), fluorides, ethylene, various hydrocarbons, ammonia, ozone, aldehydes, arsine, phosphine, pesticides

A 'bolting' lettuce, producing flowers and seed

Damage to common holly caused by exposure to salt spray

and herbicides (especially those that contain copper, polysulphides or insecticidal oils or emulsions), various heavy metal salts and dusts such as smoke and cement. Most of these are the products of industrial processes, although common salt as an airborne pollutant is commonest near the sea, while herbicides and pesticides are usually encountered as drift from commercial farm spraying. All of the chemicals listed can, in appropriate concentrations, cause direct damage to plants, although sulphur in the atmosphere may be incidentally beneficial through its fungicidal action on certain plant diseases, such as the well-known instance of its suppression of black spot of roses in industrial areas.

On a more domestic, localized scale, a number of other chemicals can cause problems in gardens. Among the commoner, in my experience, are: urine (especially from bitches and especially on lawns); oil and petrol (very often spillages from lawnmowers cause bare patches on lawns); creosote (near fences); paint (quite common in newly painted greenhouses and on wall plants when windows are painted); salt used on roads or garden paths in winter (a very common cause of injury to or death of roadside trees and hedges); zinc (damage commonly occurs on soft fruit if a cage of new galvanized wire is erected over them; lightweight plastic netting should always be used for the top of a fruit cage); gas (sections of hedges sometimes die when a leak from an underground main kills part of the root system although this is less common with natural gas than with the old town gas); and misused fungicides, pesticides, fertilizers and, of course, herbicides.

Symptoms are discussed later, but, even with very careful expert analysis, it's often difficult to be certain of the cause of particular chemical injuries. As so often with plant problems, however, commonsense does help. For example, if you don't possess a dog but know that last week you filled your lawnmower with fuel in a hurry, then petrol is more likely than urine to be responsible for the sudden dramatic appearance of a brown patch on the grass. And, if you have sufficient experience to recognize the characteristic brown marginal scorching on your holly leaves as typical of chloride injury, commonsense should enable you to deduce that the fact that you live a mile from the sea coast in an area of outstanding natural beauty makes it more likely to be the result of windblown sea salt than emission from a industrial process. Always bear in mind that, just as I mentioned in connection with hail damage (see page 93), any injury that is markedly unidirectional is unlikely to be a disease or pest. If more or less the same symptoms extend across different species on the side of plants facing the prevailing wind, chemical or other airborne cause is virtually certain.

Finally, it's worth mentioning one specific type of chemical injury that is remarkably common and yet leaves countless gardeners puzzled. Strangely distorted growth in tomato plants with swelling of the stem and leaf tissues occurs every year. It can be caused by virus but is much more frequently the result of damage from hormone weedkillers, to which tomatoes are exceptionally sensitive. The source is most commonly a selective lawn weedkiller applied nearby on a windy or very hot day (when the chemical vaporizes rapidly). It's important to realize that hormone weedkillers are also often present in minute amounts in straw, as residue from selective weedkillers used in cereal crops. When that straw forms a component of farmyard or stable manure, the contamination persists. Manure of this type should never be used on or near tomatoes.

CHEMICAL-TOLERANT PLANTS

Plants that are particularly tolerant of most types of moderate exposure to chemicals include apple, aquilegia, Brussels sprout, cabbage, erica, gladiolus, hornbeam, laburnum, lilac, lime, plane, privet, prunus, rose, sugar maple, sycamore, thuja and tsuga. In coastal gardens, the following are particularly useful as windbreaks because of their tolerance of salt spray: Austrian pine, escallonia, hebe, holm oak, hydrangea, Japanese spindle, olearia, Monterey cypress, Monterey pine and tamarisk.

Cabbage 'Primo'; cabbages are fairly pollution-tolerant

genetic or growth problems

There are some problems that, in a sense, can be said to be of the plant's own making. They are the result of some genetic modification or abnormality or some aberration of growth, usually with no evident cause. They are mysterious and occasionally serious but equally they are unavoidable, incurable and also not transmissible.

albinos

Albino individuals occur from time to time among young plants; in gardens, dahlias are among the most common. These curiosities are the result of a mutation and fall into a category called lethal mutations as they are unable to survive once the food reserve in the cotyledons is exhausted. Lacking chlorophyll, they cannot photosynthesize, cannot reach maturity and die in consequence. Rather commonly, individual shoots bearing white foliage arise through mutation on other types of plant; pelargoniums are especially commonly affected. These shoots are, in effect, parasitic on the remainder of the plant and will survive while they are attached to it. The temptation to try to strike cuttings and breed an all-white plant is often too much for many gardeners, but severing the all-white shoot will produce very disappointing results.

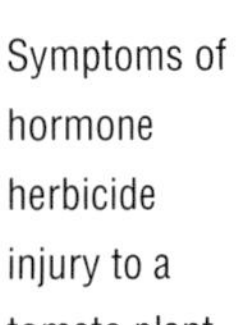

Symptoms of hormone herbicide injury to a tomato plant

blindness

Blindness is the name given to the failure of a plant to produce a flowering shoot where one might reasonably be expected and is due to either the absence or the malfunction of the growing point. It differs from the simple reluctance to flower

An albino dahlia seedling, a lethal mutation

exhibited by many types of plant that are simply too young, have been given too much nitrogenous fertilizer or have had insufficient time to become properly established. Blindness is most common on bulbous plants, although it's also rather frequent and serious on broccoli and cauliflowers, which are among the few vegetables where the flowering shoot constitutes the edible crop. There are many different causes of blindness. In bulbous plants, it's often the result of a failure to them give fertilizer after flowering or, very commonly, planting them too shallowly. Other common causes are the exposure of bulbs to high temperatures after lifting or during storage, attack by pests or pathogens (narcissus fly attacking the growing point is a frequent cause on daffodils), waterlogging or drought.

bolting

Bolting is the premature flowering and seeding of vegetable plants. It's very frustrating when crops are lost in this way. Vegetables that are very prone to bolting include beetroot, brassicas (especially Chinese cabbage and other oriental types), celery, lettuce, onions and spinach. The factors controlling it are very complex and vary from crop to crop and even between cultivars of the same crop. In general, however, in order to flower, these plants require exposure to cold temperatures at a certain critical stage of their growth and for certain lengths of time. Once they have been exposed in this way, nothing, not even prolonged periods of high temperature, can prevent flowering.

There's no real way to prevent bolting although some cultivars have been selected for resistance to it and are usually highlighted in seed catalogues. In general, however, early cultivars will bolt much more readily because they are more likely to experience the appropriate cold temperatures. Bolting will be less of a problem in a season following a mild and early spring and more serious after a late and cold one. If low temperatures occur in late spring, brassicas raised under glass for spring planting will be more prone to bolting than those plants raised outdoors as they will be further advanced and will have already reached the critical growth stage. It must be added, however, that day length also influences the onset of flowering and can interact with, or modify, the temperature-induced response. That most popular of oriental vegetables, Chinese cabbage, exemplifies this. If you sow Chinese cabbage too early, it may well receive the irreversible cold stimulus. The trick, in western Europe, is to delay the sowing as long as possible; ideally until shortly after midsummer, when the days are beginning to shorten but the temperatures are still fairly high (early July). It's also advisable to choose one of the cultivars that have been selected as more suitable to our conditions.

A rather different type of bolting is that commonly arising during periods of dry weather, when plants are under stress. A natural response of most plants under these conditions is to flower and produce seed and the likelihood of this can be lessened by giving them additional water at such times. Conversely, ornamental plants that fail to flower often do so because they are too well looked after, that is, not placed under sufficient stress, and withholding of water from them can often induce flower formation.

other growth problems

Epicormic shoot growth is the technical name for the generally inexplicable bursting into life of dormant buds, principally on woody plants. Abnormally high temperatures in winter may be one cause

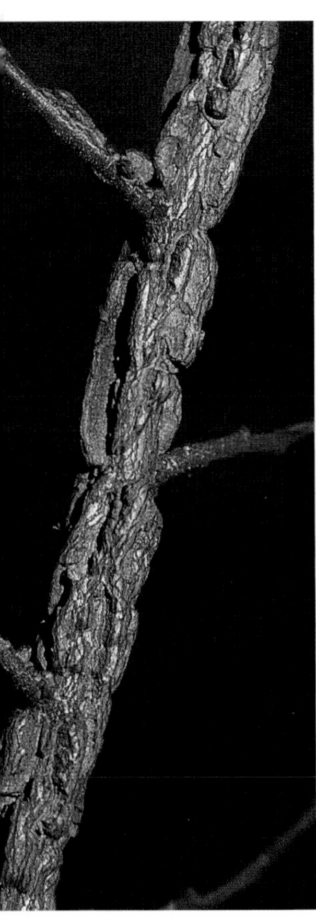

above: Winged cork on *Acer campestre*, an abnormality of unknown origin

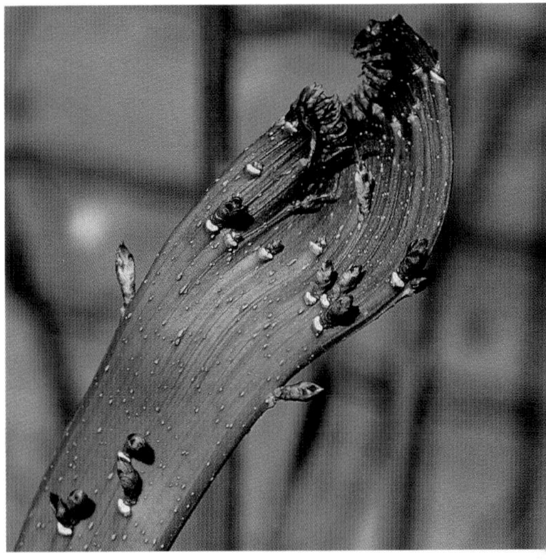

right: Fasciation on a flowering shoot of forsythia

although it's also sometimes associated with disease or pest infestations and it's particularly frequent on larch trees affected by canker and dieback.

The development of closely massed and often fused shoots, presumably arising through a failure of the cells to divide at an early stage, is called fasciation. The name derives from the Latin *fasciculus*, a bundle, a reference to the brushwood bundles ignited and used as flares by the Romans. Fasciation, which is harmless, occurs occasionally on a wide variety of trees, shrubs and herbaceous plants; forsythias and lilies are particularly prone in gardens.

Hybridization nodules are small hard swellings on the roots of some cultivars of swede and turnip. Their cause is unknown and they are harmless, but they are commonly mistaken for the superficially similar and much more serious symptoms of clubroot disease.

Lammas shoots are new growths that arise abnormally late in the season (Lammas day is the first of August, the occasion of a religious festival). They are especially common on oaks and the stimulus for their production isn't known. They are harmless although exceptionally prone to infection by powdery mildew.

Oedema, also sometimes called dropsy or intumescence, is manifested as small rough and warty outgrowths on the undersides of the leaves and on the stems of a wide range of plants, including begonias, brassicas, cacti, camellias, capsicums, pelargoniums, peperomias, solanums, tomatoes and vines. It's most frequent in greenhouses and arises as a result of overwatering and abnormally high humidity or other factors that lead to an excess of water in the plant. Tomatoes are especially prone when they are grown in the same greenhouse as cucumbers, which naturally need much more moist conditions. The moisture excess induces extra growth of discrete patches of cells and so the formation of the warts. Oedema can be prevented by not overwatering and improving ventilation.

Silvering is a descriptive term for leaf discoloration in tomatoes. The problem appears as silver-green patches on the leaves and stem and is combined with a failure to set fruit. Other than being an inherited characteristic, its cause is unknown.

Spiral growth is common on many trees and shrubs; the shoots develop in a twisted or corkscrew-like form, evidently through a mutation. It can be rather attractive, and among examples that are deliberately perpetuated as ornamental cultivars are the twisted or corkscrew willow, *Salix babylonica* var. *pekinensis* 'Tortuosa' and the twisted hazel, or Harry Lauder's walking stick, *Corylus avellana* 'Contorta'. (For the benefit of younger readers, Sir Harry Lauder, 1870-1950, was a Scots comedian who always carried a curled walking stick.)

Winged cork is extremely common on field maples and on elms, especially when they are growing as hedgerow plants. It manifests itself as abnormally thick and deeply fluted bark. The cause is unknown and, like most of these woody plant abnormalities, is quite harmless.

14 Weeds

"The problems that weeds present are pure ecology: they are the embodiment of the simple phenomenon of competition."

The tired definition of a weed as 'a plant growing in wrong place' is misleading because, in truth, it's a plant growing in the right place. A weed is a wild plant doing no more than attempt to reclaim its birthright. Or, to look at it another way, a weed is a purely artificial concept. In shaping the environment with cultivation, we have created the ecological niche in which weed species thrive. In most instances, we can only speculate about the habitat that weeds occupied before the bare earth of fields and gardens, the mown verges of field edges and lawns and the general suppression of the naturally dominant species provided conditions ideal for them. There are good reasons for believing that many now common weeds were, in reality, once rather rare species: the perversity of cultivation provides some evidence for this.

The beautiful purple-flowered corncockle (*Agrostemma githago*) was once a very common weed of cornfields (wheat fields in current terminology). Modern chemical herbicides did for it, however, and according to the latest *British Flora*, it's 'now very rare and only casual'. Presumably, it has returned to the native status it possessed before wheat fields became significant features of the landscape in the past five hundred years or so.

Weeds compete with garden plants for light, air, water and nutrients, and in most instances, if weeds were ignored by gardeners, the garden plants would slowly disappear and the garden revert to a place of wild vegetation. Why? Why do weeds almost invariably triumph? Quite simply because they have had far, far longer to adapt to the local environment. Native species have been present for millennia – and introduced species for up to two thousand years – ample time for competition and selection to enable them to find their ecological niche. Garden plants are largely exotics, fitted ecologically to some alien environment very different from that of our gardens. And, most importantly, many of them have been artificially disadvantaged further by being bred and selected for some horticulturally desirable feature such as large flowers or lush foliage, a process that has quite commonly selected *against* ecological robustness.

Given that wild plants generally have an ecological advantage over garden plants and thus have the potential to cause problems for gardeners, why don't they all do so? Why is it that only around seventy wild species are important as garden weeds in Britain, while the remaining four and a half thousand are not?

Among those that aren't weeds, a large number have specialized habitat needs – particular types of soil, of weather, temperature, shelter and so forth – that just don't arise in gardens. And the remainder don't possess the attributes required to become effective competitors in the various ecological niches that make up our beds, borders and vegetable plots. It's a feature of many of the most successful weeds that they have evolved with the capability of

Chickweed, *Stellaria* sp.

growing in a fairly wide range of habitats. They can, therefore, build up large populations of individuals able to spread from one habitat to another with few natural barriers. The key to this spread, in most cases, is a highly efficient system of reproduction and/or very rapid or vigorous growth.

Ecological similarities between weed species have more meaning than taxonomic relationships. A glance at the list of important British garden weeds included in the key on pages 208–213 reveals that the fifty main species are spread among almost thirty families, and they belong to families that also contain important garden ornamentals and crops. For instance, ground elder is in the same family as carrots, parsnips and parsley; thistles and dandelions are related to asters and lettuce; and bindweed is in the same group as the ornamental morning glory. There's little that is predictable or significant here, therefore. Their life form categories are more revealing: most vegetable garden species are annuals and most perennial lawn and path weeds are rosette-forming. Most serious perennial weeds of beds and borders, however, are basal bud plants, a characteristic that seems harmless enough because it's below ground – but that is where the key to their success lies, as I shall explain shortly.

Now we need to look in more detail at the ways in which each of the main groups of weeds fulfils the necessary criteria of efficient reproduction and vigorous growth.

annual weeds

First, annual weeds, those that produce flowers and set seed within a single season. Unlike many annual plants (including many garden ornamentals), the seeds of some annual weed species require no period of cold or enforced dormancy before they can germinate and if, as in groundsel (*Senecio vulgaris*), or some of the chickweeds (*Stellaria* spp.), this is combined with the ability to produce flowers and seeds very early in life, more than one generation may occur within a single season. Those annual weed seeds that do undergo a dormant phase may vary in the time of year when they are able to germinate. Some, like those of the red deadnettle (*Lamium purpureum*), can germinate only in the spring while others, such as those of the annual nettle (*Urtica urens*), can germinate both in spring and in autumn. Generally, the longer the period of the year over which it's able to germinate, the more successful a weed is likely to be. A few species, including shepherd's purse (*Capsella bursa-pastoris*) and annual meadow grass (*Poa annua*), can germinate in every month of the year.

Annual red deadnettle, *Lamium purpureum*

An important feature for the success of annual weeds is the number of seeds that they produce. Usually, the greater the number of seeds, the greater the likelihood of some escaping the attention of mammals, birds and other animals and, of course, of decay-causing micro-organisms, and hence the greater the chance of the weed attaining significance in the garden. The table on page 117 indicates the average number of seeds produced by a range of common annual weeds. However, these figures should be taken in conjunction with other factors. The sow thistle, for instance, produces a very large number of seeds but anyone who has observed sow thistles will know that they are a magnet for finches and other seed-eating birds and so the proportion of seeds reaching the soil may be relatively small.

Moreover, although a period of dormancy may not be essential, many weed seeds can survive for long periods and only germinate when the soil is disturbed, such as when old grassland is dug up or when moles, earthworms and other animals bring them to the surface. Once in the soil, most annual weed seeds have the potential to survive for at least ten years; not all, of course, manage this for the various reasons outlined above. Seeds of many weed species can survive for much longer periods (see table page 117) and in an unweeded garden, where new plants are growing and adding their seeds year by year, the numbers present in the soil can reach formidable proportions. The highest number of seeds recovered from a sample of soil is about 90,000 per square metre although many species have physiological systems that permit only a proportion of the seed population in the soil to germinate at any given time.

It's possible to estimate the numbers of seeds present in an area of your garden by using the reasonable approximation of ten per cent germinating in one year. Count the number of weed seedlings that emerge in a defined area (say, half a square metre) and multiply this by ten (make sure you identify each species correctly, using the key on pages 208–213). Use the table to find the longevity of the particular weed seed and this will give you an idea of how many years must elapse before the population of that species will vanish from your garden *as long as you prevent any of each year's emerging plants from seeding and adding to the total.* The validity of the results is also dependent on the species not having freely airborne seeds that are likely to blow in from nearby gardens. You will ultimately find that there's some truth in the old gardener's adage that 'one year's seeding' leads to 'seven years' weeding'.

Another feature of the seeding of annual weeds has a considerable bearing on its efficiency and on the merit of particular control measures: groundsel and annual meadow grass are examples of weeds that, in addition to all their other attributes, can continue to mature their seeds if they are hoed down during flowering. Moreover, if the weather and soil are moist at the time, they may produce new roots in response to the wounding and end up, in effect, merely having been transplanted.

Perennial stinging nettle, *Urtica dioica*

seed dispersal

It's one thing to produce large quantities of seed and quite another to ensure that it's well dispersed and so many of the most successful weeds have a very efficient means of dispersal: initially by explosive discharge, and then by wind, water or animals (either externally, by adhering to their bodies, or internally, by surviving the digestive tract).

perennial weeds

For perennial weed species, seeds are rarely of great significance as part of their means of survival or spread. The problems they cause almost invariably come from some

Seed head of dandelion, *Taraxacum officinale*

method of vegetative growth: deeply growing or creeping roots, far-spreading rhizomes, creeping stems and bulbils are the most important.

Rapid growth of a root or rhizome to great length provides a straightforward albeit awkward problem in gardens: a large amount of plant has to be removed, and when it's growing deeply in the soil, there's the added difficulty of locating all of the growth. However, this purely physical problem is relatively small compared with that produced by those weeds which can regenerate from small parts of stem or root that are left behind. Perennial weeds vary in their ability to do this. Dandelion (*Taraxacum officinale*), for example, can regenerate from any part of its taproot, whereas docks (*Rumex* spp.) can only do so from the top 7–10cm (3–4in). Plants with creeping rhizomes, such as couch grass (*Agropyron repens*), ground elder (*Aegopodium podagraria*) or horsetail (*Equisetum arvense*), present special problems. Their rhizomes have numerous nodes with buds at each one. If the rhizome is severed or otherwise disturbed, these buds are stimulated to grow and when, as is often the case, the whole structure is innately brittle, the physical eradication of the plant becomes an exceedingly difficult task; in a clay soil, it's almost an impossible one.

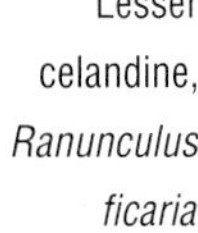

Lesser celandine, *Ranunculus ficaria*

Rather fewer important weeds have creeping roots but these too can regenerate when they are severed or damaged; creeping thistle (*Cirsium arvense*) is probably the most significant garden weed in this category. In a league of their own are the weeds that produce bulbils (tiny bulbs); these are ineradicable by physical means and when, as in the pink-flowered *Oxalis* spp., this attribute is combined with almost total resistance to or tolerance of available weedkillers, the problem is insurmountable. One member of this group deserves special mention: the common lesser celandine, *Ranunculus ficaria*. Superficially, this plant would seem the most intractable weed of all, possessing not only bulbils but also small brittle tubers and fairly prolific seed production. Fortunately, it's susceptible to chemical weedkillers, but more importantly it grows and flowers early in the spring, and all but vanishes by the start of summer and so has little impact on the growth of garden plants.

SEED PRODUCTION AND SURVIVAL OF SOME COMMON ANNUAL GARDEN WEEDS

Name	Average number of seeds produced per plant	Approximate longevity of seeds in the soil (years)
Aethusa cynapium (fool's parsley)	6000	10
Capsella bursa-pastoris (shepherd's purse)	4000	30
Cardamine hirsuta (hairy bittercress)	600	?
Chenopodium album (fat hen)	3000	30
Euphorbia peplus (petty spurge)	250	?
Fumaria officinalis (fumitory)	few	30
Galium aparine (cleavers)	few	?
Lapsana communis (nipplewort)	1000	?
Matricaria matricarioides (rayless mayweed)	7000	?
Papaver rhoeas (field poppy)	17000	80
Senecio vulgaris (groundsel)	1000	?
Solanum nigrum (black nightshade)	10000	40
Sonchus spp. (sow thistles)	18000	?
Stellaria media (chickweed)	2500	?
Urtica urens (annual nettle)	1000	?
Veronica spp. (annual speedwells)	2000	10

introduced weeds

There's a handful of plants that have achieved weed status through the simple expedient of gardeners' intentions going awry. I have stressed that weeds are wild plants that are inherently better competitors than introduced garden species because of their better ecological fitness for our environment, but there are exceptions and a few aliens clearly find our gardens ideally suitable. Quite commonly in plant catalogues, you will find descriptions of ornamentals that include the caveat 'can be invasive'. Take careful note. In the past, the lack of such a warning has unleashed some unsuspected weeds in our midst. Ground elder, or to give it its more appropriate name, bishop weed (*Aegopodium podagraria*), wouldn't be a problem in British gardens today had medieval bishops not suffered from gout. The plant was deliberately introduced here from elsewhere in Europe, almost certainly to early monastery herb gardens and almost certainly because of its use as a treatment for gout. The popular tiny-leaved but extraordinarily vigorous and tenacious little mind-your-own-business (*Soleirolia soleirolii*) might not have been introduced from the Mediterranean had its compulsive attraction to lawns, its ability to survive mowing and the fact that it's all but ineradicable been better known. And the southern European creeping bellflowers (*Campanula portenschlagiana* and *Campanula poscharskyana*) would probably not continue to be planted in rock gardens if more gardeners knew just how rapidly they will subjugate their companions.

15 The spread of plant problems

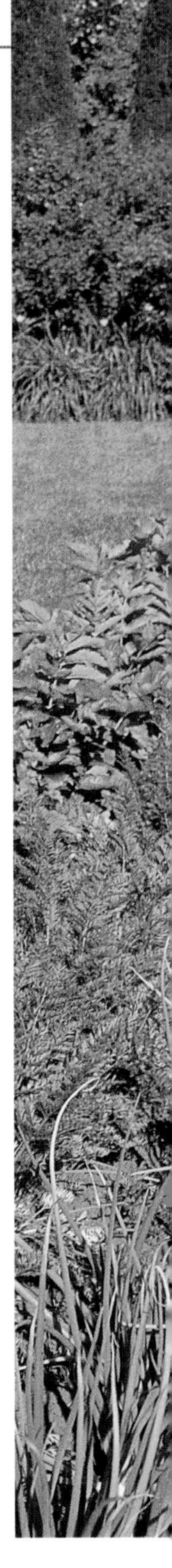

I've no doubt that most gardeners find the greatest mystery about pests and diseases relates to their sudden and unannounced appearance. You wake up one morning to find that plants which a few days earlier were in the pristine flush of health are now white with mildew, black with aphids or, worse still, bereft of much of their foliage. Some of this observation can be explained by the rapid reproduction rates of pests (see page 74): a single aphid is easily overlooked but once it produces offspring, their presence becomes apparent; and no fungal spores are ever visible to the naked eye, but their germination and growth into hyphae and mycelia soon renders the pathogen very obvious. It's also possible for pests and diseases to survive the winter hidden in and around the garden protected from the elements to emerge and cause problems in spring.

This does not explain everything about the origin of pests and diseases. What is the source of problems that have never previously been seen in your garden and what is the source of problems that have never before been seen in the country?

"The arrival of 'new' pests and diseases in the garden or in the country is by one of two methods: actively, by deliberate directed movement, or passively, by being carried."

active movement

Active movement is clearly limited to pests that can fly or can walk considerable distances. Birds are an obvious example (although wandering rabbits and deer can be fairly destructive, too). It's unlikely that any bird lives permanently in a single garden. They move freely and regularly from one to another, and if they happen to be a pest species, they will cause problems wherever they go. Of course, some birds do not even live permanently in any one country, although those pest species that aren't residents in Britain tend to be winter rather than summer visitors. For example, the winter fruits from holly bushes and pyracanthas are stripped by the blackbirds and song thrushes, which are year-round residents, along with the fieldfares and redwings, which have arrived only a few weeks previously from northern Europe.

insects

Insect migration is much less widely known about than bird migration and although Britain does not experience the biblical plagues of locusts, we do have important garden pests that arrive by deliberate migration. To be fair, the long-distance movement of any insect is always aided to some degree by the wind and so inevitably has a passive element. Garden insect pests that travel from outside the country can be divided into two main groups: those that never survive the winter in Britain and so are only here through migration; and those that do survive the British winter but which are supplemented in the following year by migratory insects. There's a third sub-group: those that normally do not breed in Britain but which migrate here occasionally, and may cause serious problems when they do.

Row cropping of garden vegetables

butterflies

Understandably, most studies of migration have been made on large insects, and the information available about butterflies and moths greatly exceeds anything else. Among pest species that never or hardly ever survive here over winter is the silver Y moth (*Autographa gamma*). This moves north and west from the Mediterranean region in summer and its caterpillars can be important vegetable pests. Probably the outstanding single example of a pest species in which overwintering pupae are supplemented by migratory individuals is the large white butterfly (*Pieris brassicae*). This insect is unusual in that the main immigrant populations arrive late, towards the end of the summer, principally from southern Scandinavia. It has been suggested that, without this supplemental immigration, this common and important pest species might not survive in Britain because parasitism by Braconid wasps of the caterpillars of the resident population is so high.

aphids and beetles

Aphids migrate over considerable distances and populations are supplemented by an influx each year. However, all aphids are weak fliers and their transport over long distances is very largely dependent on them being carried aloft in thermals.

Many beetles are also fairly weak fliers and this must explain the normal absence from Britain of such pests as the North American Colorado beetle (*Leptinotarsa decemlineata*), which is well established as a potato pest in France. Although strict

"The movement of pathogens is entirely passive, therefore, and they are dependent both on the physical elements of wind and water and the deliberate or accidental cooperation of other living things."

vigilance combined with legislation largely ensures that any beetles found here are swiftly eliminated, the fact remains that only a very few Colorado beetles are recorded in Britain each year and almost all of them have clearly been carried here through human intervention.

Some beetle species, nonetheless, do migrate and although I am not aware of any important garden pests among them, many species of ladybird, which are extremely important as aphid predators, certainly migrate in very large numbers both within Britain and from the continent. (It seems that ladybirds are very gregarious insects in general for they also take part in mass hibernations.) There's another aphid predator that also migrates in large numbers: influxes of hoverflies or syrphids are recorded from time to time on the south and east coasts of Britain, sometimes, intriguingly, in company with migrating ladybirds.

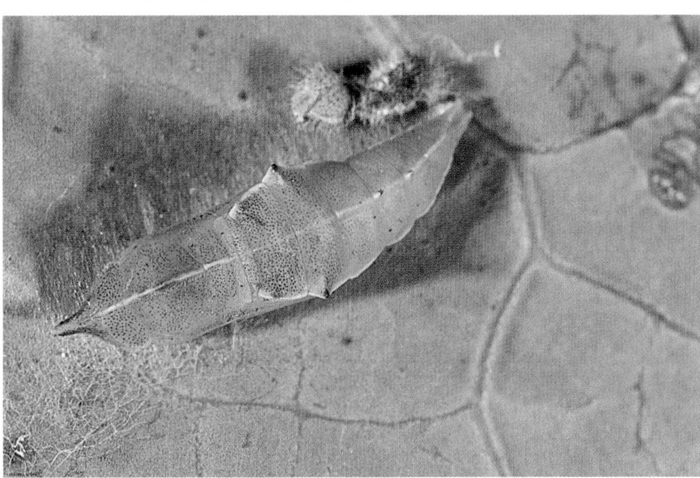

Pupa (chrysalis) of green-veined white butterfly, *Pieris napi*

Sawflies can be very important pests of some garden plants, their larvae showing a remarkable resemblance to caterpillars. The best known, the gooseberry sawfly (*Nematus ribesii*), causes havoc on gooseberries and currants. This isn't a migratory species, but its relative, the turnip sawfly (*Athalia rosae*), certainly is and it comes into my category of creatures that occasionally reach pest status solely through immigration. It's normally a rare insect in Britain but at intervals, over a period of several hundred years, huge influxes have been recorded, these invasions being followed by serious damage to crops.

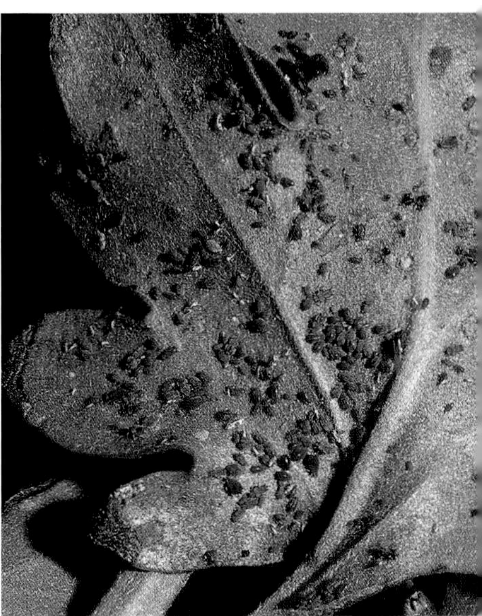

pathogens

Unlike pests, pathogens are unable to move to any significant extent. Certainly, some bacteria have motile spores and some fungi have free-swimming zoospores, but the distance they can travel of their own volition is measured in micrometres. Wind is the principal means by which fungal spores, of pathogen and non-pathogen alike, are carried from one place to another. The mildew spores that blow in from your neighbour's diseased Michaelmas daisies offer an example of the localized spread which is so important for individual gardeners. On a larger, wider scale, huge clouds of spores of pathogens such as rust fungi are borne aloft by thermals from diseased cereal crops and carried intercontinentally. Indeed, the air always contains large numbers of fungal spores,

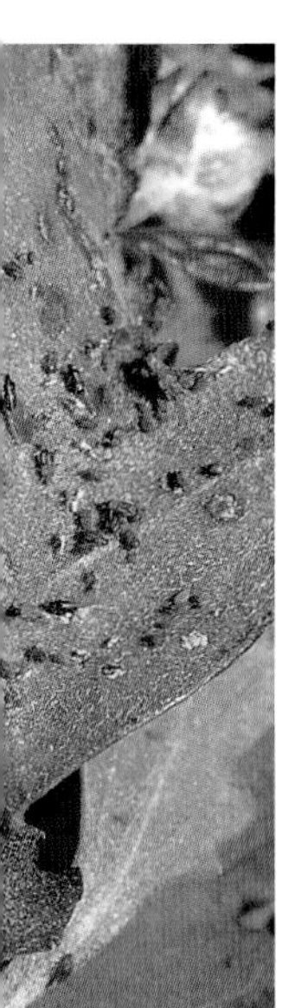

White rust (*Puccinia horiana*) and aphids (*Aphis gossypii*) on a chrysanthemum leaf

and their study has spawned the science of aerobiology. Aerobiologists use traps to sample the air. They work by drawing air at a predetermined rate over sticky glass slides which trap the spores and other particles. By positioning traps at different heights (even attaching them to aircraft) and then examining these slides microscopically, much fascinating information has accrued on the seasonal, diurnal and spatial changes in the invisible spore population of the air. Comparable studies monitor pollen to produce information for hay fever sufferers. Spore sampling can similarly be of predictive value (see page 124).

It may seem rather surprising that more diseases aren't spread long distances by the wind but a major limiting factor for many fungal spores is that they are very prone to be killed by desiccation or by ultraviolet radiation. While they can remain viable for long enough to be blown around within a garden or a neighbourhood, therefore, they remain localized and do not become national problems. Much as the Colorado beetle has not crossed the English Channel, so a number of airborne diseases, such as crocus rust (*Uromyces croci*), remain common in parts of the European continent but are absent from Britain.

passive movement

When we consider the passive spread of both pests and pathogens, a whole range of possibilities for widespread movement opens up. Surpassing all other natural pathogen-carrier relationships in global significance is that between viruses and their insect or other animal vectors (see page 68), but some fungi and bacteria are also carried by insects, although not perhaps as many as might be thought. Undoubtedly the most important in Britain is Dutch elm disease, with the spores of the cusual fungi *Ceratocystis ulmi* and *Ceratocystis novo-ulmi* being routinely carried by bark beetles (*Scolytus* spp.), see page 60.

Another important tree problem that is spread by insects is the bacterial disease fireblight (*Erwinia amylovora*), which was quite unknown in Britain until 1957. First found in Kent, it has spread widely and is now common in gardens throughout Britain. It isn't entirely clear if insects (which include bees) feed on the bacterial slime or pick it up accidentally when they are attracted to the blossoms.

Other diseases commonly spread by insects are the bacterial problem of willows called watermark disease (*Erwinia salicis*) and also rhododendron and azalea gall (*Exobasidium vaccinii*).

birds

Birds are responsible for transporting a few diseases and one of the most important is sweet chestnut canker (*Cryphonectria parasitica*), a very serious problem that is spread within the European continent by starlings. It does not occur in Britain and it isn't clear just why it has not been carried across the Channel by these migratory birds.

Birds are important, too, in the transport of the semi-parasitic plants known

Seven-spot ladybird, *Coccinella 7-punctata*

Gooseberry sawfly, *Nematus ribesii*

"The thoughtless or inadvertent carrying of pest- or disease-affected plants by people is also now hugely important."

popularly as mistletoes. One species (*Viscum album*) occurs in Britain and is common on apples and poplars; other strains, probably of the same species, affect conifers in Europe, where another mistletoe, *Loranthus europaeus*, can be a serious problem on oaks. It's easy to understand why birds have not carried these European mistletoes to Britain as the seeds aren't transported internally (from eating the fruits): instead the sticky fruits are lodged in the bark of trees by the birds so that they can eat them. They are unlikely to wait until they have crossed the Channel before finishing their meal!

the role of people

There's worldwide movement of plant produce, both as foodstuffs and as planting material, and all of it has the potential to carry problems from one area to another. With many food plants, transport takes place from tropical or warm-climate regions to cooler ones where the problems are unable to survive. When crops are being moved between areas with comparable climatic conditions, however, the threat is much more real and certainly the transport of planting material, which may still have soil attached to the roots, is potentially very serious.

It's for all these reasons that governments all over the world have enacted legislation to regulate the conditions under which plants can be transported.

The localized spread of diseased or pest-affected plants into gardens occurs extremely commonly through gardeners buying infected material. It isn't entirely fair to blame suppliers for this as many problems can scarcely be recognized at an early stage. It was largely for this reason that some old legislation called the Sale of Diseased Plant Orders was all but impossible to enforce: the theory was that anyone selling plants affected with certain problems committed an offence, but with young plants, no one could ever prove the presence of the problems.

weeds

It's fairly evident that those weeds with prolific seed production are more likely to spread further and faster than those that rely on vegetative methods. However, the ability of rhizomes to disperse plants locally should not be underestimated: that most notorious of all garden weeds, the Japanese knotweed (*Reynoutria japonica*), has been shown to travel beneath a four-lane road solely by means of rhizome growth.

Some seeds have a violent discharge mechanism designed to throw them a considerable distance from the parent plant. Hairy bittercress (*Cardamine hirsuta*) is a very familiar and important garden example. Nonetheless, to travel really significant distances, weeds depend mainly on airborne seeds or fruit or the use of carriers or vectors. Many garden weeds

Mistletoe, *Viscum album*, on black poplar

have lightweight seeds or fruits that are easily blown by the wind. Pearlwort (*Saginaprocumbens*), a common and rather pretty little weed of paving slab crevices and similar places, has minute seeds. As each weighs only 0.000012g, they are little more than dust particles and are very readily blown away. More obvious adaptations to wind dispersal come with weeds such as rosebay willowherb (*Epilobium angustifolium*), dandelion (*Taraxacum officinale*) and sow thistles (*Sonchus* spp.), which have feathery or parachute-like appendages on the seeds or fruits.

The purchase of plants in containers of compost that is contaminated with weed seeds is one of the commonest sources of 'new' weeds. Hairy bittercress is now a very widespread and important weed problem due to this method of dispersal: the fact that so many containers of compost become contaminated in nurseries and garden centres must be due to the explosive seed discharge mentioned above. However, in my opinion most of the initial unexpected arrivals of weeds in gardens originate with seeds that have been dropped by birds. A very wide range of weed seeds has been shown experimentally to pass unharmed through birds' digestive tracts. On average, food material is present inside a bird for between half an hour and three hours before being discharged – a bird can travel a considerable distance in that time. In some instances, it has been proved that the germination of weed seeds is even enhanced after their exposure to an avian digestive tract.

16 Prediction of plant problems

Symptoms of dahlia mosaic virus

Prediction means having the ability to foretell if a certain event will take place. In science it's a more or less precise judgement, and like all scientific judgements, it must be based on evidence: the better the quality of the evidence, the more accurate is the prediction. So, to continue the analogy with the weather, the more recording stations and the wider the area over which existing patterns can be seen, the more precise the forecast.

There are several categories of evidence that can be used to predict the likely occurrence of plant problems. All have their basis in a knowledge of pest, pathogen or weed biology, and some are rather more obvious than others.

plant and problem

For the problem to occur, there must be plants in your garden that are prone to it. This might seem self-evident but it does underline the fact that many problems are host-plant specific: if you don't grow dahlias, for instance, you can predict with total certainty that dahlia mosaic virus won't arise in your garden. Nonetheless, predictions aren't always so straightforward and knowledge of pathogen or pest biology is important. Just because you don't grow potatoes, you cannot predict that potato blight won't occur. If you do grow tomatoes, which are also prone to this disease, there's a fair degree of certainty that, other things being equal, potato blight will strike.

The relevant parts of the plant must be present: you can predict that problems which affect stems and leaves will be unlikely to appear if your plant is leafless and stemless. This might appear a ludicrous notion but it underlines much gardening practice. By cutting down the foliage on mildew-prone herbaceous perennials, such as doronicums, after they have flowered, there's nothing on which mildew spores can gain a foothold and the prediction of freedom from disease is a valid one. By the time that new foliage has arisen later in the summer, the peak of mildew spore production has passed. A comparable situation exists with many food plants which are harvested at certain stages of their life. One can predict with certainty that a pest or disease that attacks the flower heads of carrots, for example, will never occur in gardens because carrots are dug and used long before their flowers are formed.

problem and proximity

The problem must already exist close enough to your garden. This is critical. I have already said that no plant problem materializes *de novo*. Fungal spores, bacterial cells, insects and mites all come from somewhere. Knowledge of the proximity of the problem source, the quantity in which it occurs, its biological efficiency (how fast or how much it eats, how swiftly it grows), together with an idea of the nature and efficiency of its transport systems give another basis for prediction. For instance, a rabbit in an allotment at the other end of the street can be predicted to be more likely to turn up in your own garden and so pose a bigger threat to your lettuces than do caterpillars in a neighbouring plot. There's only one rabbit and

"Plant problems are like the weather: if you know what's coming, it never seems as bad because you have had a chance to prepare yourself. What prospect then for the plant pathological equivalent of the umbrella, the woollen gloves or the sun cream?"

it's more distant than the caterpillars, but it's larger in size and moves much further and much faster than they do.

Proximity of the problem is important not only in relation to space but also in relation to time. If it occurred in your garden or nearby last year or the year before, this increases the likelihood of there being viable organisms present now. There are numerous examples of this, some of which have already been mentioned in other contexts: for instance, the survival of weed seeds in the soil (see page 117). In the first year after seeding, there will be a large number of seeds present and so we can predict that the likelihood of the problem recurring is very high. Assuming no more seeds are added to the soil, however, the population will gradually decline, so that by the seventh, eighth and ninth years, we can fairly reasonably predict that there will be very few weeds emerging.

proximity and conditions

Knowledge of environmental conditions affecting biology can also be very important. The sooty bark disease of sycamore (*Cryptostroma corticale*) and the smut disease of sweet corn (*Ustilago maydis*) provide dramatic examples. Spores of both may persist in the soil for many years, and may even be present in the soil of your own garden, so satisfying the criteria of proximity of viable material in space and time. However, armed with the knowledge that they require very high temperatures to germinate, we can predict with a great degree of certainty that the problems won't recur unless we experience a very hot summer.

Potato blight, *Phytophthora infestans*, on tomato

time and quantity

Having a particular pest or disease in your garden, and growing a very susceptible host doesn't necessarily mean that the likelihood of damage is high: they must coincide in time. Take the example of the pea moth (see page 75): by adjusting the sowing time of the crop so that there are few plants in flower during the period when the female moth is laying eggs can significantly reduce the problem.

"It's obvious that, although it can be a highly exact science, the prediction of plant problems can also be a pretty complex one."

Coincidence in time must also mean coincidence of sufficient quantity of the pest. In gardens where subterranean keeled slugs are a problem on potatoes, for example, it might be thought that one could predict significant damage every year. Damage doesn't occur, however, if only early crops are grown; these escape, not because there are no slugs, but simply because, in the early part of the season, they haven't built up to sufficient levels to cause much harm.

Symptoms of attack by caterpillars of pea moth, *Cydia nigricana*

predicting success

Given the economic pressures on the growers of commercial crops, it isn't surprising that real, quantifiable success in devising predictive systems has come about in areas of relatively high-value crops. The first breakthrough came with downy mildew of grapevines (*Plasmopara viticola*) and related diseases, but the textbook example for British growers has been the system used to predict the likelihood of outbreaks of potato blight caused by *Phytophthora infestans*. It takes no account of the presence of the pathogen in the previous season or geographical locality, but assumes that in commercial potato growing areas, there will always be sufficient fungal spores present everywhere. The system depends on knowing precisely the conditions required for the spores to germinate and so initiate the disease. The formula is based entirely on meteorological information and, in its best-known form, it's expressed as a Beaumont period (after its originator). This is a period of 48 hours during which the minimum temperature is 10°C (50°F) and the relative humidity doesn't fall below 75 per cent. Gardeners who listen to the farming news on the radio will often hear warnings broadcast in early summer when a Beaumont period has occurred.

A different relationship between weather conditions and pathogen behaviour is exemplified by one of the earliest attempts at disease forecasting, a procedure originating in the United States to predict the likelihood of apple scab disease (*Venturia inaequalis*). Here, the critical phase of the life cycle isn't the germination of spores but their release from the dead leaves on which they have survived the winter. By knowing precisely the conditions under which this release occurs, some prediction can be made of the likelihood of disease occurring.

Comparable types of prediction systems have been developed from knowledge of the weather conditions during which aphids are most likely to fly and thus to estimate the likelihood of the appearance of the virus diseases that the aphids carry.

control

The potato blight prediction system, for instance, would have been no help to the unfortunate Irish population in the last century. Their potatoes would still have succumbed and there would still have been famine. It only works today because we have protective fungicides that can be applied to the potato foliage to prevent infection from taking place.

Gardeners may not want or need (or even have access to) the sophisticated data and warning arrangements that commercial growers employ and require (although listening to potato blight warnings on the radio can certainly be useful). However, knowing the principles behind pest and disease prediction will help an understanding of the principles of avoidance. Knowing that there's a need for a pathogen or pest to be present locally and understanding why it occurred the previous year should, if nothing else, encourage garden hygiene: clearing away diseased or damaged plants at the end of one season will help to increase the validity of predicting that the problem won't occur in your garden in the following year.

"All the pest and disease prediction in the world is of very little value without an additional and hugely important factor: there must be a control method that can capitalize on the information supplied."

top: Grapevine downy mildew, *Plasmopara viticola*

above: Potato blight foliage symptoms caused by *Phytophthora infestans*

17 Control: physical and cultural

"Pest, disease and weed control isn't something separate and distinct from the rest of horticulture: part of the definition of good gardening is that all plants are grown as well as possible, and working to keep them free from problems is, of course, an essential factor in this."

routine cultivation

Before considering problem avoidance practices, it's worth remembering the relative importance of routine gardening in keeping problems at bay. I like to think that knowing the benefits of each and every gardening operation helps you do it a bit more thoroughly. The laborious hours of winter digging might gain a little interest and seem a little more worthwhile when you appreciate the part you are playing in reducing at least some of next summer's tasks.

pans and caps

A heavy weight on the soil, be it pounding rain or gardeners' feet, will compress the soil crumbs, especially at the surface, and lead to loss of some of the pore space and air content. Plant roots will be denied the air they need, and the lack of air space will impede the through-flow of water (and any nutrients dissolved in it). It will also limit the growth of the air-requiring (aerobic) bacteria and fungi that are responsible for the degradation of organic matter. In severe cases, it might encourage the growth of anaerobic micro-organisms, which bring about a different degradation of organic matter that results in the formation of an amorphous dark material and the production of such gases as hydrogen sulphide, hydrogen and methane. Denitrification is faster when the oxygen supply is impaired and the result is an accumulation of chemicals that may not only be useless as nutrients but may be toxic or otherwise detrimental to plant growth. The inability of water to drain freely through a soil will inevitably lead to its accumulation at the surface. This will further restrict the penetration of air, further aid the disintegration of the soil crumbs and so result in a more permanent blocking of the pore spaces, called capping, in the process. This is especially serious on soils with a high content of clay minerals, which can pack impenetrably together.

As the physical weight at the surface continues, its effect spreads downwards and soil structure is impaired at ever increasing depth. Nonetheless, even a soil with a very high clay content that is trampled by a small army of allotment holders is unlikely to be converted into a totally brick-like mass for several centimetres at the surface. However, the breakdown of structure can arise at some depth, so that, for example, there's a compacted layer twenty centimetres or more below the surface, even when the intervening space may be fairly unaffected. This is called a pan or a hard pan. It restricts further downward water movement, even if the water has drained fairly freely initially. Pan formation can arise naturally in regions of very high rainfall, when soluble minerals fall

Carefully trained and pruned apple trees

with the rain, or when small, insoluble mineral particles gradually accumulate. But pans can also arise as a result of soil regularly being dug to the same depth. This particularly occurs when a mechanical cultivator with L-shaped, or similar, tines has been used repeatedly. The result is a smearing of the soil and gradual development of the impervious layer.

As the soil structure deteriorates in any of these ways, so the subterranean environment becomes less favourable to earthworms and other forms of soil animal and, ultimately, there will be a rather sharp decline in the performance of the plants growing there. This can arise, directly or indirectly, because the environment has become more conducive to pathogens and possibly some pests.

digging and forking

Digging (with a spade) or forking (with a fork) breaks up the impervious crust or cap at the soil surface and, if done deeper and more laboriously, any hidden pan also. It's a vital part of maintaining plant health and is also crucial for weed control. Annual weeds are buried by annual digging: simply turning them under as the soil is dug will be enough to kill them and should also, in most cases, ensure that weed seeds are killed too. Although many types of seed will survive for fairly long periods in the soil, they will generally only do so relatively close to the surface where the soil is well aerated. Deeper burial will asphyxiate them.

Forking, with either a large border fork or a short-handled weeding fork, will

The rotary cultivator, a much misunderstood garden tool

remove annual or shallow-rooted perennial weeds relatively easily. Deeper-rooted weeds, especially in a heavy soil, will be almost impossible to remove by this method, however, and digging with a spade will compound the problem by severing the roots and rhizomes of persistent perennial weeds, effectively taking cuttings from them. By a similar token, a rotary cultivator, which seems such an attractive option for digging large areas, will shred underground rhizomes and may make matters far, far worse. And, remember, it can also help create a pan below the surface.

trenching and ridging

Trenching (the digging of a trench into which organic matter is placed) is done either as part of the periodic process of cultivating an area in the operation called double-digging, or for the preparation of a planting position for plants like runner beans or sweet peas that require a moisture-retentive soil and a deep root run. Just as with preparing a planting position for a tree or shrub, there's a risk here. In a very heavy soil or a very light one, especially in cold places, such an organically enriched spot may act as a sump and attract excess moisture. The consequence can be that root-rotting organisms will thrive, root growth will be poor and thus the plants suffer seriously.

There's another problem related to the use of trenches, particularly with plants such as celery. These are planted in the base of a trench and soil is gradually filled in around them as they mature, the objective being to make the stalks blanched and tender. To keep the stalks clean and free from soil, 'collars' are placed around the plants. Unfortunately, they provide ideal places for slugs to congregate beneath and these will damage the stalks. I prefer my

Leek plants protected by collars to induce blanching

celery dirty but slug-free.

Much of the damage associated with very heavy, poorly drained soils can be obviated if plants (especially root vegetables) are grown on the reverse of a trench: a ridge. Planting in the better drained conditions on an elevated ridge can make the difference between success and abject failure in many gardens.

hoeing

The hoe is one of the most misunderstood of garden tools. Despite various modern innovations, it still takes one of two basic forms: the dragging action of the pull, or draw, hoe and the slicing action of the Dutch-style push hoe. The draw hoe has incidental benefits in maintaining plant health. It will certainly cut through some weeds, and when it's used, as it is most frequently, to pull soil over the crowns of potato crops, it helps protect the young shoots from late frost damage and then, later in the season, helps ensure that the potato tubers aren't exposed to the light and so turn green.

The Dutch hoe is of much more direct benefit. It should be kept sharp and it's one of the tools for which stainless steel is much the preferred material. It's important only to hoe on dry days when the severed weeds will shrivel and die quickly: hoeing on wet days is little better than transplanting. Remember, too, that some annual weeds, most notably groundsel (*Senecio vulgaris*), will continue to mature their seedheads even when the stems have been severed. They should be raked up and composted.

A Dutch hoe is also commonly used during the summer to loosen the soil surface and break up slight capping, and in dry weather, this exposure of darker, moister soil improves the appearance of beds and borders. Two contrasting beliefs have grown up around this practice. One is that the exposure of moist soil enhances water loss; the other is that maintaining a loose, friable soil surface retards water loss: both can be true, depending on the circumstances. There will be some water loss from the small amount of moist soil brought to the surface. Normally this is of no consequence, but in drought conditions, when as much moisture as possible must be conserved, hoeing should be avoided as it may encouraging wilting. A dry soil surface layer will act as a mulch and lessens water loss from below even if it isn't hoed.

While hoeing is an invaluable technique, it must always be undertaken carefully as damage can easily be done to shallowly rooted plants and, in the vegetable garden, onions in particular should never be hoed as they respond unfavourably to the disturbance.

"In my garden, the Dutch hoe is the most important means of controlling annual weeds."

A modern version of the traditional push-hoe

raking

Although the main part that raking has to play in preventing problems occurs on the lawn, the use of a rake to prepare a fine tilth for seed sowing will help ensure uniform and healthy emergence of young seedlings.

mulching

Mulching is another of gardening's misunderstood and undervalued arts. A mulch is simply a layer of material placed over the surface of the soil. In its traditional form, it is some form of organic material: a compost or manure. In modern gardening, it could also be of plastic sheet, either of familiar polyethylene style or of a type degraded in time by micro-organisms or ultraviolet radiation.

In terms of minimizing plant problems, the moisture-retaining attributes of a mulch are important. Laying a mulch over a moist soil early in the season lessens the problems caused by drying out later. But only mulch a moist soil: laying mulch on a dry soil will keep it dry. A mulch will also minimize the penetration of frost into the soil, so frost damage will also be reduced. Indeed, a thick mulch placed around the crown of a marginally hardy plant in autumn may be the sole reason it survives the winter.

"Mulching has a number of almost equal virtues: frankly I couldn't garden satisfactorily without it."

For combating problems, the value of a mulch in weed control surpasses all its other virtues. A layer of mulch over the soil surface uses the best of ecological principles in that it starves weed seedlings of air and light. A layer of organic matter at least 5cm (2in) thick will control most annual weeds. It should go without saying that if the mulch is of compost, then the compost itself must be well-made and weed-free (see page 142). A mulch of this type will be equally effective in killing seedlings of annual or perennial weeds; however, it should be borne in mind that most of the invasiveness of perennial weeds isn't vested in their seeds but in underground rhizomes, tubers or other organs (see pages 115–117) and these will have plenty of reserves of energy to enable them to emerge through even the thickest of mulches. I have traced a tiny tuber of the lesser celandine (*Ranunculus ficaria*) from its shoot, which had grown a vertical distance of 45cm (18in) to the soil surface.

The choice between an organic and a plastic mulch is usually made on the basis of three criteria: availability, cost and appearance. Few gardeners are likely to be able to afford or obtain sufficient organic matter to enable them to use this routinely as a mulch in the vegetable plot as well as in more permanent plantings. On the other hand, a plastic mulch is scarcely an aesthetically endearing embellishment to shrubberies and herbaceous borders, although it's certainly useful in the kitchen garden. In addition (although I have no personal verification of it), it's often claimed that a plastic mulch laid over an area for at least twelve and preferably eighteen months may even effect eradication of such persistent weeds as horsetail (*Equisetum arvense*). While there's little, if any, difference in either the soil-warming properties or the moisture retentiveness of clear, white or black plastic sheeting, it should be remembered that weed seedlings can grow and even flower and seed under a translucent clear plastic sheet, something that is completely impossible under a black one.

rotation

Although it isn't always recognized as such, the vegetable garden procedure known as rotation is an essential part of soil management. And it has an often overstated and misunderstood role in combating plant problems. Crop rotation is simple enough in practice. The principle is that no crop is grown on an area of soil where it, or a very similar crop, was grown the previous year. The most common rotation is the three-course: the plot is divided into three equal plots and the crops on each plot are changed year by year so that three years elapse before the same crop is grown again on a particular spot. The crops to occupy each of the three areas are chosen because they have some significant aspect of their cultivation in common and tend to be grouped into root crops, peas and beans, and brassicas and related plants.

Rotation has practical constraints because some crops take up a disproportionately large area of land, some are semi-permanent or aren't changed every year, and, of course, the system presupposes that you want more or less equal amounts of the crops in the three categories. The advantages are supposed to outweigh the disadvantages, however: rotation is claimed to ensure that the whole spectrum of soil nutrients is used by the different plants (so nutrient deficiencies don't arise), that the soil is fully and uniformly cultivated because of the differing cultivation methods for each crop and that pests and diseases have the chance to die away in the soil.

I'm not convinced about the nutritional argument. As already stated (see pages 102–105), minor nutrients are rarely deficient in British soils, whatever you do to them, and major nutrients always need annual replenishing. The cultivation argument has something to commend it, especially with a crop like potatoes which does require deep and regular movement of the soil. Finally, the pest and disease argument is largely specious. It depends on two principles: first, that many pests and pathogens are fairly specific to individual types of host plant and cannot survive on other types of plant, and second that the period over which such organisms can survive in the soil in the absence of the correct host is very limited. There are common and important exceptions to the first category – for example, the grey mould fungus (*Botrytis cinerea*) and the peach-potato aphid (*Myzus persicae*) both affect a very wide range of plants – but in general the reasoning is fairly sound. The second principle also has some exceptions as there are some organisms that can survive for very many years in the soil – resting spores of the clubroot-causing fungus (*Plasmodiophora brassicae*) lives for over twenty years and sclerotia of the onion white rot fungus (*Sclerotium cepivorum*) probably live for thirty – but, in general, this too is a reasonable notion. Even the spores of the fungus that causes potato blight (*Phytophthora infestans*), which are often believed to 'contaminate' the soil, survive for less than a year.

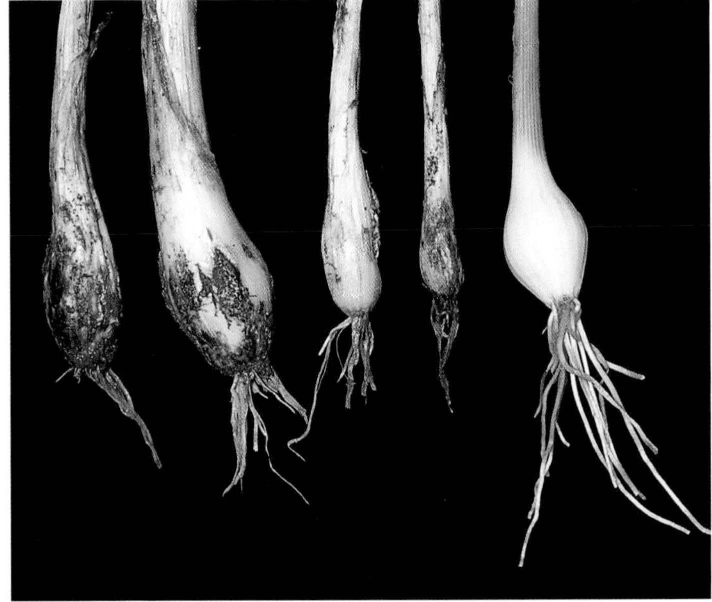

Symptoms of onion white rot caused by *Sclerotium cepivorum*

Unfortunately, much of the theory of crop rotation was established in commercial horticulture and farming, where the distances between the site in which a crop is grown in one year and that to which it is moved the next may be considerable. In a garden or allotment, the distance is likely to be a few metres at the most and the conventional three-course garden crop rotation takes no account of the fact that many pests can fly or that soil contaminated with pathogens will be moved on spades, wheelbarrows and gardeners' boots. In gardens I believe the only real pest and disease benefits from crop rotation are with potato cyst eelworm control.

rogueing

Most perennials are obtained as plants, rather than raised at home from seed, and the way that the plant is chosen and then introduced into the garden can go a long way towards ensuring it's problem-free thereafter. The technique known in commercial practice as rogueing is one that gardeners should take to their hearts. Rogueing is the removal of rogues: plants that are defective, pest-ridden or diseased. It's perhaps done most easily when buying bulbs, corms and similar material, especially where these are being bought loose. Check for and reject any that have spots or blemishes. Remember than even an insignificant blemish may be the early stages of a decay. Select only perfect individuals; even undersized specimens will probably be weak and are either unlikely to flower or more likely to succumb to pests or diseases. It's harder to examine packeted bulbs and impossible to check those bought by mail order. The maxim, therefore, should be to buy only from reputable suppliers and to return any that prove on delivery to be defective. Good suppliers will be happy to exchange them.

The inability to examine material bought by mail order also, of course, applies to plants. Small plants may be mailed in small and ingenious containers (this is an increasingly popular and successful way to market young bedding plants for example); large stock is generally sent bare-rooted in straw and hessian wrapping in the dormant season. In every case, examine the specimens carefully on their arrival.

Plants obtained, as most are, in containers from garden centres and nurseries should also be checked closely at the time of purchase. Any showing gross signs of neglect should be rejected. For example, if the roots are uncovered because the soil has been washed from the top of the pot don't buy the plant: I still see far too many roses that appear to be growing on stilts because of this. And ascertain if plants in containers have been container-grown (raised in the container from the beginning) or containerized (awful word, but meaning that they have been lifted from a field or nursery bed and placed in the container for sale). The latter may easily have experienced root damage in the process.

Small amounts of weed, moss or liverwort growth on the surface of containers should not, in itself, be a reason for rejection. It's impossible in commercial practice to keep containers free from this sort of contamination and only if it's truly extensive and the plant is showing yellowed leaves or other stress symptoms should it be a reason not to purchase. Nonetheless, it makes sense to scrape away the top few centimetres of potting compost when new container stock is being planted in your garden to avoid introducing any alien weed seeds into your own beds.

Tender greenhouse plants, which will be kept in the warm conditions in which many problems thrive, can very usefully be put in a 'quarantine' area for some time after purchase to allow any pests or diseases to become apparent and treated.

planting and aftercare

Planting should be undertaken with care. Prepare the planting position carefully and appropriately for the plant concerned. Be sure that the site for perennials is dug, manured and fertilized thoroughly; it won't be possible to repeat the task as well for many years.

Bulbous plants are perhaps planted less carefully than most, largely because there are so many to do at one time. I strongly advocate placing a small bed of sand beneath bulbs of all kinds, especially on heavier soils. This will improve drainage around the vulnerable base of the bulb and help to discourage the onset of decay. Be careful not to damage any roots attached to bulbs as this too may allow diseases and pests to enter. Make sure you adhere to the optimum planting depth for each type of bulb. Any planted too deeply will be weakened when their shoots grow to reach the surface and planting too shallowly (daffodils especially) is one of the commonest reasons for the development of the condition called blindness (see page 109). As a general guide, most bulbs should be planted with their base at a depth in the soil equal to between 2½ and 3 times their average diameter. There are exceptions: shallots and nerines, for instance, should be placed just below the surface.

When planting herbaceous perennials, shrubs and trees, spread the roots of bare-rooted specimens in the planting hole. Too often poor growth and consequent problems come from roots being allowed to spiral together and form a knot. Move the plants gently up and down as you refill the planting hole (which should be approximately twice the volume of the root extent). This will help to prevent the formation of any air pockets, which might accumulate water. With container-grown plants, I always tease out the roots at the periphery of the root ball without unduly disturbing the remainder as I find this encourages them to explore the surrounding soil rather than remain confined. Ensuring that the soil around the root system is laced with fertilizer will also encourage root growth outwards rather than inwards.

Always water in plants carefully after planting. I make it a practice to include soluble fertilizer at this stage as this helps them to overcome the inevitable transplanting shock. This is also a useful 'first-aid' procedure for damaged plants.

fertilizer

The importance of correct, appropriate and appropriately frequent feeding of plants in order to avoid specific nutrient deficiencies and to ensure that they are generally able to fend off other problems is discussed on pages 102–105. The way that fertilizer is applied can have a bearing on plant health. While it might seem that spraying fertilizer over plants or placing granules or powders as close as possible to them would ensure the most efficient uptake, this isn't necessarily so. Solid fertilizers applied before seed sowing or pricking out can, in fact, be damaging to young seedlings (they appear scorched), although this effect can be minimized by watering the seed bed thoroughly after the fertilizer has been spread. Nonetheless, it's sensible to apply about one-third of the recommended dose before sowing and water this in well. A further third can be applied after the young plants have emerged and the remainder when the plants are about a quarter grown. Dry, powdered fertilizer should never be allowed to remain in contact with plants of any type for long periods and powdered lawn fertilizer should always be watered in if rain hasn't fallen for about 24 hours after application.

High levels of both chlorides and nitrates can cause fairly general damage to young roots. This can be lessened by the technique of applying specific nitrogen and potassium fertilizers *between* the rows of plants so that the high initial salt concentrations formed as the raw fertilizers dissolve are as far as practicable from the young root systems.

watering

As with fertilizers, problems can occur with water, not only in relation to its presence or absence, but also to the way that it is applied. Many garden plants, especially seedlings, will suffer leaf scorching if they are watered in very hot sunny weather. Among houseplants, the leaves of saintpaulias (African violets) and their close relatives streptocarpus will turn brown and disfigured if cold water is splashed onto them. (In answer to the inevitable question of how they survive rain in the wild, the explanation lies in the temperature of the water: in their native East Africa, it is warm water, not cold, to which they are exposed.)

propagation

First and foremost, only propagate from plants that appear healthy. Selecting those free from obvious leaf spotting or pest infestation is a large part of the commonsense approach but it's important too to be aware of the debilitating effect that virus contamination can have.

Plants that are routinely propagated by vegetative means are especially prone to pass viruses from parent to offspring (see page 67). Never be tempted to propagate from your own potatoes or soft fruit but always buy stock that is certified virus-free. In part this is because virus contamination is almost certain to be present in mature plants grown in your garden and also because the symptoms may not be very obvious, being manifested essentially as a reduction in yield. With other types of vegetatively propagated plants, such as carnations, chrysanthemums, dahlias and orchids, it is safe enough to propagate from your own stock, provided there are no signs of viral symptoms like mosaics and mottling (see pages 66–69). Although rather fewer plant viruses are transmitted from parent to offspring in the seed, it makes sense not to save seed from stock that shows virus-like symptoms.

Lining out hardwood cuttings

"The techniques associated with propagation all have implications for plant health but, in large measure, commonsense is all that is required to avoid problems."

cuttings

Cuttings are potentially the trickiest method of propagation. The difficulties are all related to the fact that they lack roots through which water can be taken up, but are still able to lose moisture through their leaves (leafless hardwood cuttings of deciduous plants, taken during the winter-dormant period, are the only exception). Therefore, most cuttings need to be placed in a moist, if not saturated, atmosphere in order to eliminate water loss and this may create just the right conditions for potentially damaging mould growth, on both foliage and stems. Moulds are most likely to appear if the cuttings are being grown (or 'struck') in compost rather than relatively more sterile media such as sand, vermiculite, perlite or similar material. This is just one good reason for using one of these materials for the surface at least, even if there's compost beneath.

Use of a hormone-containing proprietary rooting powder will generally aid quicker rooting and thus mean that the time that the plant must be kept at very high humidity is limited. Rooting powders generally contain a fungicide addition (usually captan) to lessen the likelihood of stem-base rotting. As soon as there's an indication that new roots have formed, the ventilators in the propagator or other vessel should be opened. This will immediately create conditions less favourable for fungal growth.

layering

Layering, a simplified and fail-safe form of taking cuttings, relies on not severing the new plant from the old until it has formed roots of its own. In the interim, it can continue to utilize the parental root system, a saturated atmosphere isn't, therefore, required and, in respect of diseases and pests, the whole operation should be trouble-free.

division

Mature perennial plants are generally propagated by division, an operation that, if done routinely, offers not only multiplication but also rejuvenation. It's important, however, to ensure that only healthy (or at least healthy-looking) parts of the clump are replanted. A general rule is to reject the brown, older matter towards the centre and only replant the fresher looking parts from the periphery.

grafting

Grafting is an important method of vegetative propagation, one that few gardeners will be likely to undertake themselves but of which all gardeners make use. Grafting is one of horticulture's special arts and it offers several benefits to today's nurserymen.

First is the ability to propagate large quantities of plants from relatively little starting material (especially so when the scion takes the form not even of a length of stem but, as with roses, a mere single bud). Second is the opportunity to raise plants that have some special feature of function or appearance but which have an inadequate root system. Third is the chance, among apple trees in particular, to regulate the size of the mature plant simply by careful choice of a rootstock with specific growth-regulating abilities.

And finally, there's the opportunity in some instances to grow an otherwise desirable but pest- or disease-prone cultivar on a less desirable but resistant rootstock. Common examples used in recent times are the *Prunus* rootstock 'Pixy', which has some resistance to silver leaf disease (*Chondrostereum purpureum*), the myrobalan and F12/1 cherry rootstocks, which have some resistance to bacterial canker (*Pseudomonas syringe* pvs.), and the tomato rootstock 'K.N.V.F.', which has some resistance principally to wilt (*Verticillium* spp. and *Fusarium* spp.), and eelworms (*Meloidogyne* spp.).

Preparing a whip and tongue graft

Onion neck rot caused by *Botrytis allii* on stored onion

seeds

More garden plants are routinely propagated by seed than by any other method, and by far the majority are raised from seed that is purchased ready packeted. A very small proportion is raised from seed collected in people's own gardens.

Although most seeds, particularly bought ones, are free from contamination and problems, there are a few exceptions. Seeds are a desirable food source for many creatures, large and small, and also for many pathogenic fungi and bacteria. Additionally, some diseases that affect the emerged plant are carried on the seed; most important among these are those that affect the newly emerged seedling but a few diseases of mature plants are also carried through space and time on or, more rarely, in the seed. Viruses, too, can sometimes be seed transmitted.

Among plants commonly grown from packeted seed, onions are a notable exception to the general problem-free state. Onion seed rather frequently bears the spores of *Botrytis allii*, the cause of onion neck rot. The spores can also be carried on onion sets. This is a particularly interesting problem for it isn't manifested on the young seedling or even on the growing crop but only becomes apparent when onions are harvested and stored. For a long time it was thought that infection occurred at harvesting, and bending over the necks of mature onions was thought to be the means of admitting it. However, almost all neck rot incidence in home-grown and stored onions can be eliminated by the simple expedient of dusting the seed with a systemic fungicide, preferably carbendazim. Soaking onion sets for about 30

Seedlings in heated propagators

minutes in a spray-strength mixture of the same product is also a wise precaution. Seed of some other types of plant (peas especially) is sold already treated with insecticide or fungicide, although rather less now than formerly.

Just as with cuttings, seeds sown in a propagator will be in a moist, often relatively warm environment – excellent conditions for mould growth. There's a difference, however, in that, although fragile and delicate, at least seedlings have roots and are actively growing. Hence they have greater ability to resist or tolerate potential infection and it is much less important to use sand or other inert material on the surface of the growing medium and by far the majority of seeds in propagators are sown directly in compost.

There's one hugely important factor in sowing seeds: the compost used must always be fresh, regardless of whether it's soil-based or soil-less. Never re-use old material: not only will it have had its nutrients depleted, but it will also have had every opportunity to accumulate contaminating organisms. It's sometimes imagined that proprietary seedling composts are sterilized. They aren't. Given appropriate laboratory conditions, large numbers of species of both bacteria and fungi can be identified in any compost. The only component of any of these mixtures that has in any way been sterilized is the loam used in soil-based composts of the John Innes type. Peat certainly isn't sterile naturally and neither is it sterilized artificially. Indeed there have been a number of well-publicized occasions when peat-based composts have been shown to be the source of weed seeds and some plant diseases.

However, increased prevalence of problems shouldn't necessarily be taken as proof that the peat or compost is contaminated. Perhaps the two best-known instances of an increase in garden problems that coincided with the greater use of peat-based composts are vine weevil (*Otiorhynchus sulcatus*) and the weed, hairy bittercress (*Cardamine hirsuta*). The increase in vine weevil incidence seems simply to be due to the female weevils finding peat-based composts provide ideal conditions in which to lay their eggs. And, while hairy bittercress undoubtedly naturally occurs close to peat bogs, its abundant growth in plant containers is almost certainly due to only a few seeds being present initially but the resultant plants producing a substantial further crop.

Composts can be sterilized before use but this is really only practical for very special and critical use, such as sowing fern spores or very tiny seeds. Sterilization is most easily done in a domestic oven at 150°C (gas mark 2) for about one hour or in a microwave oven at full setting for about seven minutes. Longer treatments tend to damage the fertilizer components.

Notwithstanding possible compost problems, most difficulties with young seedlings originate from contaminated pots, seed trays or propagators, or from

SOWING SEED CORRECTLY

Pests and diseases aside, the most common reasons for the failure of seeds to germinate properly stem from them being sown incorrectly. Care should always be taken to ensure that each type of seed is sown to the correct depth, whether in compost under protection or outdoors in soil. Some seeds must be sown on the surface, usually because, like lobelia or *Begonia × semperflorens*, they are so small and have such tiny nutrient reserves that they have insufficient energy to provide the emerged seedling with the wherewithal to grow upwards, or, occasionally, as with primulas, because the germination process itself is inhibited by light.

"With few exceptions, it's very improbable that bought packeted seed will carry significant pest, disease or virus contamination. Most of the problems associated with raising plants from seed don't originate with the seeds, but with the conditions into which they are sown."

contaminated water. Pots and other containers should always be washed and scrubbed thoroughly after each batch of plants has been raised, and then when all soil has been washed off, rinsed again in a proprietary disinfectant before rinsing in clean water. I make it a practice never to use water from a rainbutt for watering young seedlings. Even though rainbutts should always be covered to provide some protection from seeds or spores blowing in, there will inevitably be some contamination from fungi and bacteria. And algae from waterbutts, while not directly pathogenic or otherwise harmful, very soon form a green scum over the surface of compost. They then prevent proper penetration of moisture and also use up some of the fertilizer content of the compost to the detriment of the seedlings.

pruning

"Every type of pruning has a bearing on the likelihood of diseases (and, to a lesser extent, pests) having an impact. Moreover, some types of pruning are performed almost entirely for their contribution to plant health."

Pruning embraces a wide range of operations, performed for a number of different purposes. All have in common the deliberate removal of parts of a plant. Those parts may range from dead flower heads through entire stems and branches to, ultimately, tree stumps.

There are several important and separate factors to consider in relation to pruning. If part of a plant has simply been damaged (a branch broken by a gale, bark scraped away by a lawnmower, a shrub trodden on), the damage itself won't spread. Problems arise, however, if the broken tissues are then invaded by disease-causing fungi as these may penetrate further into the plant and cause much more serious damage. Infection is much less likely to take place if the damaged area is 'cleaned up' promptly as this will help encourage the efficient operation of the tree's natural wound-healing processes. All branches must be cut off cleanly and broken branches cut back to the basal collar (see page 64). When pruning for any reason, always try to cut close to a bud or other growing point; don't leave a short length of stem or shoot to wither and attract infection.

It's important to recognize the difference between localized diseases and much more deep-seated or widespread problems. Most fungal cankers are classic examples of localized problems: there isn't much infection beyond what can be seen. (I should add that some bacterial cankers are rather different as bacteria may be present some distance from the canker lesion, sometimes causing different and quite distinct symptoms.) Therefore, if a branch bearing a fungal canker is cut away neatly, there should be no further spread along the same branch, and you will also limit the number of spores being produced to initiate new infections elsewhere. (This doesn't guarantee that no more cankers will occur because there may be spores in the air, blown from other trees nearby, but at least you will have made a significant difference.) By a similar token, superficial diseases like some leaf spots and mildew may be limited if the symptoms are noticed early in the season and the affected part snipped away. Later, control of mildew and especially of rusts is much harder because the diseases may become at least partly systemic (the fungus will be present, hidden in the tissues, some way from the obvious symptoms).

Understanding disease biology will help to indicate the value of pruning as a control. There's much more information on this elsewhere in the book, but one example will indicate the principle. Superficially, it might be thought that black-spot disease (*Diplocarpon rosae*) on roses is best controlled by collecting up the diseased leaves. In practice, this will have little impact because once the leaves have dropped, the black spot fungus survives on them for a short while only. During the winter, it persists instead on small, more or less invisible lesions on the shoots. Hard pruning in the spring to remove these diseased shoots is of much greater value, therefore.

There is a further consideration. A number of important diseases are caused by fungi that don't always attack living plants: they can exist both biotrophically and saprotrophically (see page 53). The fungus *Nectria cinnabarina*, which causes the familiar disease coral spot dieback, is a good example. It's equally capable of living on dead wood and is quite commonly seen on piles of old prunings and pea sticks left lying in the garden through the winter. Spores produced on these sticks are then blown to infect small dead twigs attached to living trees. On maples, for instance, normal winter wind and frost damage frequently causes the twig tips to die. Once established there, the coral spot fungus spreads downwards into the living tissues of the branch and can then cause serious dieback.

This situation carries two messages about pruning. First, don't leave old prunings in the garden; they could cause problems for you later. And second, look carefully at dead twigs and branches on trees and shrubs. If they are large, cut them off, if they are too small, numerous and twiggy to be removed wholesale, keep an eye open for any signs of coral spot or other fungal growth on them and remove any that are affected. By a similar token, the familiar operation of deadheading is performed in part to improve aesthetic appearance but also to eliminate other fungi that can gain a foothold on dead or moribund tissue and spread from there to more vigorous, healthy parts. The oft-mentioned grey mould fungus (*Botrytis cinerea*) is the best-known example.

At the other extreme from dead flowerheads are tree stumps. I am asked fairly commonly for suggestions of plants to grow over and disguise old stumps, the thought being that an attractive garden feature can thereby be created. Perhaps. But remember that professional foresters don't leave dead tree stumps in the ground. They are winched out or ground down, two drastic forms of pruning. Admittedly, this is done partly to clear the ground for planting the next crop of trees, but it's also performed in the knowledge that one of the most important of tree diseases commonly gains access to an otherwise uncontaminated site through the cut surfaces of stumps. That disease is honey fungus (or, more strictly, the honey fungi, for it's now known that more than one species of the basidiomycete genus *Armillaria* is implicated; not simply *Armillaria mellea* as once thought). Basidiospores of *Armillaria* land on the cut surface and germinate and the fungus then grows within the dead stump, establishing a powerful base from which further spread may take place through the soil. It's this stump colonization that has given rise to one of the few commercial uses of a biological control of a plant disease (see page 146), while the spread of honey fungus through the soil gives an opportunity for using physical barriers (see page 144).

weeding

Weeding is a most important gardening operation (see page 112, for how garden plants suffer from competition from weeds); weed control also complements other methods of problem regulation.

While many pests and pathogens find our garden produce more appealing than related wild species, this isn't to suggest that their natural food sources are ignored, even in gardens. Many organisms also feed on weeds, which may offer them the means of persistence through periods when the garden host plant is absent. The weeds are acting as *alternative* hosts, a situation not to be confused with their even more important role as *alternate* hosts for those organisms that necessarily require two quite different types of plant to complete their life cycle.

Among common examples of weeds acting as *alternative* hosts are species of spurge (*Euphorbia*), which very frequently harbour whitefly, wild species of *Allium*, which harbour leek rust, and willow herbs, which are attacked by *Fuchsia* rust. Other species of rust require weeds as *alternate* hosts – sedges (*Carex* species), for example, are the alternate hosts of gooseberry rust (*Puccinia caricina* var. *pringsheimiana*) – and among many pest examples are such plants as *Stachys* and *Lamium*, the summer hosts of the blackcurrant aphid (*Cryptomyzus galeopsidis*).

Soft fruit plants protected by fruit cage

composting

The making of garden compost falls into a unique category, different from all other routine gardening tasks. It employs organisms related to the garden 'miscreants': the bacteria and fungi that break down and recycle organic waste and the invertebrate creatures that aid them in this are only slightly removed taxonomically from pests and pathogens. Compost is an aid to the alleviation of problems (see page 132, mulch) and the composting process can be used to dispose of damaged plant material.

Conventional wisdom in conventional gardening books tells you that you should compost all organic waste except animal remains (because they will attract vermin), diseased plants (because the diseases will persist and spread) and some weeds (because they too will survive). I am unconventional in almost all these respects, however, because I compost all kitchen waste, almost all diseased plant material and almost all weeds. The justification lies in the fact that I know that the centre at least of my compost bins generates a temperature of 70°C (158°F), which is sufficient to kill most living things and bring about swift decomposition. The only exceptions I make (or would if I was unfortunate enough to have any) are brassicas infected with clubroot (*Plasmodiophora brassicae*), onions with white rot (*Sclerotium cepivorum*) and rhizomes of couch grass (*Agropyron repens*). The penalty for failure here – if they don't die and decompose – is too great to risk. In passing, I would add that the only plant material that routinely survives my 70°C (158°F) are tomato seeds: this isn't surprising as it's well documented that viable tomato seeds will survive the human digestive tract, and the consequences aren't important as they aren't weeds.

STORED PRODUCE

It's axiomatic of gardening that plant material is stored from one season to the next. Living plants are stored in dormant form as bulbs, corms, tubers, seeds and so on; edible produce is stored in its harvested form to prolong the period over which it can be used. Most storage options make use of any natural capability that the plant has developed to survive periods of inactivity – apples have relatively tough skins, for example, and bulbs develop papery, tough scales. Nonetheless, storage is a vulnerable time for any plant and it's important that conditions are created in which pests and diseases are least likely to capitalize on this inactivity.

Only store blemish-free, undamaged produce. The smallest lesion, the tiniest surface wound, will allow fungi and bacteria to gain access to the inner tissues and, while some will then only cause localized damage and decay, others, once established in one fruit or other product, thereby gain sufficient energy to penetrate adjoining, undamaged ones also. Simply pulling the stalk from an apple will cause sufficient damage to start the process.

Some dos and don'ts to ensure relatively few problems arise during storage:

• Don't store windfall apples or pears; they will inevitably be bruised, even if you cannot see any damage.

• Don't drop any fruit that is to be stored, either onto the ground or into the collecting basket; this too will bruise it.

• Don't pull the stalk from fruit that is to be stored; this will cause sufficient wounding for infection to occur.

• Don't store any produce that shows the merest hint of pest or disease attack.

• If vegetables have to be washed before storage, do this with the greatest care; ensure that they are well dried afterwards, but don't do this by exposing them to any form of heat, including the sun.

• Grade your crops for size: smaller fruit and vegetables commonly keep better and longer than larger ones.

• Remember that some vegetables (carrots, parsnips and swedes, for instance) may be better left where they are, to store in the ground, with straw or other covering as frost protection.

• If vegetables have to be trimmed or cut before storage (to remove leaves, for instance) always do this with a clean knife.

• Ensure that bulbs or corms lifted from the ground for storage are well dried by arranging them on slatted trays in a well-ventilated shed or outhouse. After drying, carefully rub away any dry soil and dead leaves and then reject any showing disease or pest blemishes.

• Always harvest produce when it's at, or just below the peak of maturity.

• If you intend to grow crops specifically for storing, always choose varieties listed in catalogues as suitable for this purpose. For example, some have very much thicker skins than others.

• Cool, dry, well-ventilated conditions are needed for storing all plant products. Ornamental bulbs and tubers (but not edible produce) can also be protected by dusting with a combined fungicide and insecticide dressing. Seeds are best stored in paper packets in a fridge, ideally within a screw-top glass jar with a small sachet of moisture-absorbing silica gel.

Ornamental flower bulbs protected by fungicide in storage

SPECIFIC CONTROL MEASURES

"Although very diverse in nature, techniques that are performed specifically to guard against or eliminate pests and diseases can be grouped into the two main categories: barriers and traps."

Barriers

The fruit cage is the most familiar of all barriers and in many gardens is essential if soft fruit is to be protected from birds. Similar cages can be used equally successfully to protect vegetables but must be lighter in weight and portable to fit in with the need for vegetables, unlike fruit crops, to be moved each year. A rigid frame is very desirable, and can be made of treated wood or, as with many commercial cages, of aluminium. For a rigid, solid structure, my preference is for a wooden frame with sides of small-mesh, galvanized wire netting and lightweight plastic net on top. Galvanized netting should never be used for the roof of a cage because zinc residues will be washed from the wire by rain and cause damage to plants (strawberries are especially prone). Most proprietary cages have plastic netting all round.

Temporary lightweight netting is much more appropriate for vegetables and can be used very effectively to keep large white butterflies (*Pieris brassicae*) off brassicas while the much finer mesh of horticultural fleece will protect crops from smaller pests. A different type of barrier is useful with carrots and underlines the value of knowing something of pest biology. The female carrot fly (*Delia antiqua*) flies very close to the ground and a 'fence' of plastic sheeting approximately 60cm (24in) high around carrots can be most effective in keeping them out.

Other barriers are less sophisticated. Finely spiny twigs, crushed egg shells or dusty substances, such as ash, will deter slugs and snails, provided they form a complete boundary around sensitive plants. Dusty materials must, of course, be renewed after rain. Organic gardeners seem particularly inventive at developing comparable methods.

Sometimes, more permanent barriers can be used to prevent the invasion of soil-borne problems. Heavy-duty plastic sheeting, buried vertically to a depth of 60-100cm (24-36in) along boundaries will stop the roots or rhizomes of such problems as ground elder (*Aegopodium podagraria*) and couch grass (*Agropyron repens*) or even the rhizomorphs of honey fungi (*Armillaria*). It will also keep out sucker growth from neighbouring trees such as lilacs.

Barriers are also of some value in keeping out larger, mammalian pests although they need to be carefully and firmly constructed. Wire mesh fencing 2m (6ft) high is required to exclude deer although shorter wire netting will keep out rabbits, provided it is buried to about 30cm (12in) depth or, and more easily, turned outwards over the surface of the soil at right angles and firmly pegged down.

Traps

Traps like traditional mousetraps are of some value in sheds and other garden stores, and they will continue to trap small rodents as frequently as they are put down; they shouldn't be used outdoors in the garden where they may harm pets. Mole traps can be very effective, especially those of the calliper variety, but they should be placed and checked by an expert. Other relatively crude, but nonetheless effective, traps include dishes filled with beer to lure snails and slugs to an intoxicated end and sunken jars to trap beetles, although these are likely to catch as many beneficial as harmful creatures. Slugs and snails are encouraged to cluster under upturned grapefruit skins, and inverted plant pots filled with hay or straw and placed atop canes among chrysanthemums and dahlias will attract earwigs, which hide there during the daytime. Jars filled with sugary water are used to trap wasps but should be used with circumspection. Wasps might be troublesome to humans for short periods of the year but the relatively minor damage they cause to fruit is more than off-set by their value in catching other insects (including many pests species) to feed to their young. Honey should never be placed in wasp traps. Much honey is imported and, while perfectly safe for humans, may contain diseases harmful to British bees, which are also attracted to the traps and could transfer the problems to native bee populations if they then fly free.

Perhaps the simplest and most effective of insect traps are the proprietary yellow cards, which are coated with very powerful adhesive and hung up in greenhouses. Many insects are attracted to the colour yellow and while, like most traps, these cards cannot discriminate between the good and the bad, they are valuable in keeping whiteflies in check. They should not, of course, be used in combination with any flying biological control agent, which will also be caught. Bands of adhesive can also be 'painted' around the perimeter of greenhouses to trap crawling pests and a similar principle is used in the grease bands on fruit trees to catch the flightless female winter moths (*Operophtera brumata*, *Alsophila aescularia* and *Erannis defoliaria*) as they climb up the trunks in autumn.

Not all traps are equally effective, however. A long-standing method used for the control of another fruit-tree pest, the codling moth (*Cydia pomonella*), involved strips of hessian sacking or other material being tied around the tree trunk. The theory was that this would induce the caterpillars that migrate *down* the tree to pupate within the cloth. The material would then be removed and destroyed with its contents. This overlooked the fact that by the time the caterpillars were pupating, the damage had already been done and that most codling moth attack in most years originates from moths flying into the garden from neighbouring areas.

Codling moth is, nonetheless, susceptible to one of the most sophisticated types of traps: the pheromone lure. This fairly modern development utilizes synthetic chemicals that mimic natural pheromones (sex attractant substances produced by insects to entice potential mates). In its horticultural form, the pheromone trap comprises a small, sheltered weatherproof platform coated with adhesive, in the centre of which a small phial of synthetic pheromone is placed. The device is hung from the branches of an apple tree and male codling moths, attracted to the lure, become ensnared on the adhesive. In consequence, the female moths have no mates and no eggs are laid. In commerce, pheromone traps tend to be used to monitor pest populations to ascertain if chemical pesticide sprays are required. In gardens, the traps themselves are used as the control. Although the codling-moth pheromone trap is the most widely used and most effective, similar traps exist for the control of plum fruit moth (*Cydia funebrana*), carnation tortrix moth (*Cacoecimorpha pronubana*), cyclamen tortrix moth (*Clepsis spectrana*) and pea moth (*Cydia nigricana*).

Deterrents

Finally, I must mention those procedures that are intended to prevent damage to plants or gardens without causing any harm to potential pests, especially those mammals and birds which have legal protection. These procedures are generally called deterrents and while specific chemical deterrents are obtainable (see page 161), the list also embraces a range of devices from the traditional scarecrow to sophisticated modern appliances like the electronic scarers that emit a very high-pitched sound, inaudible to humans but evidently irritating to cats. Low voltage electric fencing has also proved very effective at keeping badgers out of gardens. Among other, more bizarre techniques which are claimed to be very effective at deterring deer or other potential intruders are: small bags of (unwashed) human hair hung on boundary fences; a synthetic product that simulates the aroma of foxes; and even artificial tiger and lion dung.

Humane rodent trap

18 Control: biological

"Biological control methods make use of natural systems, and it's worth remembering that our gardens already contain natural systems that can be enhanced without anyone needing to buy anything."

If the notion of controlling pests and diseases without chemicals has an emotive, popular appeal (despite an often illogical basis), then the idea of adapting a natural process to gardening ends is even more attractive. This is the principle behind biological control. In reality, there's nothing new under the sun and as long ago as the thirteenth century, farmers in China were placing ants in their litchi trees in the expectation that the ants would attack potential pests. Over the past century or so, an ever-increasing number of biological controls have found their way into commercial horticulture and agriculture, and over the past ten years, many of these have been adapted to garden use.

Most of the early biological controls for amateurs were employed solely against greenhouse pests, partly because higher temperatures were needed for them to work properly but also because they involved agents that had to be confined if they weren't to fly or crawl away. More recently, systems for use on some outdoor pests have become available, too. There are still no biological controls for diseases for private gardens, although a few are used commercially and involve artificially introducing species of fungi antagonistic to pathogenic species into or onto plants. In Britain, the best known of these is the saprotrophic species *Peniophora gigantea*, which is antagonistic to the root- and trunk-attacking fungus *Heterobasidion annosum*. When trees are felled in commercial forestry, a suspension of *Peniophora* spores in water is brushed over the cut surface. The spores germinate, *Peniophora* mycelia colonize the stump and effectively prevent it from being colonized by the wood-rotting fungus *Heterobasidion annosum*. The information derived from studies such as I made into clubroot (see page 6) may lead to commercial exploitation of this type.

One of the difficulties of making biological controls available for small-scale home garden use has little to do with the way that they operate, let alone concerns over their safety; it's to do with the fact that the 'preparation', which is a living organism, has a limited shelf-life. This has been overcome in several ways. Some organisms, such as the nematodes used to control some soil pests, have been found to be amenable to various preservation methods and remain viable for long periods. Some large companies have adopted the system of selling through garden centres what is in effect an empty carton containing a prepaid card, which is then mailed by the purchaser to arrange delivery on a pre-chosen date. Direct mail order is also tailor-made for marketing this type of product.

Because of the relatively small-scale and labour-intensive production processes, as well as the complexities of marketing, biological controls will always tend to be relatively expensive compared with chemicals.

Hoverfly (*Syrphid*) on thistles

To work effectively they are also, by and large, more demanding of rather precise conditions, especially of temperature, at the time of application. Because of these factors, many gardeners try biological controls once or twice but then abandon them. This is unfortunate but understandable.

existing controls

Before spending money on biological control methods, it's worth considering what is present in the garden. Among numerous types of beneficial insects which are likely to be in our gardens already are various species of ground beetle, hoverflies, lacewings and ladybirds, and many groups of flies, among which the ichneumonids, which parasitize caterpillars, are some of the best known. Try to keep garden pesticide use to a minimum so as not to harm these creatures, and particularly avoid chemicals that persist in the environment for some time. Quite often, and understandably, gardeners tend to use pesticides most when they see the most pests. By then though, the bulk of the damage to the plants may have already been done and the pest populations could be about to collapse as predators build up. Thus, by using pesticides at this point, you may be doing more harm than good.

companion planting

Placing small groups of flowering plants, especially those that produce yellow or orange flowers, among crop plants seems to have some value in attracting insects, and there's a notion that they might then turn their attention to prey on pests that are feeding nearby. This seems to be the principle behind some so-called companion planting, which holds that growing one type of plant is beneficial to another growing in close proximity. There are no logical scientifically-based explanations of the phenomenon, and I remain slightly sceptical, especially as there seems to be no reason why yellow and orange flowers shouldn't be equally effective at attracting the pests.

control types

Biological controls for garden pest control fall into three main groups:

Predators are species of insect, mite or other creature that prey on pest species, devouring them whole. Mites, beetles, lacewings and midges are among the principal groups involved.

Parasites live on or in the bodies of pests, feeding on them and eventually killing them before they then complete their own developmental cycle. Far and away the most important are the parasitic wasps.

Pathogens cause disease in pests. Bacteria are the most important. They are either made into a spray formulation for killing caterpillars, or introduced into pests via nematodes which penetrate their bodies.

ADVANTAGES AND DISADVANTAGES OF CONTROL TYPES

Advantages

- Biological control methods are natural in that they utilize a preference that a creature displays in the wild. It's important to appreciate, however, that in a few instances, such as *Cryptolaemus montrouzieri,* they aren't British native species, although there's no reason to believe that this creates any problems.
- No chemicals of any type are involved – a boon for gardeners who, for whatever reason, are concerned about the use of chemicals.
- Phytotoxicity problems are eliminated and there's no possibility of plants being damaged by chemical use. Some plant species may be susceptible to chemical scorching, for instance, and in hot weather, even resilient plants may sometimes be affected adversely.
- Treatments are often fairly specific in that a particular control agent will only affect a particular pest or group of pests. This is rarely the case with chemicals.

Disadvantages

- Biological controls are relatively expensive compared with most chemicals.
- In small greenhouses, such as those in gardens, the predator or parasite may rapidly eliminate the pest and then itself die out. Repeat applications (and, therefore, repeat purchases) may be necessary. In commercial greenhouses, there will always be sufficient pests remaining for the predator to continue.
- It may be necessary to predict the occurrence of a pest problem some time in advance because few control agents are available off the shelf: they must be ordered from the suppliers.
- No chemicals or general traps (such as sticky yellow cards) should be used to control other pests affecting the same plants as these will also kill the biological control agents.
- There are relatively few methods that can be used outdoors.
- There are no biological control methods available for gardeners to use against plant diseases.

Whitefly scales parasitized by *Encarsia formosa* on tomato leaves

right: Mealy bug predator, the ladybird *Cryptolaemus montrouzieri*

BIOLOGICAL CONTROLS

Specific garden problems with a biological control available in Britain are given in this table. In different parts of the world, other controls are also used. In the United States, for instance, several different ladybird, mite and lacewing species as well as praying mantids and pirate bugs (*Orius insidiosis*) are widely available, and a greater range may be expected to be offered to British gardeners in the future, too.

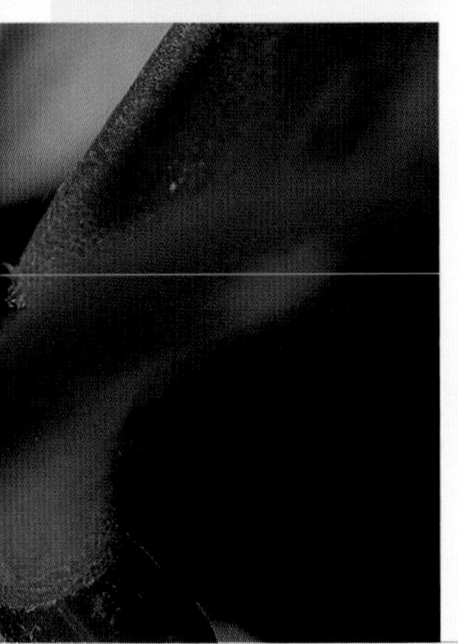

Pest	Organism: uses and limitations
Aphids	*Aphidoletes aphidimyza* (predatory midge) Greenhouse use at a minimum air temperature of 10°C (50°F)
Aphids	*Aphidius matricariae* (parasitic wasp) Greenhouse use at a minimum air temperature of 10°C (50°F)
Aphids and other pests	*Chrysoperla carnea* (lacewing) Greenhouse/outdoor use at a minimum air temperature of 10°C (50°F)
Caterpillars	*Bacillus thuringiensis* (bacterium) Greenhouse/outdoor use; applied as a spray. Kills all caterpillars, not only pest species
Fungus gnats	*Hypoaspis miles* (predatory mite) Greenhouse use at a minimum air temperature of 12°C (54°F)
Glasshouse whitefly	*Encarsia formosa* (parasitic wasp) Greenhouse use at a minimum air temperature of 18°C (64°F)
Glasshouse whitefly	*Delphastus pusillus* (predatory ladybird beetle) Greenhouse use at a minimum air temperature of 15°C (59°F)
Mealy bug	*Cryptoleamus montrouzieri* (predatory ladybird beetle) Greenhouse use at a minimum air temperature of 20°C (68°F)
Red spider mites	*Phytoseiulus persimilis* (predatory mite) Best in a greenhouse at a minimum air temperature of 10°C (50°F)
Scale insects (soft scale only)	*Metaphycus helvolus* (parasitic wasp) Greenhouse use at a minimum air temperature of 22°C (72°F)
Slugs	*Phasmarhabditis hermaphroditica* (nematode-carrying bacteria) Outdoor use at a minimum soil temperature of 5°C (41°F)
Soil pests (some)	*Steinernema carpocapsae* (nematode-carrying bacteria) Outdoor use at a minimum soil temperature of 14°C (57°F)
Thrips	*Amblyseius cucumeris* (predatory mite) Greenhouse/outdoor use at a minimum air temperature of 10°C (50°F) and high humidity
Vine weevil (larvae)	*Heterorhabditis megadis* (nematode-carrying bacteria) Outdoor use at a minimum soil temperature of 12°C (54°F)
Vine weevil (larvae)	*Steinernema carpocapsae* (nematode-carrying bacteria) Outdoor use at a minimum soil temperature of 14°C (57°F)

19 Control: chemical

"Knowing something about garden chemicals is vital if you are to use them correctly and effectively because, while using the wrong fungicide or pesticide generally means little more than that the treatment is ineffective, using the wrong herbicide can result in serious harm to your garden plants."

You won't spend long in your local garden centre or store before realizing that the number of chemicals on sale to gardeners is vast. Many of them are fertilizers, offering a wide range of different blends, primarily of the three main ingredients of nitrogen, phosphate and potash, but quite commonly with other nutritional elements, too. Details are given on pages 102–105 about how using these might relate to the solving or avoiding of plant problems. Apart from fertilizers, you'll also encounter row after row of bottles, packets, aerosols and sachets offering the promise of brighter flowers and more plump fruit and vegetables than you would ever have thought possible. This chapter looks at how to make sense of these products, how effective they all are, how to select them for particular problems and how to use them.

First, it is useful to clarify a few terms. The expression 'garden chemicals' is used here to mean fungicides, pesticides or herbicides (weedkillers) and the word 'pesticide' is used in its restricted sense – a chemical that kills pests, without including fungi. Note that, although a pesticide is usually an insecticide (kills insects), this isn't invariably so: a few are acaricides (kills mites), molluscicides (kills slugs and snails), rodenticides (kills rodents), or are substances that don't kill anything but act as repellents.

Rose powdery mildew, *Sphaerotheca pannosa*

In selecting chemicals for garden use, there are two important factors to consider. First, you need to know the range of problems that a particular product will control or, to use the more correct phraseology, how broad spectrum it is. Second, you need to know something of the way that it achieves its effects because this will dictate how and when you should apply it.

selectivity

Apart from the broad divisions of chemicals into the categories indicated above, there are very important subdivisions. I'll deal first with weed control because, while a mistaken choice in fungicides or pesticides generally means little more than that the treatment is ineffective, a mistaken choice of herbicide can result in serious harm being caused to your garden plants. The key word here is selective, or selectivity. To what extent is the product effective against certain types of weed and ineffective against other weeds or garden plants? To what degree does it select its targets?

While most herbicides are undeniably better at killing some plant species than others, they are inherently non-selective. Applied at certain times of the year or at certain stages of growth, they will kill or damage most plants with which they come into contact. Genuine selectivity of herbicides between different types of plant is rare, the major exception being the weed-

killers that are sold for use on lawns. These have been developed from chemicals used to control weed growth among cereal crops (cereals are types of grass) and they can discriminate between broad-leaved (dicotyledonous or magnoliopsid, see page 27) plants and narrow or grass-leaved (monocotyledonous or liliopsid) types. So they will kill broad-leaved weeds in lawns but they won't kill weed grass species. The most important among these chemicals are 2,4-D, mecoprop, dicamba, dichlorprop and MCPA.

The effect of selectivity can sometimes be achieved by using the chemicals in a certain way. Glyphosate, for instance, is a total weedkiller and will kill all green plants. But it's only taken up through green tissue and so won't affect the woody base of a tree or shrub if it is sprayed around it. Paraquat and diquat are also total weedkillers and will scorch off weed seedlings in a trice but can be used quite safely to control weeds in areas where daffodils or other bulbs are planted, provided they are used after the bulb foliage has died down.

Genuine selectivity among pesticides and fungicides is rather more widespread, mainly because there are more significant differences in physiology, structure and metabolism between the various groups of pests and fungi than there are between garden plants and weeds. There is, therefore, more scope for chemicals to act in different ways. This also creates an interesting divergence of practicality. For example, the ability of a fungicide to kill only mildews can be a confounded nuisance: the damage that it causes to the wider and beneficial fungal population is almost insignificant, but the fact that it is ineffective against rust, grey mould or cankers is a serious drawback, meaning that you have to use several different treatments to ensure that all these problems are also dealt with. Conversely, selectivity of pesticide action is a welcome attribute because almost all pests belong to larger groups of animals, within which the majority are harmless or beneficial. The ability to kill aphids, for instance, while leaving other insects unharmed is a highly important attribute for any garden pesticide and there's one chemical that can do this: pirimicarb. But the perverse logic that attends some organic gardening dogma means that strict adherents to the organic creed aren't permitted to use pirimicarb because it is a purely artificial product, unlike the undiscriminating, but naturally occurring, derris or pyrethrum.

Kentish snail

"On a broad perspective all chemicals fall into one of two main categories: they either work at the surface of the plant or they are absorbed to some degree into its sap and operate within."

how chemicals work

You don't need to know the biochemical details of how garden chemicals operate; at this level it is sufficient to understand that they are many and varied, and, in some instances, especially with fungicides, that they mimic or are based on the sort of systems that plants possess as part of their natural defence mechanisms (see page 61). However, it's important to understand the two basic modes of action: surface or internal. Different terms are used to describe these in the different groups. Herbicides are generally referred to as contact or translocated, pesticides as contact or systemic, and fungicides as protectant, eradicant or systemic. Sometimes the word translaminar is used; this describes movement across a leaf but not much deeper into a plant's tissues. And some herbicides are also described as pre- or post-emergence.

All of these terms are fairly self-explanatory. **Contact** suggests that the chemical comes into physical contact with its 'target' and then achieves its effect on its surface or just below it: erosion or damage to an insect's outer cuticle, for example. **Translocated** or **systemic** indicates that the chemical is absorbed and moved within the tissues. **Protectant** describes a chemical that is applied in advance of an expected attack to prevent damage, and **eradicant** is a chemical that is able to eliminate some existing invasion or infection. A pre-emergence herbicide kills seeds or newly germinated seedlings before they appear above the soil surface, whereas a post-emergence herbicide kills the emerged plant. Of course, not all of these terms are mutually exclusive. Many eradicant fungicides, for example, are systemic because they must seek out fungal infection deep within the tissues.

The importance and significance of the two broadest categories – systemic/translocated and non-systemic/contact – vary with different problems. The practical importance of translocated herbicides is that they are absorbed through green foliage and then move downwards into the roots or rhizomes and so offer the only realistic way of killing such deep-seated plants as bindweed (*Convolvulus* spp.), docks (*Rumex* spp.) and some thistles (*Cirsium* spp.). However, their effect isn't guaranteed because other factors affect their efficacy. For instance, one of the most widely used translocated herbicides is glyphosate which isn't fully absorbed unless six hours without rain elapse after its application. Moreover, the effectiveness of its absorption varies with the prevailing temperature and the age of the plant and its growth stage, and some plants are inherently more tolerant of it: Japanese knotweed (*Reynoutria japonica*) is notoriously almost unaffected whatever the conditions.

Field bindweed, *Convolvulus arvensis*

The greatest merits of systemic insecticides lie in their control of sap-sucking pests like aphids, whiteflies and scale insects. Being present in the sap on which the pests feed means that the chemical is delivered directly to where it is most effective. For systemic fungicides, the advantages are rather less specific. Certainly, other things being equal, they facilitate the control of those fungi, most notably obligate-biotrophic species, that develop an intimate contact with their host tissues by growing within the cells (see page 58). But because fungal growth tends to be more nebulous than pest attack and the areas of its greatest concentration aren't always obvious, they also permit the control of pathogens that might escape direct action.

RESPECTIVE MERITS OF SYSTEMIC AND NON-SYSTEMIC PESTICIDES AND FUNGICIDES

Systemic

- Little accuracy is required in spraying; the chemical will reach inaccessible parts of plants.
- Once the spray has dried, it is unaffected by rain or other weather conditions.
- The product is usually required in only very small amounts.
- It is relatively easy to eradicate established problems, even when they are well-entrenched.
- By their nature, systemic products must be harmless to plants. However, because it permeates the plant tissues, the chemical may be in harvested edible produce so the minimum stated safe intervals between application and harvest must be closely adhered to.

Non-systemic

- The product must be sprayed precisely because only the sprayed parts will be protected; therefore, significant problems are likely to arise with pests or pathogens under leaves or in other inaccessible places.
- The product is permanently liable to be washed off by rain.
- The product is usually required in relatively large amounts.
- Chemicals often have only a protective action and can only eradicate problems that are on the exposed surface.
- Some products can sometimes cause damage to plants, especially in hot weather.
- The product may be present on the surface of edible crops which must therefore be washed before consumption.

types of chemical controls

fungicides

The use of chemicals to attempt to control problems in horticulture and agriculture originates in classical times: Pliny mentioned olive oil dregs among other putative remedies. However, it has only been within the past three hundred years that chemicals of proven effectiveness first began to be used. Mercuric-chloride was employed as a wood preservative in 1705 and copper sulphate was tried as a treatment for seed-borne diseases later in the eighteenth century. The first approach to modern treatment came in 1802 with the use of sulphur to control powdery mildew on fruit trees, and this forms the basis of a preparation known today as lime sulphur. The recommendation was to sprinkle the trees with a mixture of lime water and urine (details of the application technique aren't given!), and follow this by washing them with a concoction primarily containing sulphur and lime.

Sulphur remains a key ingredient of fungicides, and although sulphur-containing organic chemicals were very significant during the middle years of the twentieth century, more recently, elemental sulphur has seen a return to favour, especially among organic gardeners.

Until the advent of organic fungicides, the only serious rival to sulphur was copper, the fungicidal properties of which were discovered by an accident that has passed into horticultural folklore. In 1882, a mixture of copper-sulphate and lime was being used in a vineyard in the Medoc region of France to render grapevines unappealing to pilferers. The Professor of Botany at Bordeaux, Pierre-Marie-Alexis Millardet, noticed that the vines treated in this way were unusually free from downy mildew (*Plasmopara viticola*). From this chance observation came the development of a product containing copper-sulphate and slaked lime; known as Bordeaux Mixture, it remains a garden fungicide today. A number of other inorganic copper-containing fungicides were developed subsequently and some are still available for garden use.

Since the early use of mercuric chloride for preserving timber, the fungicidal properties of other mercury-containing compounds have been widely recognized but their high level of human toxicity means that they have now fallen from favour and all have been withdrawn. The last mercury-containing product sold for garden use was calomel (mercurous chloride), which was available to protect brassica plants against clubroot disease and cabbage root fly until the 1980s.

The modern fungicide era began with the development of a large number of synthetic organic compounds from the 1930s onwards, most importantly a group called dithiocarbamates. A few have survived and the garden fungicides captan (now only obtainable as an additive to hormone-rooting powders to prevent the rotting of cuttings) and mancozeb (effective against

Glasshouse whiteflies, *Trialeurodes vaporariorum*, on a tomato leaf

some rust diseases and foliage blights) are of this type.

All of the fungicides mentioned so far were primarily protectant in action although a few have some eradicant properties. While some of the earlier fungicides offered a hint of systemic properties, in that a chemical applied to one part of a plant seemed to affect fungal infection in another, the real breakthrough in the search for systemic fungicides came in the 1960s. A series of compounds was developed, most famously those allied chemically to a substance that was marketed under the name benomyl. From around 1970, and for some twenty years, benomyl and its relatives provided the answers to a huge number of plant diseases in both commercial cropping and home gardens. It was a golden age for the chemical companies. Few of these products remain today, however, for the simple reason that fungal pathogens gradually developed resistance to them and their effectiveness was, therefore, eroded. The only chemical of the benomyl type still available to gardeners for widespread use is carbendazim, although the related thiophanate-methyl is obtainable as a treatment for clubroot (as a replacement for calomel).

A number of other systemic fungicides of chemically different types are still obtainable and are widely used, including myclobutanil, penconazole and triforine, but compared to the 1970s the range of fungicides that gardeners can buy is now greatly depleted.

insecticides

Like fungicides, the range of insecticides available for garden use has fallen dramatically from its peak in the 1960s and 1970s. Here, too, there has been something of a return to favour of products of natural origin, such as rotenone (derris), an extract from the roots of species of the tropical plants *Derris* and *Lonchocarpus*, and natural pyrethrum, which is extracted from the flowers of *Tanacetum cinerariaefolium* and originated in the nineteenth century. Both of these products, however, illustrate the care needed in choosing to follow any particular gardening dogma. Both are generally accepted by organic gardeners although both have serious side-effects in their toxicity to creatures other than insects. They are, for instance, extremely harmful to fish.

A more recent development among products of natural origin are insecticidal soaps, a re-invention of the soft soap sprays that were used until the late 1920s. Manufactured from natural plant and animal oils, these are effective but often broad spectrum in action and some have phytotoxicity, too.

Interestingly, among the most important modern synthetic garden insecticides are the synthetic pyrethrins, a group of chemicals that are chemically similar to pyrethrum and which have been developed following British research in the 1960s. They are among the safest of modern synthetic insecticides with low mammalian toxicity and relatively short persistence in the environment. Permethrin, bifenthrin and resmethrin are widespread examples.

Pirimicarb has already been mentioned for its special selectivity to aphids. It is one of a group of insecticides called carbamates. The only other representative available to gardeners is bendiocarb, which has much wider effectiveness and is used especially for the control of 'crawling pests'. Another member of the same chemical group, carbaryl, was withdrawn in 1996 after some doubts about its safety.

The only survivor for garden use of the large group of organochlorine insecticides is HCH, formerly known as BHC or lindane. However, because it is persistent in the environment (see right), many gardeners find it unappealing.

The largest group of modern garden insecticides are the organophosphorus products. Some are systemic or translaminar in action but most have considerable persistence and so again many gardeners prefer to use them only as a last resort. Malathion, fenitrothion and pirimiphos-methyl are common examples.

herbicides

In gardening books and catalogues produced before about 1940, there are references to pest- and disease-controlling chemicals, but very little about weedkillers. A few products containing arsenic were available and a few others (ironically, often branded 'non-poisonous') contained such toxic substances as sodium chlorate or mineral oils for relatively small-scale use. Weed control was by and large as it had always been, a physical operation. What changed matters was the synthesis of materials that were chemically very similar to naturally occurring plant hormones.

These hormone herbicides had two huge appeals, especially to commercial growers and farmers: they were operative at very low doses and they were extremely effective at discriminating between broad-leaved weeds and grasses or cereals. It's fair to say that the subsequent development of many other synthetic herbicides, many of them hormone analogues, revolutionized much of commercial arable farming. And inevitably, some of these products found their way into gardening where 2,4-D, dichlorprop, MCPA and others continue to be used, especially on lawns. Apart from the selective hormone herbicides, the two other significant products for garden use are the contact herbicide paraquat (avail-

able to gardeners in mixture with diquat) and the translocated, non-selective chemical glyphosate, which was developed in 1971 and provides the only sure way of eradicating deep-rooted perennial weeds.

resistance

Using a chemical to control a pest or disease imposes a selection pressure on the organism, exactly as any other constraint on its life would do. Any individuals that are less affected by the chemicals, through some inherent feature of their make-up, will survive (in Darwinian terms, those best fitted to survive will do so). If this attribute has a genetic, heritable basis, as often it does, so the resistant or tolerant individuals will produce resistant or tolerant progeny and, in time, a population will arise that is mostly unaffected by the original selection pressure. This is one way that resistance to pesticides and fungicides can arise among pests and pathogens.

Because many synthetic chemicals, however, are dissimilar to anything occurring naturally, it commonly happens that there's no existing genetic basis for resistance. The organism, historically, has had no 'need' to be resistant because it will never, naturally, have encountered such a selection pressure. Nonetheless, resistance can still arise through the mutation of existing genes and there are many examples of resistance developing relatively quickly to totally new products. In gardens, common examples are the resistance shown by the grey mould fungus *Botrytis* to those fungicides based on carbendazim and the

Thistles, *Carduus tenuiflorus*

PERSISTENCE

A further feature of garden chemicals that needs to be taken into account before deciding that they are appropriate for a particular purpose is their persistence. A persistent chemical is one that remains active in the environment (especially in the soil) for a long time before it's diluted or chemically changed to an inactive state. The realization that many organochlorine insecticide compounds remain in the environment and in plant and animal tissue for long periods began the modern environmental movement in the 1960s. These substances (which included the well-known and once very popular insecticide dichlorodiphenyltrichlorethane, better known as DDT) enter ecological food chains and are passed in turn from one type of animal to the predators that feed on it. This is why birds of prey commonly die from their toxic effects a long time after they are first applied to the environment for insect control.

The persistence of garden and farm chemicals is often expressed in terms of their half-life: the period over which a given quantity of chemical degrades or is otherwise reduced to half its original amount. There's no justification for using any garden insecticide or fungicide that has a long half-life; no product of any sort should be used which is not inactivated within a season. Herbicides used on paths and other unplanted areas to keep them weed-free for up to a year, including amitrole, simazine, ammonium thiocyanate, atrazine and MCPA, should represent the absolute extremes of persistence in gardens.

Persistence in the soil is no virtue in a substance that must come into contact with or be absorbed by the foliage of mature plants, although it's of value with pre-emergence products that act by preventing the germination of weed seeds. At the other end of the spectrum are those substances that are inactivated very quickly after contact with the soil. The widely used contact herbicide paraquat is very strongly adsorbed on to soil particles and can be used to kill emerging seedling weeds while enabling the soil to be sown or planted immediately afterwards. And the remarkably successful and widely used translocated herbicide glyphosate, so effective against persistent perennials, is also strongly adsorbed on to soil particles and is broken down by soil micro-organisms to produce phosphoric acid, carbon dioxide and ammonia, all of which, somewhat ironically, are used by plants as nutrients.

rather widespread resistance of whiteflies to many common pesticides. Such phenomena are added reasons for gardeners using chemical controls in moderation.

bacteria and viruses

Symptoms of pear stony pit virus

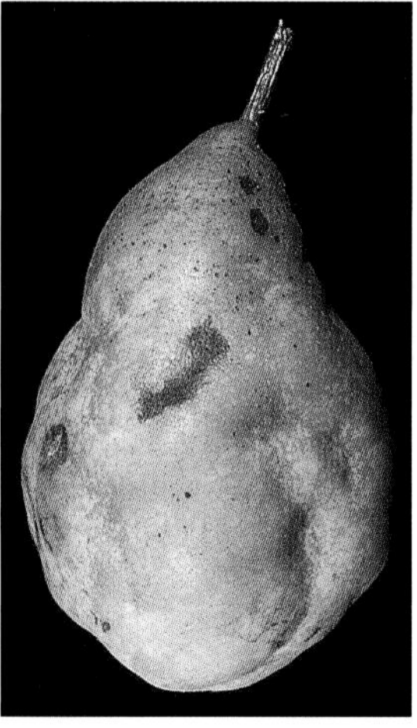

Chemical control of bacteria and viruses in plants is at a different level from the control of fungal diseases. A few fungicides, most notably those based on copper, have some incidental anti-bacterial action, but specific bactericides (or antibiotics) cannot legally be used on garden plants (nor to any extent on commercial ones) for the simple reason that their presence in the environment could cause human bacterial pathogens to develop resistance to them and thus their clinical use would be rendered ineffective.

The position with chemical control of virus diseases (in animals as well as plants) is even more bleak. Although there have been many experimental demonstrations that particular chemicals could diminish the effects of viral infections, there are very few practical applications of this even in clinical medicine, and none in gardens. Nonetheless, chemicals do have an important role in combating virus diseases of plants, especially in commerce, through the insecticidal control of vectors (see pages 67–69).

PLEASE NOTE

"Garden chemicals of any type must be used exactly and only according to the directions on the labels."

Although a fungicide won't control a pest and a pesticide won't control a disease, the labels of some proprietary products state that they may be used to treat both pests and diseases. For example, a number of substances sold for use on roses are said, with justification, to control mildew, blackspot, rust and aphids. The explanation is they contain more than one chemical and only one operation is needed to achieve a multiple effect. The existence of such mixed chemicals shouldn't tempt you to try mixing your own blends: many chemicals are incompatible with each other and at best you may diminish their effects; at worst you could seriously damage your plants.

formulation

On returning to the garden centre, it's now possible to rationalize the choice of controls offered by understanding that different products do different tasks by virtue of the different chemical ingredients (the so-called active ingredients) that they contain. But, before finally making a selection, there's one other feature to consider: the formulation. Most garden chemicals are sold in concentrated form for dilution by the user. This concentrate may be either a liquid or a solid (usually a wettable powder which is finely dispersed as a suspension in water). It's essential to use the appropriate dilution as recommended by the manufacturers. Preparing a mixture of double the suggested rate won't double the effect and could be positively harmful or even dangerous. A few garden chemicals are sold as dusts, granules, pyrotechnic mixtures (usually called 'smokes') or aerosols for application without further dilution.

Both liquid and solid concentrates are usually used to make up sprays for application to foliage, although the diluted product may sometimes be used for drenching onto soil or compost or for soaking bulbs, corms or other planting material. Dusts are also sometimes applied to soil or to places where insects or other pests may be concentrated but are also valuable for treating overwintering ornamental bulbs, corms or tubers. Smokes are used exclusively in greenhouses for the eradication of overwintering pests or pathogens.

Chemical	Principal mode of action	Notes	Garden uses
HERBICIDES chemicals to kill weeds			
Amitrole (Aminotriazole)	Translocated	Only in mixture with other total herbicides	Total
Atrazine	Contact/residual	Only in mixture with amitrole	Total
Chlorpyralid	Translocated	Only in mixture with other selective herbicides	Selective for broad-leaved plants
2,4-D	Translocated	Only in mixture with other selective herbicides	Selective for broad-leaved plants
Dalapon	Translocated	The only selective herbicide available to gardeners	Selective for grasses
Dicamba	Translocated	Only in mixture with other selective herbicides	Selective for broad-leaved plants
Dichlobenil	Residual	Unique in action and method of application (as granules in cold weather)	Selective for seedlings and young plants
Dichlorophen	Contact	Alone and in mixture with selective herbicides for lawn use	Selective for moss (but also used as a fungicide)
Dichlorprop	Translocated	Only in mixture with other selective herbicides	Selective for broad-leaved plants
Diquat	Contact	Only in mixture for unplanted areas or for control of annual weeds	Total
Diuron	Residual	Only in mixture with selective herbicides for lawn use	Total
Ferrous sulphate	Contact	Only in mixture with selective herbicides for lawn use	Selective for moss
Glyphosate	Translocated	The most widely used translocated herbicide	Total
MCPA	Translocated	Only in mixture for use on lawns or unplanted areas	Selective for broad-leaved plants
Mecoprop	Contact	Only in mixture with other selective herbicides for lawn use	Selective for broad-leaved plants
Paraquat	Contact	Only in mixture for unplanted areas or for control of annual weeds	Total
Simazine	Residual	Only in mixture for unplanted areas	Total
Sodium chlorate	Residual	Only for unplanted areas	Total

Rose slugworm sawfly larvae, *Endelomyia aethiops*

FUNGICIDES chemicals to control diseases

Chemical	Principal mode of action	Notes	Garden uses
Ammonium carbonate	Contact	Only in mixture with copper sulphate	See copper sulphate
Ammonium hydroxide	Contact	Only in mixture with copper sulphate	See copper sulphate
Bupirimate	Systemic	Only in mixture with triforine	See triforine
Captan	Contact	Only in hormone rooting powders	To protect cuttings from rotting
Carbendazim	Systemic	The most widely used systemic fungicide, taking the place of the now withdrawn benomyl	A very wide range of diseases of edible and ornamental plants and lawns
Copper oxychloride		Contact	See copper sulphate
Copper sulphate	Contact	Only in mixture with ammonium hydroxide as Bordeaux Mixture and with ammonium carbonate as Cheshunt Compound	A wide range of diseases on edible and ornamental plants. Especially useful against blight and rusts
Dichlorophen	Contact	As a fungicide, only in hormone rooting powder. (But also widely used as a moss killer)	To protect cuttings from rotting
Mancozeb	Contact		Especially against blight and rusts
Myclobutanil	Systemic		Especially against rose diseases and apple scab
Penconazole	Contact	Replaced the chemically similar propiconazole	Especially against rust diseases on ornamental plants
Sulphur	Contact	Alone as liquid or powder and also in mixture with other chemicals	Especially against mildew and as protection for stored ornamental bulbs
Thiophanate-methyl	Systemic	Chemically similar to carbendazim	Only as a root dip formulation for brassica transplants for clubroot control
Triforine	Systemic	Only in mixture, with bupirimate or with sulphur and insecticide	Especially for rose diseases; also used for fruit but not vegetables

INSECTICIDES chemicals to control pests, especially insects

Chemical	Principal mode of action	Notes	Garden uses
Bendiocarb	Contact/systemic		Ant and other crawling pest control
Bifenthrin	Contact		Most pests on edible and ornamental plants
Bioallethrin	Contact	Only in mixture with permethrin	See permethrin
Borax	Contact		As ant bait
Butoxycarboxim	Systemic	Formulated on impregnated cardboard 'pins' for insertion into compost in pots	Control of sap-sucking pests in containers
Chlorpyrifos	Contact		Ant and other crawling pest control
Cypermethrin	Contact		Ant and other crawling pest control
Deltamethrin	Contact		Ant and other crawling insect control
Fenitrothion	Contact		Controls a range of pests, especially sawflies and raspberry beetle
Heptenophos	Systemic	Only in mixture with permethrin	See permethrin
Horticultural soaps (natural fatty acids)	Contact		Aphids, whitefly, red spider mite and soft scale on edible and ornamental plants
Imidacloporid	Contact/systemic		Aphids, vine weevil, sciarids
Lindane	Contact		To control soil pests

Chemical	Principal mode of action	Notes	Garden uses
Malathion	Contact	Alone and in mixture with permethrin	A wide range of pests, especially sap-sucking types on edible and ornamental plants
Permethrin	Contact	The most widely used garden insecticide; alone and in mixture with other chemicals. Also available as smokes for greenhouse whitefly control	Most pests on edible and ornamental plants
Piperonyl butoxide	Contact	Only in mixture with permethrin	A wide range of pests on edible and ornamental plants
Pirimicarb	Contact	Available alone and in mixture with fungicides	Almost specific to aphids
Pirimiphos-methyl	Contact		A wide range of pests on edible and ornamental plants
Pyrethrins	Contact	General name for a group of chemically similar substances	See permethrin
Pyrethrum	Contact		A wide range of pests on edible and ornamental plants
Quassia	Contact	Only in mixture with rotenone	See rotenone
Resmethrin	Contact	Only in combination with pyrethrins	See permethrin
Rotenone (derris)	Contact	As liquid or powder, also in mixture with rotenone	A wide range of pests on edible and ornamental plants
Tar oils	Contact		Overwintering pests on deciduous trees and shrubs in the dormant season
Tetramethrin	Contact	Only in mixture with permethrin	See permethrin
Trichlophon	Contact		Ants

Chemical	Principal mode of action	Notes	Garden uses
MOLLUSCICIDES chemicals to control slugs and snails			
Metaldehyde	Anaesthetic	As liquid and pellets	Slugs and snails
Methiocarb	Gastric action	Only as pellets	Slugs and snails
REPELLENTS chemicals to deter pests without killing them			
Aluminium ammonium sulphate			Pets and birds
Naphthalene			Cats and dogs
Pepper dust			Cats and dogs
MISCELLANEOUS PRODUCTS			
Brodifacoum		As bait	Mice
Coumatetralyl		As bait	Rats and mice
Difenacoum		As bait	Rats and mice
Sulphur		Smoke	Moles

A well-grown crop of cauliflowers

Problem identification and treatment

Part two

This section deals with the identification and treatment of the many different problems that gardeners are likely to come across.

In '100 common problems' (pages 164-183) you will find photographs and details of 100 problems that in my experience are those most likely to cause concern to gardeners. Overall, they are also the commonest and certainly include the most serious. There will, nonetheless, be a few surprises – less common or less serious conditions that always elicit comment when they do arise.

The 'Keys' (pages 184-219) are another way that you can diagnose problems that you encounter in your garden. Use them to identify the pest, disease, disorder or weed and then refer to the relevant index to find out how to combat it.

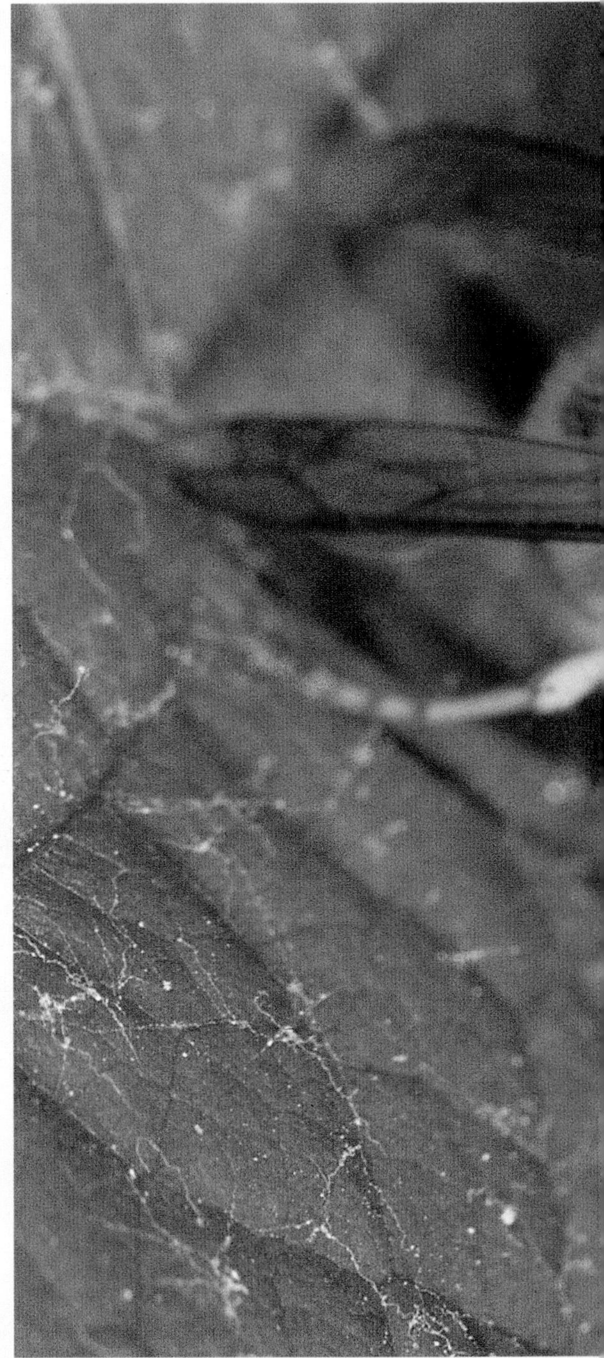

Common wasp, *Paravespula vulgaris*, on grapes

100 common problems

1 what is it?
Adelgids
what does it affect?
Conifers
what causes it?
Species of sap-sucking insects, mainly Adelges
how to treat it
If severe, spray trees with malathion or other contact insecticide in early summer. Cut out and destroy any disfiguring pineapple-like galls.

2 what is it?
American gooseberry mildew
what does it affect?
Gooseberries and blackcurrants
what causes it?
Fungus *Sphaerotheca pannosa*
how to treat it
Spray with systemic fungicide when symptoms are seen. Don't plant in shady sites; don't plant bushes very close together. Choose resistant gooseberry varieties such as 'Invicta' and 'Jubilee'.

3 what is it?
Antirrhinum rust
what does it affect?
Antirrhinums
what causes it?
Fungus *Puccinia antirrhini*
how to treat it
Spray every two to three weeks when symptoms are seen with an appropriate approved rust fungicide. Destroy all plants promptly at the end of the season. Choose modern rust-resistant varieties.

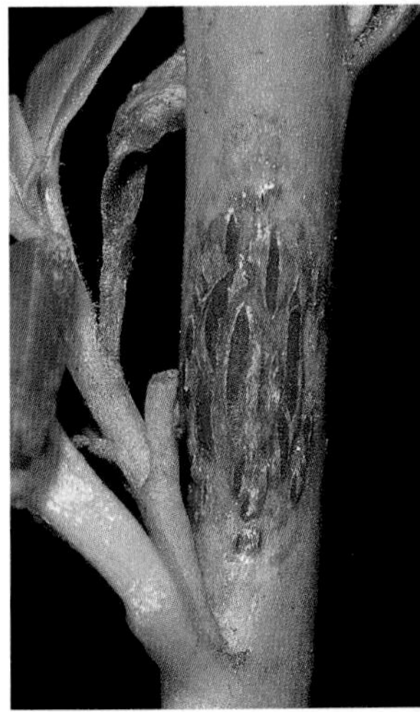

4 what is it?
Ants
what does it affect?
Any plants growing in light, free-draining soils
what causes it?
Several species of both red and black ants
how to treat it
Try to build up the organic matter content of the soil by regular applications of manure or compost – ants are discouraged by moist conditions.

5 what is it?
Aphids
what does it affect?
Almost all plants, although individually aphid species are often restricted to certain types
what causes it?
Many species of small sap-sucking insects
how to treat it
Spray with an appropriate approved insecticide when first infestations are seen, to prevent build-up of large populations.

8 what is it?
Apple and pear powdery mildew
what does it affect?
Apples, pears, quince, medlar but similar problems affect other fruit trees
what causes it?
Fungus *Podosphaera leucotricha*
how to treat it
Pinch off mildew-affected shoot tips as soon as they appear in spring. Spray trees with an appropriate approved fungicide as buds turn pink and repeat three times at two-week intervals. 'Discovery' and 'Greensleeves' are among varieties with resistance.

6 what is it?
Apple and pear brown rot
what does it affect?
Apples and pears although almost identical diseases affect plums and tree fruit
what causes it?
Fungi, especially *Sphaerotheca* species
how to treat it
Clear away damaged fruit promptly, pick up windfalls and remove any dead shrivelled fruit hanging on the trees over winter.

9 what is it?
Apple sawfly
what does it affect?
Apples
what causes it?
Ant-like insect *Hoplocampa testudinea*
how to treat it
Collect and destroy fallen young fruits (fruitlets) early in the season.

7 what is it?
Apple and pear canker
what does it affect?
Apple and pears; comparable diseases on many other trees
what causes it?
Fungus *Nectria galligena*
how to treat it
Cut out branches bearing cankers, especially on young trees. Little can be done for severely affected old trees but don't plant new young stock nearby.

10 what is it?
Apple and pear scab
what does it affect?
Apples and pears
what causes it?
Fungi *Venturia inaequalis* (apples) and *Venturia pirina* (pears)
how to treat it
Prune out damaged shoots in winter. On young trees, spray with an appropriate approved fungicide from bud burst and repeat twice at two-week intervals.

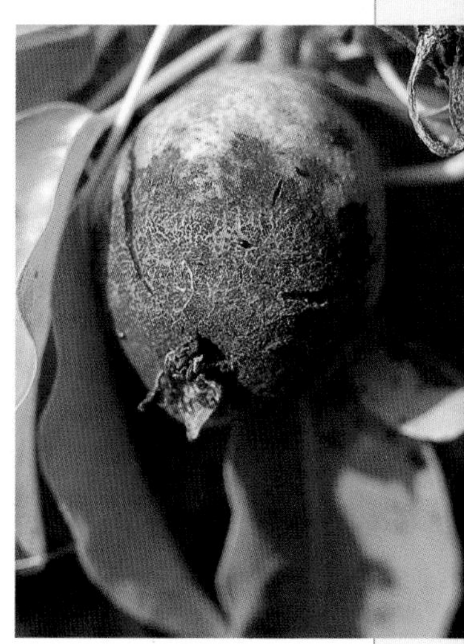

11 what is it?
Aster wilt
what does it affect?
China asters (not Michaelmas daisies)
what causes it?
Probably several different fungi in soil
how to treat it
Grow asters on land on which they haven't been grown for several years; if all soil becomes contaminated, rest it from asters for five years and grow plants in containers.

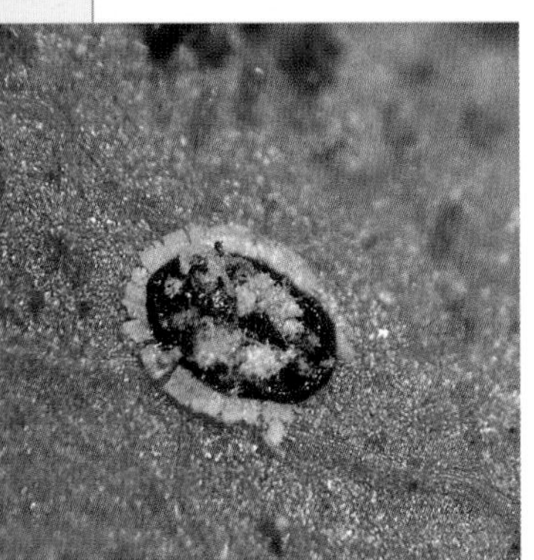

12 what is it?
Bay sucker
what does it affect?
Bay laurel
what causes it?
Sap-sucking insect *Trioza alacris*
how to treat it
Cut out severely distorted foliage and spray small plants with systemic insecticide.

13 what is it?
Pea and bean root and foot rot
what does it affect?
Peas and beans
what causes it?
Fungi in soil, especially *Fusarium* species
how to treat it
Destroy badly affected plants and use a strict rotation, not growing peas and beans on the same land more than one year in three or four.

14 what is it?
Big bud
what does it affect?
Blackcurrants
what causes it?
Virus-like organism transmitted by gall mite *Cecidophyopsis ibis*
how to treat it
Cut out and destroy affected shoots. Replace plants with new ones as the yield will inevitably begin to decline.

15 what is it?
Birds
what does it affect?
Many plants but especially fruit bushes (buds and fruit), leafy vegetables (foliage), peas (seeds) and crocuses (flowers)
what causes it?
Several bird species but bullfinches, sparrows and wood pigeons are most serious
how to treat it
Use a year-round fruit cage for soft fruit and erect temporary netting to protect vegetables; don't use black cotton as it can kill the birds if they become entangled.

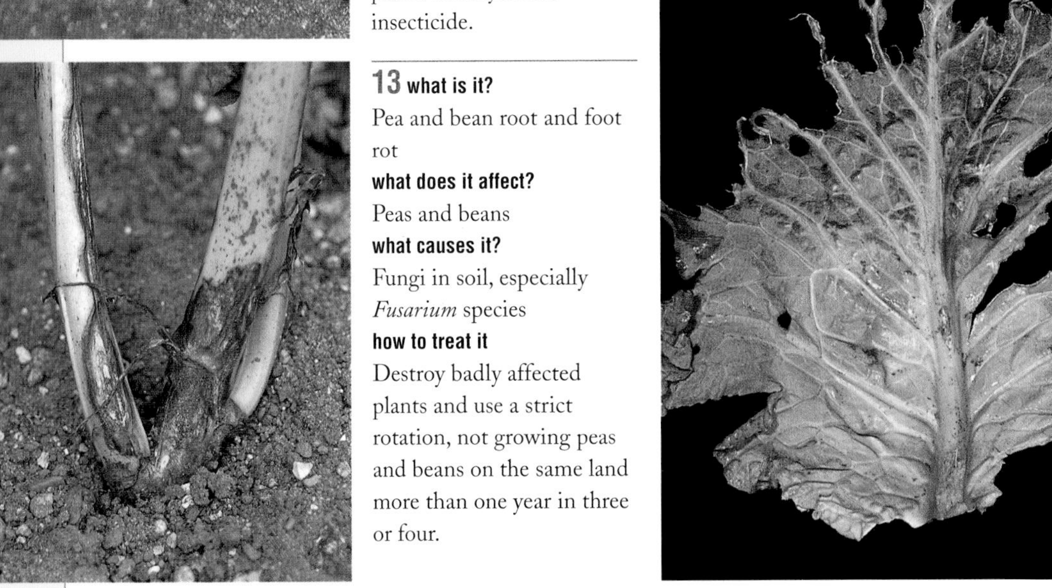

16 **what is it?**
Brassica caterpillars
what does it affect?
Brassicas, also nasturtiums and occasionally other plants
what causes it?
Principally large white butterfly (*Pieris brassicae*) and small white butterfly (*Pieris rapae*). Comparable caterpillars affect many other plants
how to treat it
Pick off small numbers of individuals (use gloves); spray severe infestations with biological bacterial spray. Protect crops with proprietary fleece.

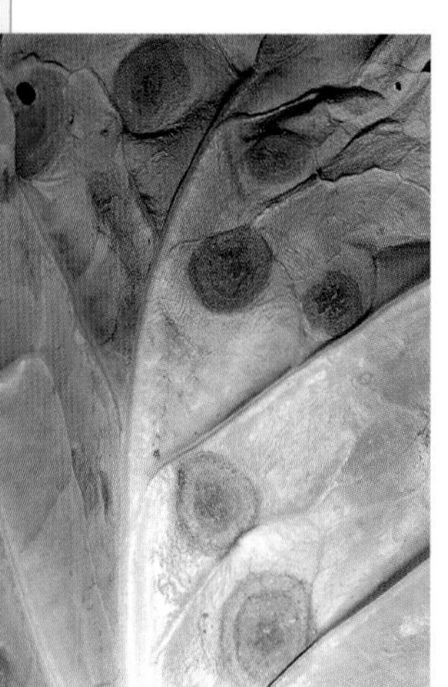

17 **what is it?**
Brassica leaf spot
what does it affect?
Brassicas
what causes it?
Several different fungi and some viruses; comparable problems on many other plants
how to treat it
Pull off severely affected foliage. Clear away crop debris promptly at the end of the season.

18 **what is it?**
Brassica powdery mildew
what does it affect?
Brassicas; comparable problems on many other plants
what causes it?
Many species of mildew fungi
how to treat it
Pull off severely affected foliage and maintain the moisture content of the soil. Spraying is not worthwhile.

19 **what is it?**
Broad bean chocolate spot
what does it affect?
Broad beans
what causes it?
Fungus *Botrytis fabae*
how to treat it
Don't apply nitrogen fertilizers. Maintain wide spacing between plants and don't plant in damp, shaded sites.

20 **what is it?**
Broad bean rust
what does it affect?
Broad beans
what causes it?
Fungus *Uromyces viciae-fabae*
how to treat it
Destroy affected plants at the end of the season.

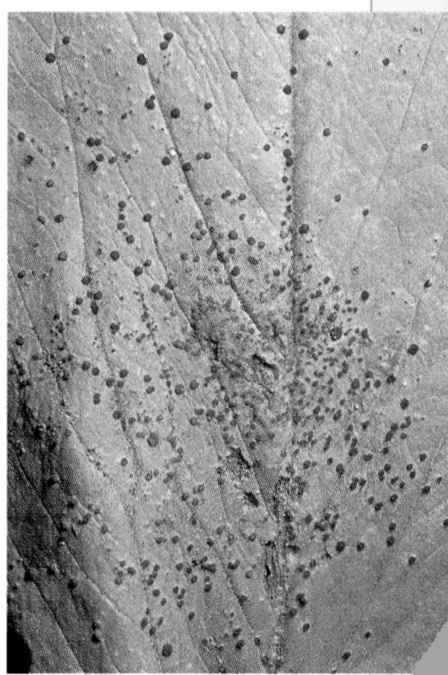

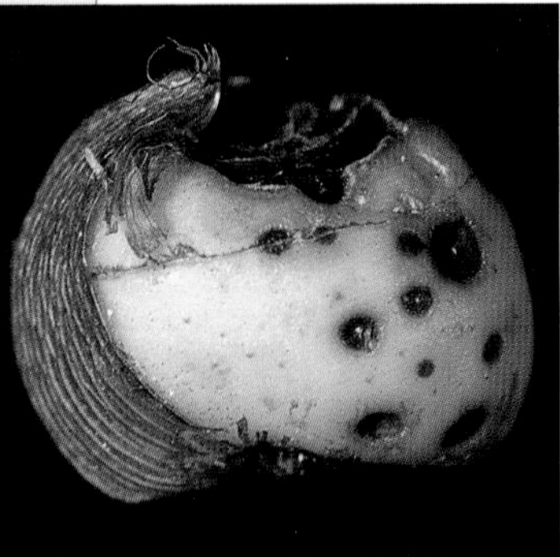

21 what is it?
Bulb rot
what does it affect?
Plants that form bulbs, corms, tubers or rhizomes
what causes it?
Many different fungi and bacteria
how to treat it
Carefully check new purchases and old, lifted stock; destroy any that show defects.

24 what is it?
Carrot fly
what does it affect?
Carrots, parsnips, parsley and related plants
what causes it?
Fly *Psila rosae*
how to treat it
Grow resistant carrot varieties such as 'Fly Away'; erect 60mm-high plastic 'fence' around crops to deter low-flying females.

22 what is it?
Cabbage root fly
what does it affect?
Brassicas
what causes it?
Fly *Delia radicum*, related to house fly
how to treat it
Destroy affected plants. Place proprietary collars around transplants when planting to deter egg-laying females.

25 what is it?
Cherry blackfly
what does it affect?
Fruiting and ornamental cherries
what causes it?
Sap sucking insect *Myzus cerasi*
how to treat it
Apply tar oil spray to dormant trees in winter.

23 what is it?
Capsid bugs
what does it affect?
Apple, plum and pear fruits; also foliage on many other plants
what causes it?
Sap-sucking insects
how to treat it
Clear away plant debris at the end of the season; use tar oil spray in winter on fruit trees.

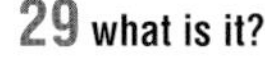

26 what is it?
Clubroot
what does it affect?
Brassicas and related ornamentals, including wallflowers
what causes it?
Fungus *Plasmodiophora brassicae*
how to treat it
Destroy affected plants before the roots rot. Raise plants in individual pots and plant out in complete ball of compost. Proprietary fungicide dip for bare-rooted plants offers some protection. Add lime to raise pH to above 7.

29 what is it?
Crown gall
what does it affect?
Many woody and herbaceous plants
what causes it?
Bacterium *Agrobacterium tumefaciens*
how to treat it
Cut out if disfiguring; otherwise no treatment necessary.

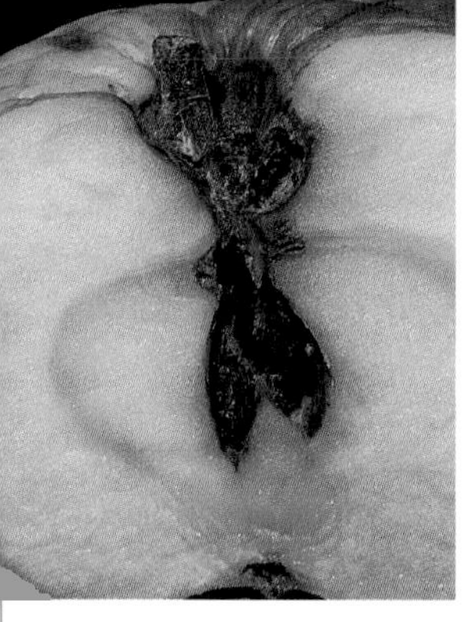

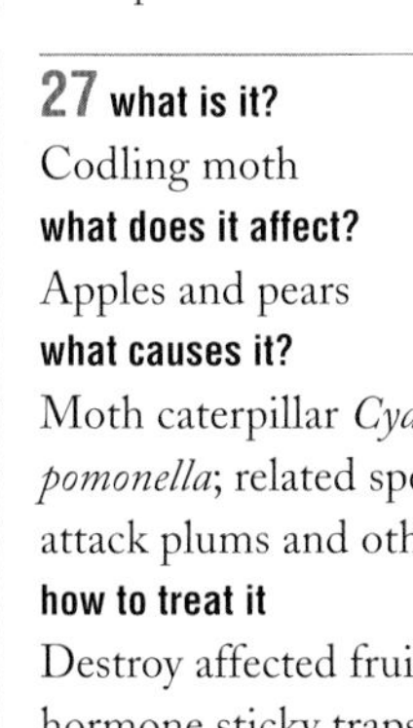

27 what is it?
Codling moth
what does it affect?
Apples and pears
what causes it?
Moth caterpillar *Cydonia pomonella*; related species attack plums and other fruit
how to treat it
Destroy affected fruit; use hormone sticky traps in trees.

28 what is it?
Coral spot
what does it affect?
All woody plants except conifers
what causes it?
Fungus *Nectria cinnabarina*
how to treat it
Cut out affected shoots, cutting well into healthy wood. Don't allow old woody prunings or debris to accumulate in the garden.

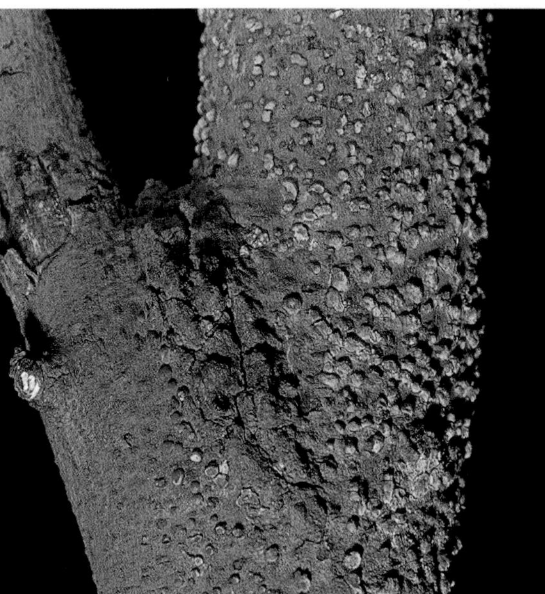

30 what is it?
Cucumber mosaic virus (above)
what does it affect?
Cucumber family especially but also many other plants
what causes it?
Virus that is spread by aphids
how to treat it
Destroy badly affected plants.

31 what is it?
Currant and gooseberry leaf spot
what does it affect?
Gooseberries and currants
what causes it?
Fungus *Drepanopeziza ribis*
how to treat it
Collect up and destroy fallen leaves.

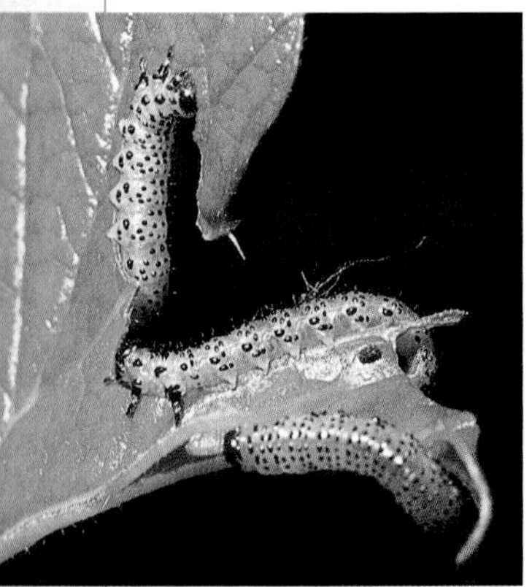

32 what is it?
Currant and gooseberry sawfly
what does it affect?
Gooseberries and currants
what causes it?
Larvae of ant-like insect *Nematus ribesii*
how to treat it
Spray with contact insecticide at very first signs of symptoms.

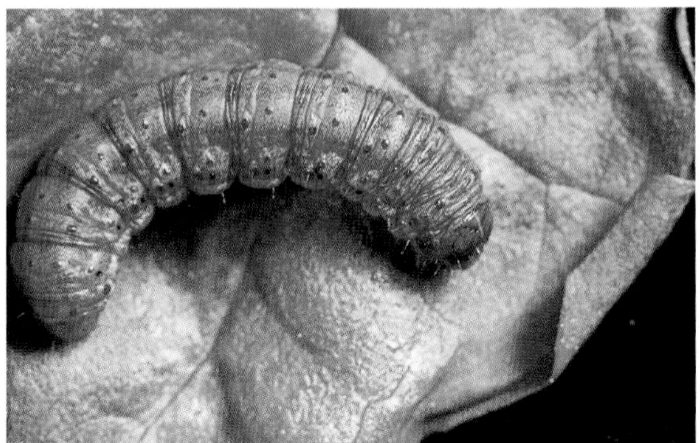

33 what is it?
Cutworms
what does it affect?
Leafy vegetables and other plants
what causes it?
Soil-inhabiting moth caterpillars
how to treat it
Cultivate soil regularly to bring insects to surface.

34 what is it?
Damping off
what does it affect?
Seedlings of all kinds
what causes it?
Several different soil fungi
how to treat it
Destroy affected batches of seedlings. Always use fresh compost and wash and disinfect seed trays.

35 what is it?
Die-back
what does it affect?
Woody plants of all kinds
what causes it?
Many different fungi and some bacteria; sometimes associated with cankers
how to treat it
Cut out affected branches or shoots, cutting back into healthy wood.

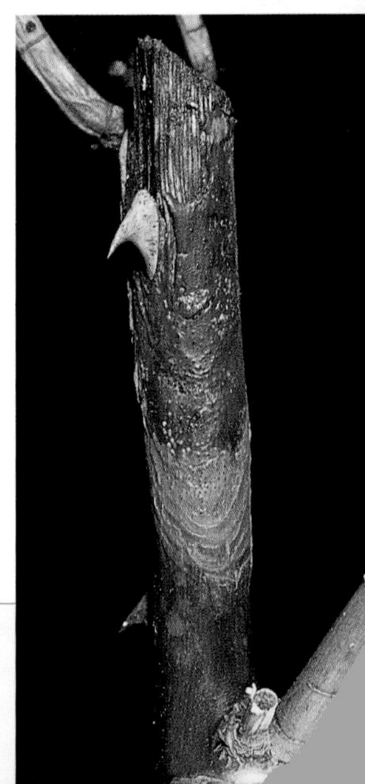

36 what is it?
Fairy rings
what does it affect?
Lawn turf
what causes it?
Fungus *Marasmius oreades*
how to treat it
Spike and feed affected areas of turf; fungi can't be eradicated permanently.

37 what is it?
Fireblight
what does it affect?
Woody members of the rose family
what causes it?
Bacterium *Erwinia amylovora*
how to treat it
Cut back affected branches, cutting well into healthy wood.

38 what is it?
Flea beetles
what does it affect?
Leafy vegetables, many types of seedlings and other plants
what causes it?
Beetles, species of *Phyllotreta*
how to treat it
Clear away plant debris regularly and don't allow plants to dry out for prolonged periods in hot weather.

39 what is it?
Flower breaking
what does it affect?
Wallflowers and tulips, sometimes other flowers
what causes it?
Virus
how to treat it
Destroy affected plants.

40 what is it?
Grey mould rot
what does it affect?
Most fruit and vegetables
what causes it?
Fungus *Botrytis cinerea*
how to treat it
Destroy affected plants and maintain careful hygiene in the garden and greenhouse; improve ventilation in the greenhouse.

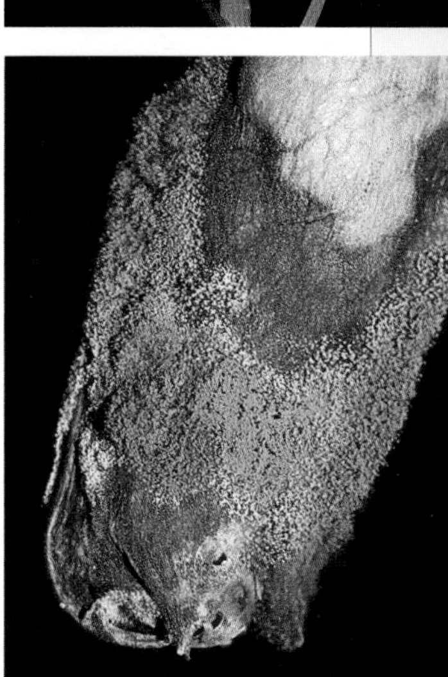

41 what is it?
Hollyhock rust
what does it affect?
Hollyhocks
what causes it?
Fungus *Puccinia malvacearum*
how to treat it
Pull off first affected leaves as soon as they are seen; spray with a proprietary rust fungicide.

42 what is it?
Honey fungus
what does it affect?
All woody plants and some herbaceous perennials
what causes it?
Fungi, species of *Armillaria*
how to treat it
Use proprietary drenches to limit spread of fungus in soil, bury vertical barriers around affected source tree stumps, always dig or grind out stumps when trees are felled.

44 what is it?
Leaf cutter bees
what does it affect?
Roses and some other plants
what causes it?
Species of solitary bee *Megachile centuncularis*
how to treat it
None – damage must be tolerated.

43 what is it?
Leaf curling aphids
what does it affect?
Plums and related fruit trees
what causes it?
Sap-sucking insect *Brachycaudus helichrysi*
how to treat it
Apply tar soil spray in winter.

45 what is it?
Leaf hoppers
what does it affect?
Many types of plant
what causes it?
Sap-sucking insects
how to treat it
None – damage must be tolerated.

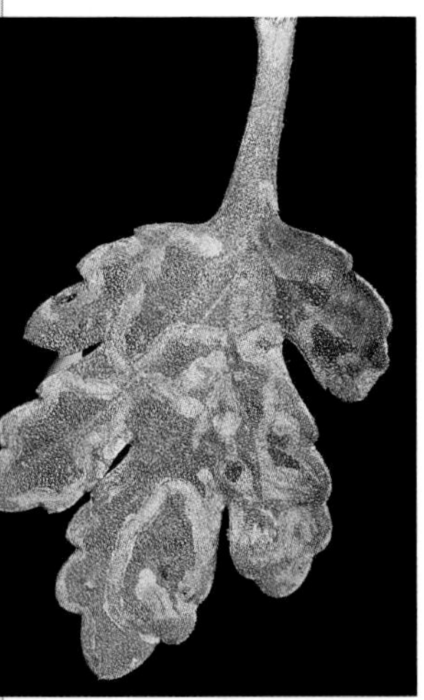

46 what is it?
Leaf miner
what does it affect?
Many types of plant
what causes it?
Larvae of flies and some other insects
how to treat it
Pick off and destroy affected leaves.

47 what is it?
Leaf spot
what does it affect?
Almost all plants
what causes it?
Many different species of fungi and bacteria
how to treat it
Generally no treatment; damage is disfiguring but insignificant. A few exceptions have individual entries.

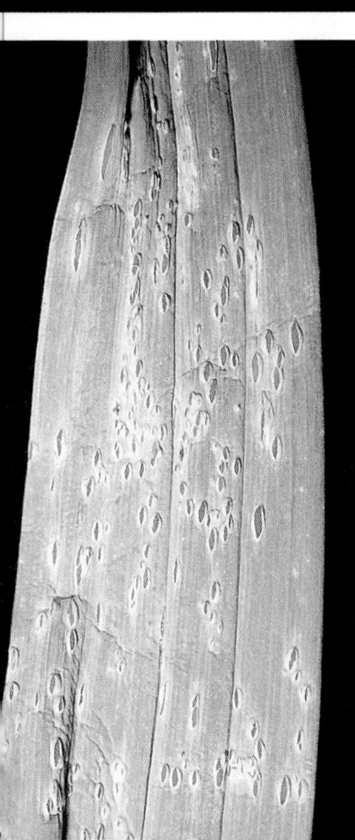

48 what is it?
Leek rust
what does it affect?
Leeks, chives and related members of onion family
what causes it?
Fungus *Puccinia allii*
how to treat it
Clear away all debris at end of season. Spray leeks with a proprietary potato blight fungicide.

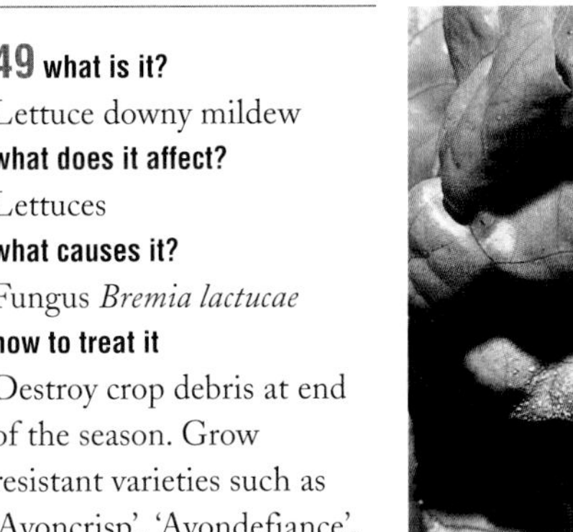

49 what is it?
Lettuce downy mildew
what does it affect?
Lettuces
what causes it?
Fungus *Bremia lactucae*
how to treat it
Destroy crop debris at end of the season. Grow resistant varieties such as 'Avoncrisp', 'Avondefiance', 'Debby' and 'Lakeland'.

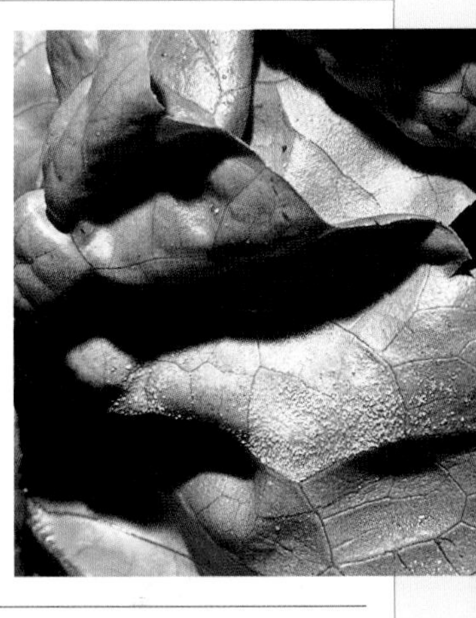

50 what is it?
Lichen
what does it affect?
Many types of woody plant, especially in wet, mild areas
what causes it?
Many different species of lichen
how to treat it
Use tar oil spray on deciduous plants in winter; scrape off evergreens if severely smothering.

51 what is it?
Lime-induced chlorosis
what does it affect?
Roses, strawberries, raspberries and many other plants, especially those requiring acidic soils
what causes it?
Inability of the plants to take up iron from the soil in alkaline conditions
how to treat it
Apply fertilizer containing sequestered iron at least once a season.

52 what is it?
Mealy bug
what does it affect?
Many plants, especially succulents in greenhouses
what causes it?
Sap-sucking insects
how to treat it
Destroy severely affected plants. Use biological control in greenhouses.

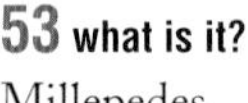

53 what is it?
Millepedes
what does it affect?
Seedling plants and fruit and vegetable produce
what causes it?
Several species of many-legged diplopods
how to treat it
Avoid accumulations of debris in gardens; dust non-edible plants and produce with an appropriate approved insecticide dust.

54 what is it?
Moles
what does it affect?
Lawns and any plants growing in moist, light soils through which they tunnel
what causes it?
Single species of subterranean mammal, *Talpa europaea*
how to treat it
Use proprietary repellent devices or set traps.

55 what is it?
Onion neck rot
what does it affect?
Onions, when stored
what causes it?
Fungus *Botrytis allii*
how to treat it
Dust seeds or sets with systemic fungicide before planting.

56 what is it?
Onion white rot
what does it affect?
Onions and related plants
what causes it?
Fungus *Sclerotium cepivorum*
how to treat it
Set aside special bed for growing onions and avoid contamination of this area with surrounding soil.

57 what is it?
Parsnip canker
what does it affect?
Parsnips
what causes it?
Several different fungi cause distinct symptoms
how to treat it
Grow variety 'Avonresister'.

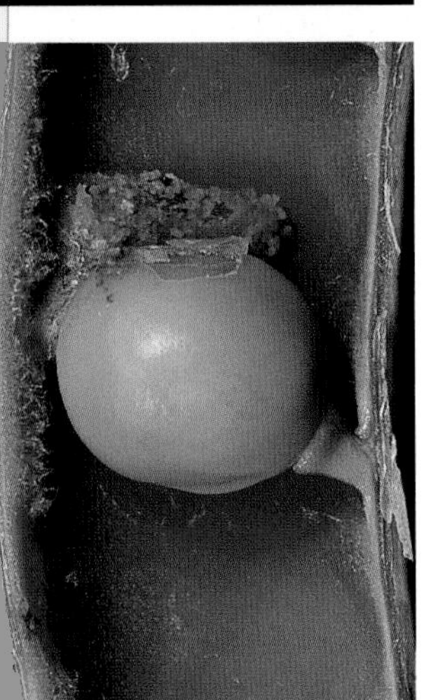

58 what is it?
Pea moth
what does it affect?
Peas
what causes it?
Caterpillars of moth *Cydia nigricans*
how to treat it
Adjust sowing time so that peas are not in flower in early and midsummer when females are laying eggs.

59 what is it?
Peach leaf curl
what does it affect?
Peaches, nectarines, almonds
what causes it?
Fungus *Taphrina deformans*
how to treat it
Chemical sprays are of little value and in areas subject to bad attacks, little can be done. Apricots are unaffected.

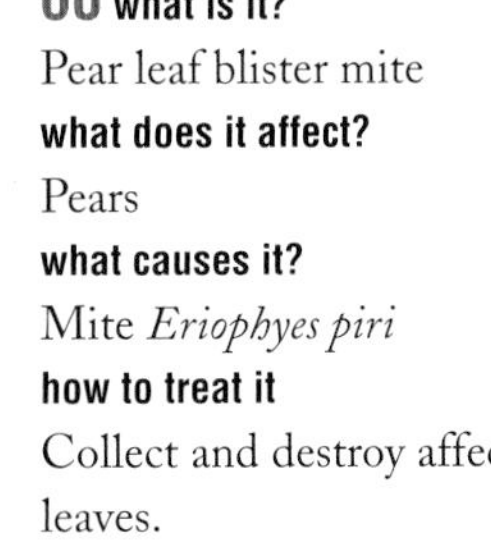

60 what is it?
Pear leaf blister mite
what does it affect?
Pears
what causes it?
Mite *Eriophyes piri*
how to treat it
Collect and destroy affected leaves.

61 **what is it?**
Pelargonium rust
what does it affect?
Pelargoniums
what causes it?
Fungus *Puccinia pelargonii-zonalis*
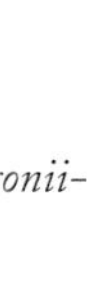
how to treat it
Spray plants with an appropriate approved rust fungicide. Do not take cuttings from affected plants.

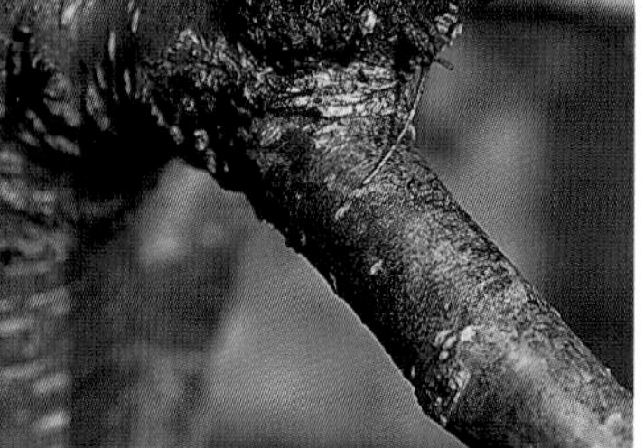

62 **what is it?**
Plum and cherry canker
what does it affect?
Plums, cherries and related plants
what causes it?
Bacterium *Pseudomonas syringae*
how to treat it
Cut off affected branches. If the disease is in the main trunk, nothing can be done and the tree should be felled.

63 **what is it?**
Plum rust
what does it affect?
Plums and related plants
what causes it?
Fungus *Tranzschelia discolor*
how to treat it
None – rarely causes serious long-term harm.

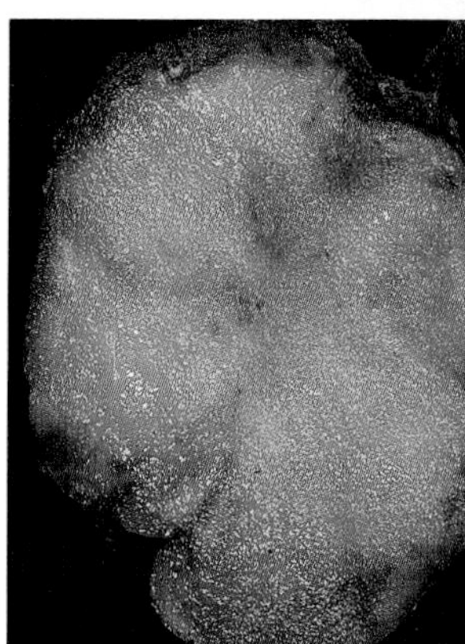

64 **what is it?**
Potato blight
what does it affect?
Potatoes and tomatoes
what causes it?
Fungus *Phytophthora infestans*
how to treat it
If severe attacks the previous year and/or the weather is very wet in early summer, spray with copper-based fungicide. If crop is affected, immediately cut off and destroy tops and lift the tubers. Check stored tubers regularly. Varieties 'Cara', 'Estima', 'Maris Peer' and 'Pentland Crown' are fairly resistant.

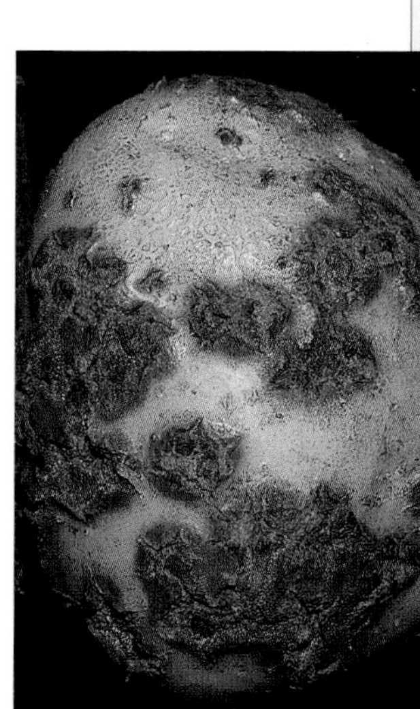

65 **what is it?**
Potato common scab
what does it affect?
Potatoes and several root crops
what causes it?
Actinomycete *Streptomyces scabies*
how to treat it
Incorporate organic matter in light soils, water crop when in flower. Grow resistant varieties such as 'Accent', 'Swift', 'King Edward' and 'Wilja'.

66 what is it?
Powdery mildew
what does it affect?
Almost all plants; some are given separate entries
what causes it?
Fungi of several closely related types
how to treat it
Remove badly damaged foliage and spray plants with approved systemic fungicide. Maintain moist conditions by watering and mulching. Select resistant varieties wherever possible.

67 what is it?
Pyracantha scab
what does it affect?
Pyracanthas
what causes it?
Fungus *Spilocaea pyracanthae*
how to treat it
Spray with an appropriate approved fungicide three times between mid-spring and midsummer. Avoid the variety 'Mohave' which is very susceptible.

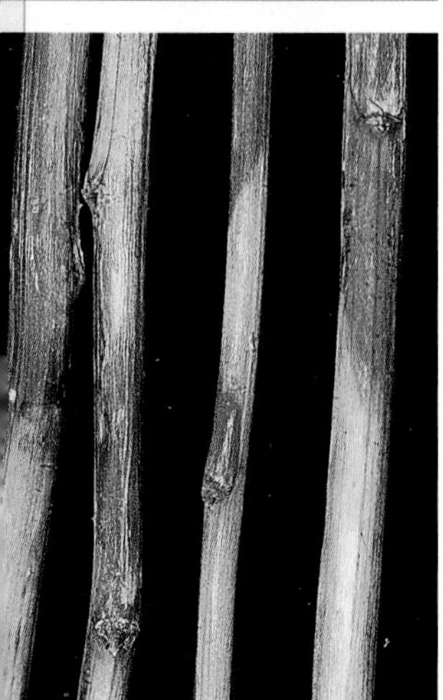

68 what is it?
Raspberry cane blight and midge
what does it affect?
Raspberries
what causes it?
Fungus *Leptosphaeria coniothyrium* with midge *Resseliella theobaldi*
how to treat it
Cut out and destroy affected canes.

69 what is it?
Red currant blister aphid
what does it affect?
Red currants
what causes it?
Sap-sucking insect *Cryptomyzus ribis*; related species affect other plants
how to treat it
Spray with tar oil in winter dormant period.

70 what is it?
Red spider mites
what does it affect?
Many types of plant in hot, dry conditions
what causes it?
Very tiny species of several different mites
how to treat it
Maintain moist conditions wherever possible; avoid planting susceptible plants, such as soft fruit and conifers, in very hot, dry places.

71 what is it?
Red thread
what does it affect?
Lawn grasses
what causes it?
Fungus *Laetisaria fuciformis*
how to treat it
Improve lawn fertility; apply soluble summer lawn fertilizer with a high nitrogen content.

72 what is it?
Rhododendron bud blast
what does it affect?
Rhododendrons and azaleas
what causes it?
Fungus *Pycnostysanus azaleae*, probably associated with leaf-hopper insect
how to treat it
Pick off and destroy affected buds.

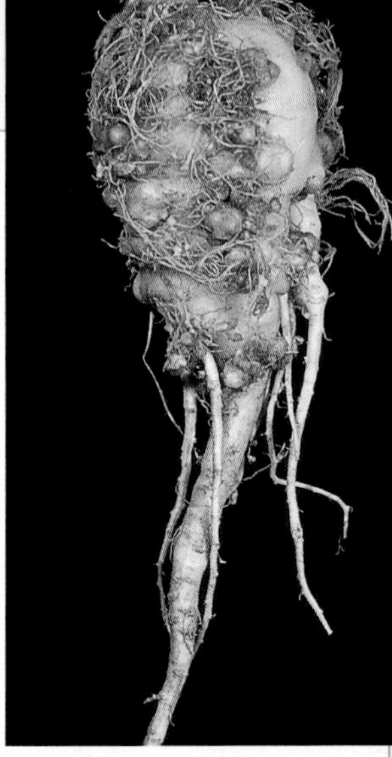

73 what is it?
Root knot eelworms
what does it affect?
Root crops and many other plants
what causes it?
Eelworm species of *Meloidogyne*
how to treat it
Destroy affected plants.

74 what is it?
Rose aphids
what does it affect?
Roses
what causes it?
Several different species of sap-sucking insects; related species affect many different plants and some are given separate entries
how to treat it
Spray with any approved insecticide as soon as the first insects are seen; repeat occasionally if populations build up again.

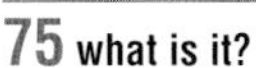

75 what is it?
Rose black spot
what does it affect?
Roses
what causes it?
Fungus *Diplocarpon rosae*
how to treat it
Spray with an appropriate approved fungicide as soon as leaves unfold in spring and repeat two or three times during the season. Hard prune bush roses in early spring and destroy prunings.

76 what is it?
Rose powdery mildew
what does it affect?
Roses
what causes it?
Fungus *Sphaerotheca pannosa*
how to treat it
Spray with appropriate approved fungicide as soon as symptoms are seen and repeat three or four times during the season. Maintain moisture in soil by mulching. Most modern rose varieties have some resistance.

77 what is it?
Rose rust
what does it affect?
Roses
what causes it?
Fungi, species of *Phragmidium*; comparable diseases affect some other plants
how to treat it
Spray with appropriate approved fungicide as soon as symptoms are seen and repeat three or four times during the season. Collect and destroy fallen affected leaves. Most modern varieties have some resistance.

78 what is it?
Runner bean rust
what does it affect?
Runner and French beans
what causes it?
Fungus *Uromyces appendiculatus*
how to treat it
Remove and destroy severely affected plants.

79 what is it?
Scale insects
what does it affect?
Many different plants but common on grapevines, trees and shrubs and also house plants
what causes it?
Several different species of sap-sucking insects
how to treat it
Apply tar oil spray to dormant deciduous woody plants in winter.

80 what is it?
Silver leaf
what does it affect?
Many trees and shrubs but always most serious on plums
what causes it?
Fungus *Chondrostereum purpureum*
how to treat it
Cut off badly affected branches. Fell and burn badly affected trees. Only prune plums and related plants in spring, not in autumn or winter.

81 **what is it?**
Slugs and snails
what does it affect?
All plants with soft and fleshy tissues
what causes it?
Several different species of gastropod molluscs
how to treat it
Use repellents, such as powdery materials, or spiny or prickly matter; set traps, such as dishes of beer; collect manually by searching after dark; use proprietary slug pellets (but protect from interference by pets and wild life).

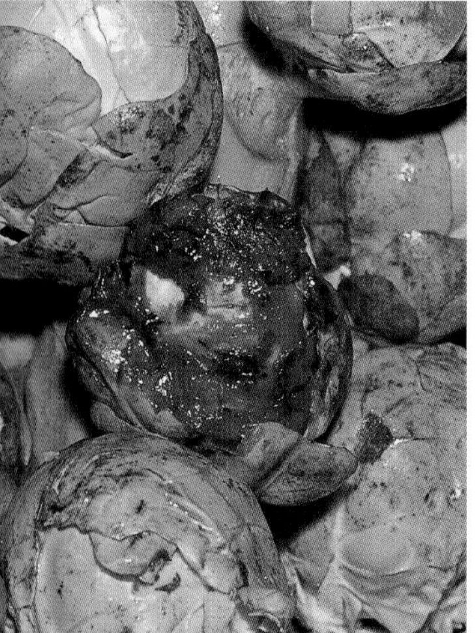

82 **what is it?**
Soft rot
what does it affect?
Many soft fruit, vegetables and other plants
what causes it?
Bacteria, especially *Erwinia carotovora*
how to treat it
Destroy affected plants.

83 **what is it?**
Sooty mould
what does it affect?
Most plants following infestation by sap-sucking insects
what causes it?
Several species of dark-coloured mould fungi
how to treat it
Wash off affected foliage; try to control insect infestations.

84 **what is it?**
Spangle galls
what does it affect?
Oaks, comparable problems on some other trees
what causes it?
Ant-like gall wasps
how to treat it
None needed, merely disfiguring.

85 **what is it?**
Splitting
what does it affect?
Many different fruit and vegetable crops
what causes it?
Periods of dryness followed by improved moisture and rapid growth
how to treat it
Uses mulches, watering and other means to help maintain uniform moisture content in soil.

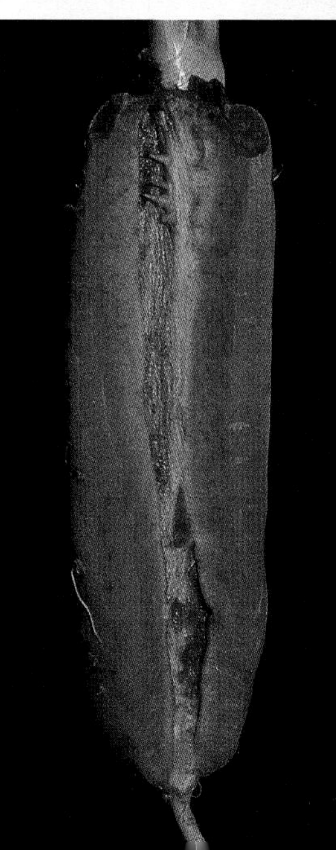

86 what is it?
Squirrels
what does it affect?
Many fruit, vegetable and ornamental plants when growing near to trees
what causes it?
Grey squirrel *Sciurus carolinensis*
how to treat it
Protect crops with netting.

88 what is it?
Strawberry leaf spot, blotch and scorch
what does it affect?
Strawberries
what causes it?
Fungi, *Mycosphaerella fragariae*, *Gnomonia fragariae* and *Diplocarpon earlianum*
how to treat it
Cut off and destroy dead foliage as soon as cropping is complete; avoid damp and shady sites for strawberry crops.

89 what is it?
Tar spot
what does it affect?
Sycamores and some other related *Acer* species
what causes it?
Fungus *Rhytisma acerinum*
how to treat it
None needed, merely disfiguring.

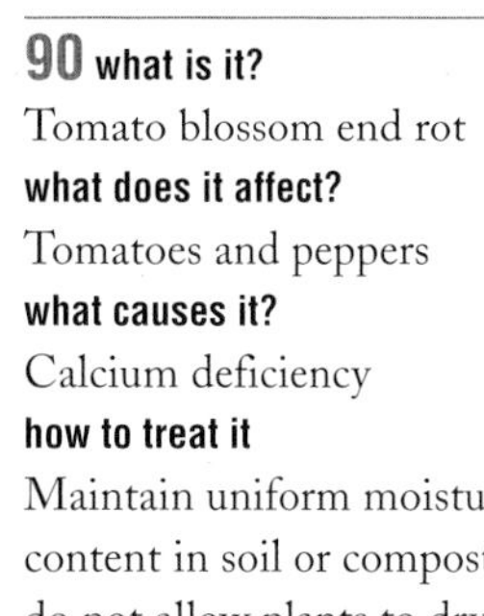

87 what is it?
Strawberry fruit rot
what does it affect?
Strawberries
what causes it?
Rhizopus, *Mucor* and other mould fungi
how to treat it
Use straw or proprietary mats to avoid fruit coming into contact with soil. Do not over-water plants.

90 what is it?
Tomato blossom end rot
what does it affect?
Tomatoes and peppers
what causes it?
Calcium deficiency
how to treat it
Maintain uniform moisture content in soil or compost; do not allow plants to dry out.

91 **what is it?**
Tomato chemical injury
what does it affect?
Tomatoes; also less seriously, other plants
what causes it?
Hormone weedkiller
how to treat it
Destroy affected plants. Never use lawn or other hormone-containing weedkillers close to tomato plants and never mulch tomatoes with manure containing straw.

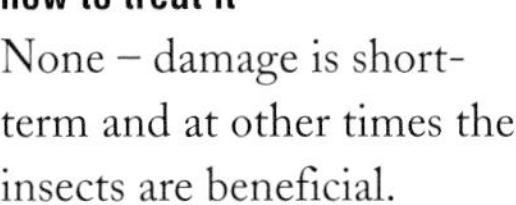

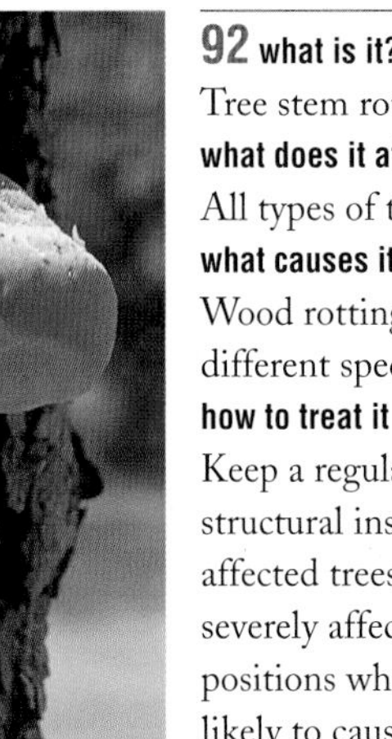

92 **what is it?**
Tree stem rot
what does it affect?
All types of tree
what causes it?
Wood rotting fungi of many different species
how to treat it
Keep a regular check for structural instability in affected trees; fell them if severely affected and in positions where they are likely to cause damage if they are blown down.

93 **what is it?**
Vine weevil
what does it affect?
Evergreen shrubs (adults), many ornamental plants, especially in containers (larvae)
what causes it?
Weevils (beetles), species of *Otiorhynchus*
how to treat it
Mulch heavily beneath shrubs; use biological control to reduce larvae numbers.

94 **what is it?**
Wasps
what does it affect?
Ripening fruit
what causes it?
Several species of wasp (*Vespa*)
how to treat it
None – damage is short-term and at other times the insects are beneficial.

95 **what is it?**
White blister
what does it affect?
Lunaria, brassicas and related plants, salsify and related plants
what causes it?
Fungi, species of *Albugo*
how to treat it
Destroy affected plants.

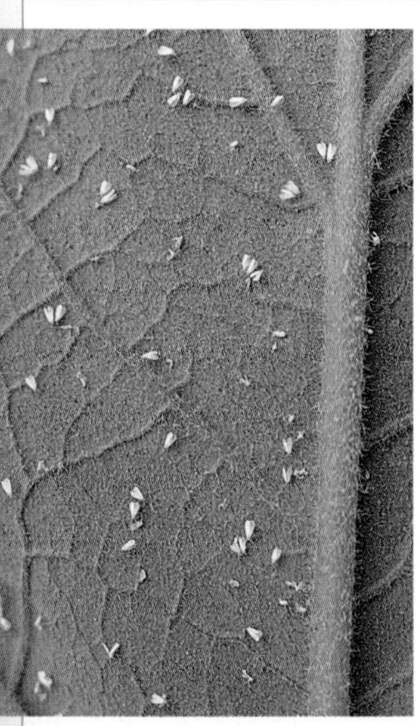

96 what is it?
Whiteflies
what does it affect?
Many different types of plant, especially brassicas outdoors and many in greenhouses
what causes it?
Sap-sucking insects of several different species
how to treat it
Outdoors, destroy crop debris promptly; in greenhouses, use biological control.

97 what is it?
Wireworm
what does it affect?
Root crops and sometimes other plant roots
what causes it?
Larvae of tipulids (crane flies)
how to treat it
Cultivate soil regularly, especially when newly dug from grassland.

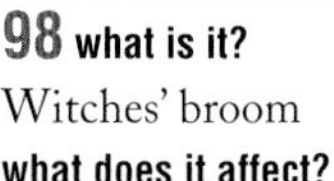

98 what is it?
Witches' broom
what does it affect?
Many types of trees but especially common on birch
what causes it?
Several different fungi, especially species of *Taphrina*; also some mites, insects, bacteria and viruses
how to treat it
None needed, merely disfiguring.

99 what is it?
Woodlice
what does it affect?
Seedlings and soft, fleshy plant parts
what causes it?
Several species of isopod crustaceans
how to treat it
Clear away plant debris promptly. Use an approved insecticide dust when colonies are found.

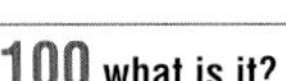

100 what is it?
Woolly aphids
what does it affect?
Several different trees and shrubs and other plants but especially common on apples.
what causes it?
Sap-sucking insects, especially *Eriosoma lanigerum*
how to treat it
Spray apple trees and other dormant deciduous trees and shrubs in winter with tar oil.

Keys to plant problems

using the keys

Correct identification is the key to understanding and combating any problem; the key to identification is to know what to look for and how to look for it, as any Sherlock Holmes enthusiast will tell you. Of course, as Dr Watson discovered, there's no substitute for experience: what was elementary to Holmes, with his vast and deep fund of experience, was pretty obscure to the less knowledgeable Watson. And so it is with garden problems: the more you see, the more will you learn and the better you will be able to make sense of the next mystery that comes along.

I've devised the keys in the hope that anyone, even those with little or no experience, will be able to identify their garden problems. Inevitably, I've been selective and have concentrated on those problems that my experience suggests you are most likely to encounter. While I can't promise that you won't occasionally come across something out of the ordinary, or that sometimes a fairly common disorder may give rise to unexpected symptoms or occur on an unexpected plant, I've tested the keys pretty thoroughly and feel confident that they will guide you in the right direction with most problems you are likely to encounter.

The keys are of what is called the dichotomous type. The principle is simplicity itself. You start at number 1 in each case and are required to make choices, usually from two possibilities (a or b), occasionally from more. Each time you make a choice, you will be directed to a further pair of choices and, ultimately, I hope, to the correct identification.

Using the keys correctly depends on careful observation – of the plant and in the choices. Don't try to make a particular problem fit somewhere that is not suggested in the keys. If the key says 'Symptoms on conifers only', for example, this means just that – *symptoms on conifers only* – and a superficially similar problem on an oak tree won't be correctly identified.

There is one key to weeds, and ten keys to plant problems (pests, diseases and disorders), each based on a different part of the plant. With the latter, therefore, you must first decide where on the plant the main symptoms occur. This will direct you to the most appropriate key. If there are symptoms on different parts of the same plant, using more than one key makes sense – if the symptoms are all part of the same problem, this gives you a double chance of getting it right, if they represent two different problems, you will not miss anything. In this case, it's best to look at the key that deals with the main symptom first. If, for instance, a tree has tiny spots on the leaves but huge, sap-oozing lesions on the branches, it's clear that the lesions are the main symptom so choose Key E (stems) before Key D (leaves).

weeds key

In the weeds key, I've selected the weeds that you are most likely to find in gardens. I've deliberately excluded a number of species that, while important as weeds, are usually only serious on farmland or in waste places. And, of course, there will inevitably be some other wild plants that occur occasionally as garden weeds or that may, for local reasons, be significant is very restricted areas. You should also remember that in individual gardens, vigorous and neglected cultivated plants (generally planted by a previous owner) can also take on weed status. They won't be identified using this key. Nonetheless, I feel pretty confident that it will direct you to the identity of about 90 per cent of the garden weeds you are likely to encounter.

The key doesn't require the presence of flowers to complete an identification, being based solely on leaf shape and growth habit. This is because many weeds, such as thistles, don't flower until they have reached a fairly large size (which they might do in wild or new gardens but are unlikely to be allowed to in cultivated plots), and a few, like couch grass, seldom flower and one, horsetail, is unable to flower, being a more primitive type of spore-bearing plant. I have, however, given details of flower colour and form with the keyed-out species description to help you to confirm your identification. Because several weeds have rather variable leaf shapes, you will find certain species key-out at more than one place.

aids to identification

I hope that the reason why I've subdivided plants into their various parts will be reasonably obvious from what has been said about the way that pests and pathogens go about their business: for instance, the ability to attack soft tissues, such as flowers, most leaves or fragile young seedlings, requires very different 'equipment' from that required to penetrate bark and wood, and the ability to attack roots suggests the presence of a creature that can live in the soil, a very different environment from the open air.

Here are some of the questions I ask myself when identifying a problem. Remember that there are many other symptoms than those listed below, and some are highly characteristic of specific problems. I stress again: examine affected plants very carefully.

Which species or varieties are affected?

Many problems are specific to particular hosts.

Do the symptoms occur on isolated plants, on odd plants irregularly dispersed or in patches?

If odd, scattered plants are affected, this could suggest the problem has a common origin: perhaps it infected the plants in a seed tray or transplant bed before they were put out in the garden.

If plants in patches are affected, perhaps the problem originates in a defined area of soil, although the possibility of it having spread outwards from a single individual should also be considered.

Are the symptoms unidirectional over the plant or more uniform?

A unidirectional distribution might suggestion a problem originating in only one part of the root system or, very commonly, from a windborne pest or disease.

Is mould growth present?

This is a sound indicator of a fungal problem, provided that it can be distinguished from the white, woolly wax that some pests produce to protect themselves.

Are the symptoms confined to young or old shoots, leaves or other parts?

Damage only on young leaves could be due to something having happened in the bud or as the leaves emerged, or it could be the effects of something insufficiently robust to attack more mature tissues. Some symptoms of nutrient deficiency are conspicuously and characteristically present on old leaves as food materials are exported to satisfy the needs of vigorously expanding new growth. Symptoms occurring at the tips of shoots or branches may be due to an airborne pathogen, pest or pollutant but death of shoot tips usually requires examination of the other end of the plant for it suggests root damage. Any impairment of root function will mean that nutrients and water are transported less effectively and the most peripheral parts of the plant will be those to suffer first.

Are there holes in the leaves? If yes, their nature, size, number and shape can betray much information.

Generally, discrete more or less rounded holes are of insect origin. Fungal or bacterial attack can result in holes but usually only after the initial production of spots of dead tissue, the centres of which then drop out (they are called 'shot-holes'). Holes with a crisp edge suggest recent feeding activity (the pests themselves may still be present nearby). A tiny brown rim, visible under a magnifying lens (a vital piece of equipment for every serious gardener) indicates that the damaged tissue has begun to heal and the causal pest has moved on. It also implies that any control measure will be a case of shutting the stable door too late.

The size and number of holes is often a good indication of the size and number of pests. The almost lace-like holing caused by multitudes of tiny flea beetles is a good example of this. The stripping of foliage to leave only veins is a common symptom of caterpillar or sawfly larva attack for they are often unable to eat the tougher tissue of veins. Sinuous pieces removed from leaf margins is characteristic of weevil activity, while for large irregular holes in the centres of leaves, accompanied by a slimy, silver deposit, diagnose snail or slug damage.

Are there spots and what do they look like?

Spots on leaves can be in a huge range of sizes, shapes and colours, and tend to be given different names. A large irregular spot is called a blotch, a very extensive area of browned tissue is scorching, and a black, sunken lesion is often called anthracnose ('charcoal-like'). Very tiny, pin-point spots are often of bacterial origin, while the presence of concentric patterning, sometimes accompanied by minute pimples, indicates a fungal cause.

Is there general discoloration?

A pattern of discoloration, rather than any real spots of dead tissue, is generally the result either of virus attack or of a specific nutrient deficiency. However, the normal coloration of the leaves of many ornamental plants is similar to this discoloration effect (indeed, some are caused by the presence of virus in the tissues). In addition, always be cautious of diagnosing any symptoms of abnormal coloration on deciduous plants in autumn when they will impossible to distinguish from normal seasonal effects.

Is there decay?

Decay is always the result of fungal or bacterial action although it may follow damage from another cause. Very soft, slimy (and especially smelly) decay is usually bacterial; firmer rot, whatever its colour, is usually fungal.

I hope you will find it both enjoyable and instructive identifying your problems using the keys. Having reached an identification, look for the word (or words) printed in **bold**. In the pest, diseases and disorders keys, it will sometimes will be the entire name – **powdery mildew**, **rabbits**, **voles** for instance, sometimes only a part – honey fungus **rot**, bay **sucker**, botrytis grey mould **rot**, for example. In the weeds key, it will be one of the broad groups of weed types – **annual**, **invasive perennial** and so on. Turn then to the 'Index to pests, diseases and disorders' or 'Index to weeds', where all the words in bold are listed and described and you will be given some general guidelines on how, if at all, the problem should be treated.

please note

Regarding the keys to pests, diseases and weeds on pages 187–213, I believe this is the first time that anything comparable to, or as comprehensive as, these keys has been attempted. So if in using them you find anomalies or have suggestions that could be incorporated in subsequent editions of the book, do please let me know.

Pests, diseases and disorders Keys A-J

Where are the main symptoms?

on or in soil or compost close to plants	**Key A**	p187
on sown seeds or seedlings	**Key B**	p188
on buds	**Key C**	p188
on leaves	**Key D**	p189
on twigs, shoots, branches, stems or trunks	**Key E**	p196
on flowers	**Key F**	p200
on fruits or nuts	**Key G**	p201
on vegetable fruit (peas, beans, tomatoes, peppers, etc)	**Key H**	p203
on bulbs, tubers, corms or rhizomes	**Key I**	p204
on roots	**Key J**	p206

Key A soil or compost

1	a	Small invertebrate pests present	go to 7
	b	No pests present	go to 2
2	a	Obvious 2-3cm diameter hole(s) in soil	**voles** or **mice**
	b	Other	go to 3
3	a	Soil generally disturbed, no claw marks	**ants**
	b	Other	go to 4
4	a	Soil pulled away, especially from seed beds, claw marks often present	**cats**
	b	Soil in small heaps	go to 5
5	a	Soil heaps at least 5cm high	**moles**
	b	Soil heaps less than about 5cm high	go to 6
6	a	Heaps of fine soil about 1cm high	burrowing **bees**
	b	Soil extruded as small 'toothpaste-like' casts and often with dead leaves partly pulled into soil	**earthworms**
7	a	Minute, white, centipede-like creatures; overall plant growth poor	**symphylids**
	b	Other	go to 8
8	a	Dark-coloured flies running over surface; white, legless larvae with dark heads sometimes present among roots and at bases of stems	sciarid **flies** (fungus gnats)
	b	Other	go to 9
9	a	Minute, wingless insects jumping from surface of soil or potting compost	**springtails**
	b	Ovoid, usually greyish pests with up to 14 legs	**woodlice**

Woodlice, *Porcellio scaber*

Key B sown seeds or seedlings

1	a	Seedlings fail to emerge satisfactorily	go to 2
	b	Other	go to 3
2	a	Seeds disappeared from soil	**mice**, **voles** or **birds**
	b	Seeds present, ungerminated	fungal **rot**, usually after sowing in cold, wet conditions
3	a	Seedlings pulled out of soil	**birds** or **cats**
	b	Other	go to 4
4	a	Seedlings emerge then collapse and die	go to 5
	b	Other	go to 6
5	a	Seedlings die in patches, and with blackening and rot of the stem base and/or fluffy grey mould growth present	damping off (**rot**)
	b	Usually isolated plants affected, blackened and shrivelled stem base	black leg **rot** or root and foot **rot**
	c	Stems damaged or severed at soil level, roots damaged	cutworm **caterpillars**
6	a	Poor growth and plants have tough wiry stems	wirestem **rot**
	b	Other	go to 7
7	a	Leaves and growing points eaten away, usually slime trails present	**slugs** or **snails**
	b	Other	go to 8
8	a	Leaves with tiny holes	go to 9
	b	Other	go to 10
9	a	Leaves minutely pitted; minute, pale, wingless jumping insects present	**springtails**
	b	Small, round holes, especially on brassicas; tiny, dark-coloured hopping insects present	flea **beetles**
10	a	Greyish spots on cotyledons	black leg **rot**
	b	Leaves variously discoloured	nutrient **deficiency**
	c	Yellow specks on upper leaf and cotyledon surfaces; off-white mould beneath	**downy mildew**

Key C buds

1	a	On cabbage heads or Brussels sprout buttons	go to 2
	b	On other plants	go to 4
2	a	Heads with soft and slimy rot; usually no mould growth	bacterial soft **rot**
	b	Heads rotted, mould present	go to 3
3	a	Fluffy, grey mould growth present; stems may rot completely	grey mould **rot** or other root and foot **rot**
	b	Pure white mould present	sclerotinia **rot** disease
4	a	Dormant buds burst into unseasonal growth	disturbed growth **disorder**
	b	Other	go to 5
5	a	Abnormally enlarged or distorted	go to 6
	b	Other	go to 7
6	a	On blackcurrants	blackcurrant **gall mite**
	b	On broom, forming large irregular galls	broom **gall mite**
	c	On hazelnut and related plants	nut **gall mite**
	d	On conifers; galls like miniature pineapples	**adelgids**
	e	On other plants	**eelworms**
7	a	Ragged and torn but not holed; flowers may be similarly affected	**birds**
	b	Other	go to 8
8	a	Infested with insects	go to 9
	b	Not infested with insects	go to 11

Flea beetles, *Phyllotreta* sp., on calabrese

9	a	Colonies of yellow, green, pink or dark-coloured winged and wingless insects; foliage sticky and sooty	**aphids**
	b	Other types of insect	go to 10
10	a	Colonies of small, flattened insects; buds discoloured, fail to develop normally, often sticky; especially apples and pears	**suckers**
	b	Variously damaged; small caterpillars present	**caterpillars**
	c	Brightly coloured insects present (red on lilies); buds holed	**beetles**
11	a	Shrivelled, no pin-like bodies; buds may die and/or drop suddenly	go to 12
	b	Other	go to 13
12	a	In spring	**frost** or sudden temperature change
	b	At other times	**drought** or root **rot** or other damage
13	a	On rhododendron; tiny, black, pin-like bodies	rhododendron bud blast (**rot**)
	b	On other plants	go to 14
14	a	Small, discrete holes present	go to 15
	b	No small, discrete holes	go to 16
15	a	No slime trails; may be silky webbing	**caterpillars**
	b	Slime trails present	**slugs** or **snails**
16	a	Mould growth present	go to 17
	b	No mould growth; buds waterlogged and discoloured (especially on roses)	balling (thin-petalled varieties do not open properly in wet weather)
17	a	White, velvety mould	**powdery mildew**
	b	Grey, fluffy mould	botrytis grey mould **rot**
	c	Orange or yellow, velvety mould	**rust**

Key D leaves

1	a	Symptoms on lawn grasses	go to 2
	b	Symptoms on other plants	go to 8
2	a	Grass yellowing, browning and dying, often in patches	go to 3
	b	Variously coloured growths on or among grass	go to 7
3	a	Yellow patches, often numerous and attracting attention of starlings or other birds	leatherjackets (crane**flies**)
	b	Other	go to 4
4	a	Large areas of brown, withered grass during dry weather; large, white larvae below surface	chafer **beetles**
	b	Other	go to 5
5	a	Occasional more or less round, discrete patches of dead grass	dog urine or chemical spillage (**disorder**)
	b	Other	go to 6
6	a	Yellow-brown patches, 5-8cm diameter, in mild, wet weather in late summer or early autumn	dollar spot (**turf rot**)
	b	Pale, bleached patches from late summer, gradually increasing in size	ophiobolus patch (**turf rot**)
	c	Irregular reddish patches, to 45cm diameter, in late summer, with red, needle-like bodies among grass	red thread (**turf rot**)
	d	Rounded patches, to 30cm diameter, in winter, grass turns yellow-white-pink and rots	snow mould (**turf rot**)
	e	Ring patterns of light (dead) and dark grass, often with toadstools present	fairy ring (**turf rot**)
7	a	Grass smothered with variously coloured (especially yellow or grey), slimy, often sponge-like bodies	**slime moulds** (also see 6c and 6d)
	b	Gelatinous, green bodies among leaves	**algae**
	c	White or greyish, often branched or flap-like growths	**lichen**

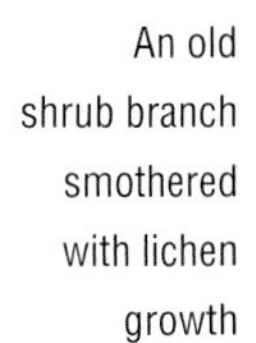

An old shrub branch smothered with lichen growth

8	a	Invertebrate pests (including apparently lifeless tiny, limpet-like bodies) and/or tufts of white, woolly or mealy wax present; no mould	go to 9
	b	Invertebrate pests absent	go to 33
9	a	Insects (six legs) present	go to 10
	b	Other pests present	go to 28
10	a	Insects (including tiny limpet-like bodies) obvious; no white woolly wax	go to 11
	b	White, woolly or mealy wax present; insects not immediately apparent but concealed beneath	go to 24
11	a	Leaves sticky and often sooty	go to 12
	b	Other	go to 15
12	a	Insects – tiny, white, winged, especially on leaf undersides	**whiteflies**
	b	Other	go to 13
13	a	Insects – small green, pink, yellow or dark coloured, winged and wingless; cast white skins and ants may be present	**aphids**
	b	Other	go to 14
14	a	Insects – legless, in form of brown, waxy scales	**scale insects**
	b	Insects – small and flat, leaves and young shoots distorted; shoot tips may be curled like tiny cabbages	**suckers**
	c	Other	go to 24
15	a	Insects – small, jumping or hopping on plants; leaf surface finely eroded	**leafhoppers**
	b	Other	go to 16
16	a	Holes and irregular pieces eaten away; sinuous insects present; no slime trails; excreta ('frass') may be present	go to 17
	b	Other	go to 18
17	a	Small to large, sinuous insects; foliage may be drawn together with webbing	**caterpillars**
	b	Medium-sized, dull-coloured, sinuous insects; foliage rapidly stripped to leave a skeleton of veins (especially on Solomon's seal and gooseberries)	**sawflies**
18	a	Tiny, jumping insects; many small holes in foliage, especially on young plants close to soil level	flea **beetles**
	b	Other	go to 19
19	a	Large, often brightly coloured (sometimes 'metallic' or striped), long-legged insects, usually few in number; holes in foliage (not on rhododendron)	**beetles**
	b	Dark brown, long-snouted insects, eating leaf margins, especially on evergreens	vine **weevils**
	c	Other	go to 20
20	a	On rhododendron	go to 21
	b	On other plants	go to 22
21	a	Small insects with green wing cases and red stripes; buds may be shrivelled and have pin-like protrusions	rhododendron **leafhopper**
	b	Small, long-legged insects with lace-like wings, on undersides of leaves in summer; foliage yellow mottled above, brown 'rusty' below	rhododendron bug (**lace bug**)
22	a	Leaf surface eroded	go to 23
	b	Masses of spit-like substance concealing green, large-eyed insects	**froghoppers**
23	a	Shiny, black, slug-like insects (on pears, cherries and other rosaceous trees); leaf surface with translucent 'windows'	pear and cherry slugworm **sawflies**
	b	Green-yellow, slug-like insects (on roses)	rose slug **sawflies**
	c	Fine, pale flecking; tiny, narrow-bodied insects	**thrips**
24	a	On conifers	**adelgids**
	b	On other plants	go to 25
25	a	On brassicas, leaves infested by dense colonies of grey-green insects covered in white, powdery wax	cabbage **aphid**
	b	Other	go to 26
26	a	On clipped hedges, especially box and beech	**aphids**
	b	Other	go to 27
27	a	On bay, leaf edges thick and curled	bay **sucker**
	b	Also on bark and twigs, especially apple	woolly **aphids**
	c	On alder twigs	alder **sucker**
28	a	White, woolly wax present; many-legged woodlouse-like pests beneath	**mealy bug**
	b	Other	go to 29
29	a	Large, brown or black, slimy pests present	go to 30
	b	Other	go to 31
30	a	Pests with shells	**snails**
	b	Pests without shells	**slugs**
31	a	Minute pests (use hand lens), often cobwebs present; leaves bronzed or flecked	red spider **mites**
	b	Larger, many-legged pests	go to 32

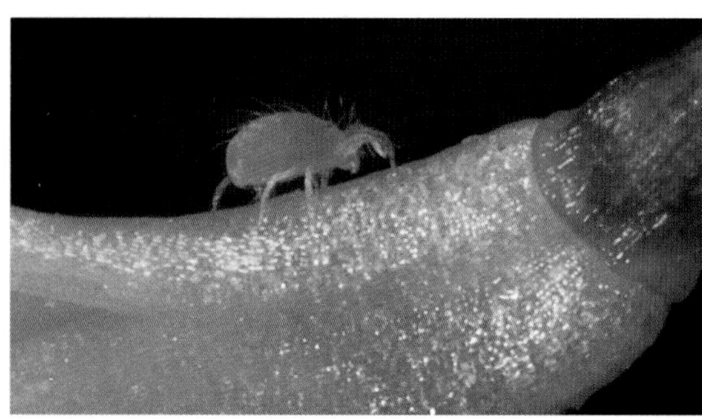

32	a	Snake-like black or pink pests with numerous (around 100) legs	**millipedes**
	b	Ovoid, usually greyish pests with fewer (up to 14) legs	**woodlice**
33	a	Leaves drop prematurely in absence of other obvious symptoms	check roots for symptoms; if none, probably **wilt** disease or **drought**; if symptoms found, go to Key J
	b	Other	go to 34
34	a	Leaves wilt (droop) but remained attached to plants	go to 99
	b	Other	go to 35
35	a	Symptoms on leaf blades (including leaves within vegetable heads)	go to 36
	b	Symptoms mainly confined to leaf stalks	go to 54
36	a	Within cabbage heads or Brussels sprout buttons, small, dark patches	calcium **deficiency**
	b	Symptoms on exposed leaves	go to 37
37	a	Distorted, bloated, plant growth poor, especially on bulbous plants	stem **eelworm** (although this is difficult to diagnose; check for symptoms roots (Key J) and stems (Key E) too
	b	Other	go to 38
38	a	Mould growth	go to 39
	b	No obvious mould growth	go to 64
39	a	Velvety, white or yellow mould and leaves puckered	go to 87
	b	Other	go to 40
40	a	At least some mould on upper surface	go to 41
	b	Mould confined to lower surface	go to 61
41	a	Black, soot-like mould (sooty mould)	go to 43
	b	Other	go to 42
42	a	Tiny, brown, black, orange or yellow pustules, often coalescing	**rust**
	b	Other	go to 47
43	a	Leaf surface finely eroded; cast insects' skins may be present beneath	**leafhoppers**
	b	Other	go to 44
44	a	Shoot tips curled like tiny cabbages	**suckers**
	b	Other	go to 45
45	a	Cast white insect skins present	**aphids**
	b	Other	go to 46
46	a	Brown, waxy scales present	**scale insects**
	b	Other	sap-sucking insects (**aphids**, **scale insects**, **whiteflies** or **suckers**)
47	a	Dense, powdery or velvety, white mould, in discrete patches or overall	**powdery mildew**
	b	Other	go to 48
48	a	Dense, powdery white and felted brown mould (gooseberries and currants)	American **(powdery) mildew**
	b	Other	go to 49
49	a	Fairly dense, white-grey mould with leaf rot (on potatoes or tomatoes)	blight
	b	Other	go to 50
50	a	Tiny, brown, black, orange or yellow pustules (dirty white on chrysanthemum), often coalescing	**rust**
	b	Greyish or off-white, fluffy mould, usually with some leaf rot or shrivelling	go to 51
51	a	On tulips, leaves die back from tips	fire disease **rot**
	b	Other	go to 52
52	a	On ornamental bulbous plants, leaves brown and rotten; plants stunted and fail to flower; bulbs turn soft and pulpy	grey mould **rot** is the commonest cause; other possibilities are smoulder on *Narcissus* or other fungal **rot** diseases
	b	Other	go to 53

opposite:

Red spider mite, *Tetranychus urticae* magnified 20 times

Cyst eelworm, *Heterodera* sp., magnified 100 times

53	a	On leeks	white tip (**rot**) is a possibility but botrytis grey mould **rot** and other **rot**-causing fungi produce similar symptoms
	b	On other plants	botrytis grey mould **rot** is the most likely
54	a	Mould present	go to 55
	b	No mould	go to 57
55	a	Dense, pure white, cottony mould, sometimes with tiny, black bodies within, associated with rot	sclerotinia **rot** disease (but on onions, more likely to be white **rot**)
	b	Other	go to 56
56	a	On peonies, soft brown region at leaf base	peony grey mould **rot**
	b	Other	stem and leaf **rot**
57	a	Stalks split	go to 58
	b	Other	go to 60
58	a	On celery	go to 59
	b	On other plants	water shortage (**drought disorder**)
59	a	Leaf stalks split but not discoloured	water shortage (**drought disorder**)
	b	Leaf stalks discoloured and split; leaves yellowed; no root damage	boron **deficiency**
	c	Leaf stalks and centre of crown blackened (black heart)	calcium **deficiency**
60	a	Leaves and/or leaf stalks with dark blisters containing blackish powder	**smut**
	b	Leaf stalks with soft and slimy rot	bacterial soft **rot**

61	a	On tomatoes, pale yellow patches on upper surface with grey-brown mould beneath	leaf mould **rot**
	b	Other	go to 62
62	a	On rhododendron, yellow patches on upper surface with grey-brown mould beneath	rhododendron **powdery mildew**
	b	Other	go to 63
63	a	On other plants, pale, often angular patches on upper surface with off-white, grey or faintly mauve mould beneath; common on brassicas and lettuce	**downy mildew**
	b	Brown, black, orange or yellow tiny pustules (dirty white on chrysanthemum), often coalescing and with corresponding pale spots on upper surface	**rust**
64	a	Tiny, orange and white, crater-like (pock-like) bodies	**rust**
	b	Other	go to 65
65	a	Spots, blotches and/or holes or areas of dead tissue at centre or margin	go to 106
	b	No spots, blotches, dead tissue or holes but some abnormal colour	go to 66
	c	Other	go to 86
66	a	Leaves turn at least partially yellow	go to 67
	b	Other	go to 80
67	a	Leaves turn more or less uniformly yellow	go to 68
	b	Leaves turn diffusely yellow with other colours also	go to 72
	c	Leaves turn yellow in patterns or irregular patches	go to 77
68	a	On trees, especially conifers, leaves yellowed and sparse; shoots may die back; roots close to stem base may die and patches of dead bark develop on stem	phytophthora root **rot**
	b	Other	go to 69
69	a	On bulbous plants only	go to 70
	b	On all plants	go to 71
70	a	Leaves yellow and bulb and/or stem base rotten	fungal bulb **rot**
	b	Leaves turn yellow and shrivel; young shoots and/or other parts with gradually spreading brown blotches	*Narcissus* leaf scorch
71	a	Leaves yellow in absence of other obvious symptoms	go to 82
	b	Leaves more or less uniformly yellow but veins dark green	iron **deficiency**
72	a	Leaves small, pale but with yellow, red or purplish tints, on older leaves first; plant generally feeble but no obvious root damage	nitrogen **deficiency**
	b	Other	go to 73

73	a	Leaves red, purple and yellow, roots damaged	go to Key J
	b	Other	go to 74
74	a	Leaves with blue-green tint; later may turn yellow and wilt	copper **deficiency**
	b	Other	go to 75
75	a	On bulbous irises, leaves with yellow but darkening streaks; terminal parts turn red-brown and shrivel	ink disease (leaf **rot**)
	b	Other	go to 76
76	a	On carrots, leaves prematurely yellowed and then blackened and killed; roots stunted	leaf blight (leaf **rot**)
	b	Leaves more or less uniformly yellow but veins dark green	iron **deficiency**
77	a	Leaves with inter-veinal yellowing, giving pronounced marbled effect	magnesium **deficiency** or **virus**
	b	Other	go to 78
78	a	Leaves with pronounced inter-veinal yellowing (lower first)	manganese **deficiency** or **virus**
	b	Other	go to 79
79	a	Leaves with other patterns, streaks, lines, rings, mosaic or mottling	**virus**
	b	Leaves with yellow margins; plants stunted	nutrient **deficiency** or yellow edge (**virus**) disease (strawberries)
80	a	Leaves turn abnormal colour, mainly other than yellow	go to 81
	b	Other	go to 86
81	a	Leaves turn shiny and silvery (especially on plums)	silver leaf (**dieback**) disease
	b	Other	go to 82
82	a	On deciduous plants in autumn	probably normal senescence before leaf fall; it is almost impossible to identify other causes at this time
	b	In absence of other obvious symptoms	check roots for symptoms; if none, see 100a and 58b; if found, go to 83 and Key J
83	a	On carrots, parsley and related plants	go to 84
	b	On other plants, leaves with blue-green coloration, often marginal scorching and plant generally feeble; on older leaves first; no root damage	potassium **deficiency**
84	a	Leaves with red-purple coloration, roots damaged	go to Key J
	b	Other	go to 85
85	a	Roots tunnelled, larvae may be present	carrot **flies**
	b	No root damage	**virus**
86	a	Leaves puckered (not simply curled) or with small, fleshy protuberances	go to 87
	b	Other	go to 91
87	a	Leaves irregularly puckered and distorted; often with some irregular yellowing of leaf tissue	**virus**
	b	Other	go to 88
88	a	Leaves puckered; may be reddened and may have a powdery white or yellow coating	**leaf curl** disease
	b	Other	go to 89
89	a	On azaleas, leaves distorted into small galls, may also be on flowers	azalea **gall** disease
	b	Other	go to 90
90	a	Small, fleshy pimples or finger-like eruptions (especially on trees)	**gall mites**
	b	On oak, more or less disc-like protuberances on lower surface	**gall wasps**
91	a	Leaves rolled or curled	go to 92
	b	Other	go to 112
92	a	On potatoes	go to 93
	b	On other plants	go to 96

Damage caused by walnut leaf gall mite, *Eriophyes erineus*

opposite: Nitrogen deficiency symptoms on brassica leaf

93	a	Leaves rolled; shoots spindly and feeble; many very small tubers	calcium **deficiency**
	b	Other	go to 94
94	a	Leaves rolled (lower first) stiff and brittle; may rattle if shaken	leaf roll **virus**
	b	Other	go to 95
95	a	Leaves rolled (upper first) and wilt; stem base black and slimy; roots rotten	black leg **rot**
	b	Older (outer) leaves curled upwards at edges; leaves yellowed between veins	manganese **deficiency**
96	a	On tomatoes	go to 97
	b	On other plants	go to 98
97	a	Leaves curled upwards, no other symptoms (including roots)	this is quite normal, especially on outdoor tomatoes, as a means of limiting water loss – no action is necessary
	b	Leaves and/or other parts, thickened, twisted or otherwise distorted	hormone weedkiller **disorder** or **virus**
98	a	Leaves rolled in absence of other obvious symptoms	on roses, leaf rolling **sawfly**; on other plants, check root symptoms; go to Key J
	b	Older (outer) leaves curled upwards at edges; leaves yellowed between veins	manganese **deficiency**
99	a	On large shrubs and trees, large caterpillars tunnelling within	leopard moth or goat moth **caterpillars**
	b	Other	go to 100
100	a	Dark streaks in stem when cut through some distance above soil level	**wilt** disease
	b	Other	go to 101
101	a	No other obvious symptoms	check roots for symptoms; if none, probably **wilt** disease or **drought**; if found, go to Key J
	b	Other	go to 102
102	a	On fleshy herbaceous plants or rhubarb, inner leaves wilt first; crown interior brown and may be rotten	crown **rot**
	b	Other	go to 103
103	a	On herbaceous plants (including vegetables), stem rotted at base	root and foot **rot**
	b	On woody plants	go to 104
104	a	Swollen lesion on stem below region of wilting leaves	**canker**
	b	Other	go to 105
105	a	Hole or other damage below region of wilting leaves	insect (probably **caterpillars** or **beetles**) or mechanical damage **disorder**
	b	Shoot (and leaves if present) more or less shrivelled, fungal growths may be present	**dieback**
106	a	Leaves with brown, dry or shrivelled tips or edges but not with pieces removed; leaf centre usually fairly normal	go to 107
	b	Other	go to 114
107	a	In hot or dry conditions (especially house plants)	dry air **disorder**
	b	Other	go to 108
108	a	On outdoor plants in spring	**frost**
	b	Other	go to 109
109	a	On *Narcissus* and other bulbous plants, leaves with red-brown scorch, spreading downwards from tip; gradually shrivel and die; flower stalks and flowers may also have brown discoloration	leaf scorch (**spot**)
	b	Other	go to 110
110	a	On lettuce, leaves shrivelled at margins	marginal leaf **spot**
	b	Other	go to 111

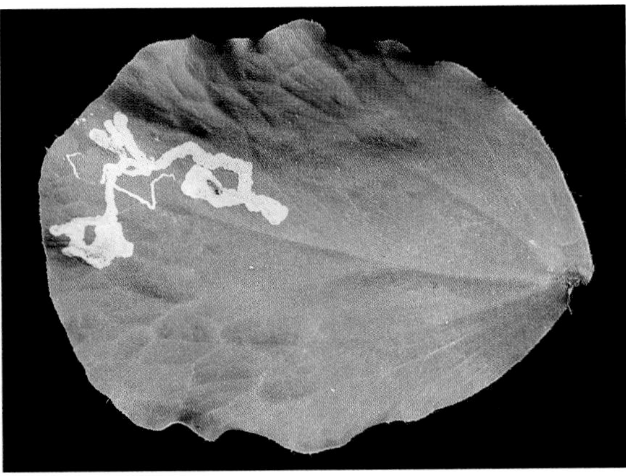

Leaf miner damage to sweet pea leaf

111	a	Leaves with brown, shrivelled, sometimes slightly purple margins	potassium **deficiency**
	b	Leaves with black and shrivelled tips	boron or calcium **deficiency**
112	a	Leaves abnormally narrowed	go to 113
	b	Other	go to 114
113	a	On cauliflower, appearing whip-like	molybdenum **deficiency** (whip-tail)
	b	On plums	**virus**
114	a	Irregular lesions or sinuous tunnel patterns inside leaf tissues (may need careful examination; held up to the light, a dark patch – a larva – may be visible within)	leaf miners (**flies**)
	b	Other	go to 115
115	a	Small, white spots, like tiny blobs of milk, often in concentric groups	**white blister** disease
	b	Other	go to 116
116	a	Scabby lesions or outgrowths	oedema **disorder**
	b	Other	go to 117
117	a	At least some holes or surface erosion present with or without spots	go to 118
	b	Only spots (which may be of various sizes, regular or irregularly shaped) present	go to 130
118	a	At least some holes present or pieces removed from margins	go to 119
	b	Leaf surface merely eroded	go to 126
119	a	Holes not associated with spots or blotches	go to 120
	b	Holes associated with brown or other coloured spots or blotches, some of which may be intact	go to 139
120	a	Excreta ('frass') present	**caterpillars**
	b	No frass present	go to 121
121	a	Slime trails present	**slugs** or **snails**
	b	Slime trails absent	go to 122
122	a	Foliage stripped to leave a skeleton of veins	**caterpillars** or **sawflies** (especially on Solomon's seal and gooseberries)
	b	Other	go to 123
123	a	Sinuous pieces eaten from leaf margins	**weevil** (on evergreens, almost certainly vine weevil)
	b	Other	go to 124
124	a	Semi-circular, scallop-shaped pieces removed from margins, especially on roses	leaf-cutter **bees**
	b	Other	go to 125
125	a	Many small holes in foliage, especially on young plants close to soil level	flea **beetles**
	b	Other	go to 127
126	a	Leaf surface eroded and with translucent 'windows' (especially on *Prunus* species)	slugworm **sawflies**
	b	Other	go to 127
127	a	Leaf surface coarsely eroded (on roses)	rose slug **sawflies**
	b	Other	go to 126
128	a	Leaf surface with fine, pale flecking, no signs of insect activity	**thrips**
	b	Other	go to 129
129	a	Leaf surface with fine pale flecking, cast skins of insects usually present on undersides	**leafhoppers**
	b	On freesias, leaf surface with rows of tiny, white flecks	freesia streak **virus**
130	a	Yellowish spots on upper surface coincide with small, coloured, powdery pustules on underside	**rust**
	b	Other	go to 131
131	a	Leaves with yellowish spots or blotches	go to 132
	b	Spots other than yellow (although may have a surrounding yellow halo)	go to 133
132	a	On bluebells, ovoid spots with tiny, brown pustules	**rust**
	b	Spots entirely yellow	**virus**

Caterpillar of the cabbage moth, *Mamestra brassicae*

133	a	No other obvious symptoms present on plant (eg. stem rot or spots, cankers, rot, shoot dieback)	leaf **spot** disease (depending on shape and size of lesion, may be called a leaf blotch or angular leaf spot or given an individual name) or, if markedly uni-directional, airborne chemical pollution
	b	Other symptoms present on plant	go to 134
134	a	On bulbous plants, associated with bulb rot or other bulb symptoms	bulb **rot**
	b	On other plants	go to 135
135	a	On herbaceous plants, associated with rot at base of stem	root and foot **rot** or black leg **rot**
	b	Other	go to 136
136	a	On trees	go to 137
	b	On fruit or vegetables	go to 138
137	a	On weeping willow, associated with die-back of shoots and tiny shoot cankers	**anthracnose**
	b	On *Prunus* species; branches display gumming or other canker symptoms	bacterial **canker**
138	a	On runner or French beans, associated with pod spots and reddening of leaf veins	**anthracnose**
	b	Other	go to 139
139	a	On cucumbers, associated with fruit spotting	**anthracnose**
	b	On fruit	go to 140
140	a	On cane fruit, associated with stem spots	cane and leaf **spot** or purple blotch (**spot**)
	b	Other	go to 141
141	a	On apples or pears, associated with crusty fruit lesions and possibly tiny twig cankers	**scab**
	b	Other	go to 142
142	a	On cherries, plums and related stone fruits, branches display gumming or other canker symptoms	bacterial **canker**
	b	On other plants	'shot-hole' symptom of fungal or bacterial leaf **spot**

Key E twigs, shoots, branches, stems or trunks

1	a	Insects (including apparently lifeless, limpet or mussel-like bodies) and/or tufts of sticky, white woolly or powdery wax present	go to 2
	b	Other	go to 5
2	a	White woolly or powdery wax present	go to 3
	b	Other	go to 4
3	a	White, woolly wax, sometimes associated with hard, irregular woody swellings; small insects more or less concealed beneath and often around pruning cuts	woolly **aphids** or if on conifers, **adelgids**
	b	White, woolly wax; insects not evident or apparently lifeless and tiny, limpet or scale-like	**scale insects**
	c	White, powdery wax covering small, pale woodlouse-like insects, especially on houseplants	**mealy bugs**
4	a	Insects small, green, pink, yellow or commonly dark coloured, winged and wingless, especially at shoot tips; cast white skins and ants may be present	**aphids**
	b	White froth covering small, wingless insects	**froghoppers**
5	a	Symptoms only associated with woody stems, trunks or branches	go to 6
	b	Other	go to 47
6	a	Abnormal woody or leafy protuberance or lesion	go to 7 (but if bracket- or hoof-like, see 39; if on conifers and like tiny, brown pineapples, **adelgids**)
	b	Other	go to 9

Canker symptom of weeping willow anthracnose caused by *Marssonina salicicola*

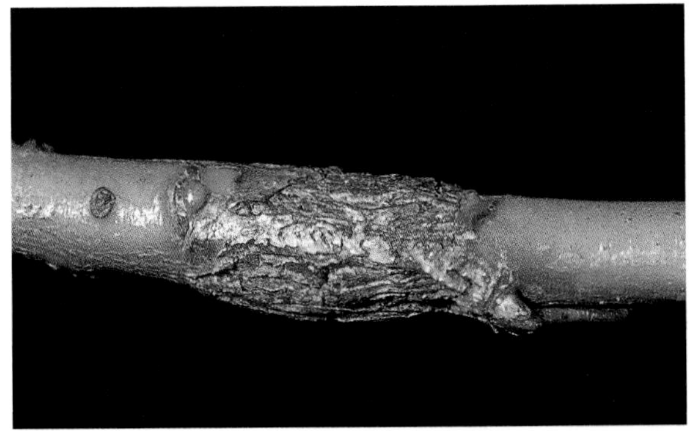

7	a	Unusual, twiggy branches growing from or rooted in main branch	go to 8
	b	Other	go to 16
8	a	Masses of proliferating twiggy shoots, often like large birds' nests	witches' brooms (**gall**)
	b	Leathery, green-leaved parasitic plant growing on branch, often almost spherical in overall shape	mistletoe (**harmful plants**)
9	a	Plant overgrown by or supporting growth of other, apparently separate and distinct plant	go to 10
	b	Other	go to 13
10	a	Overgrowing plant with no true leaves	go to 11
	b	Overgrowing plant with true leaves	go to 12
11	a	Irregular, small, usually greyish (but sometimes yellow or other coloured), leaf-like growths	**lichen**
	b	Reddish, thread-like shoots draped over branches	dodder (**harmful plants**)
12	a	Overgrowing plant evergreen, often filling the crown	ivy (**harmful plants**)
	b	Overgrowing plant more or less deciduous with small, white flowers and feathery seedheads	clematis (**harmful plants**)
	c	Overgrowing plant more or less deciduous, strongly twining with yellow flowers	honeysuckle (**harmful plants**)
13	a	Bark with green powdery covering, especially on more shaded side	**alga**
	b	Other	go to 14
14	a	Orange or orange-brown swellings; slit-like lesions or blisters, especially on pines but also on mountain ash, cane fruits and other plants	**rust**
	b	Other	go to 15
15	a	Stem with pronounced S-shaped kink (two-needled species of pine only)	twisting **rust**
	b	Other	go to 16
16	a	Hard, fairly regular and often relatively large swelling without holes or cavities; never any dying back of branch	crown **gall**
	b	Other	go to 17
17	a	More or less circular, elongated or target-shaped lesion, often with dying back of branch beyond lesion	**canker**
	b	Other	go to 18
18	a	Ragged lesion; may be oozing liquid	go to 19
	b	Other	go to 21
19	a	Bark torn away and some woody tissue exposed beneath; may ooze gum or resin	mechanical injury **disorder**
	b	Other	go to 20
20	a	Regular, if ragged lesion, not usually with any woody tissue exposed; often more than one lesion on same branch or plant; may ooze resin, gum or coloured slime	bacterial **canker**
	b	Other	go to 21
21	a	On large branches, indefinite, wet area on bark, may ooze liquid, branch may be dying back	wet wood or slime flux **disorder**
	b	Other	go to 22
22	a	Branches dying back extensively in absence of any other obvious symptoms	check for root and trunk symptoms; if found, go to Key J; if not, go to 31
	b	Other	go to 23
23	a	Symptoms only on raspberry canes	go to 24
	b	Other	go to 29
24	a	Insect larvae present	go to 25
	b	Other	go to 26
25	a	Canes with small pink or orange-red larvae under discoloured areas of bark, especially near cracks and wounds	cane midge (**flies**)
	b	Canes with pink-red caterpillars in shoots and buds, canes shrivelled and dying back	raspberry moth **caterpillars**
26	a	Canes silvery in winter, purple blotches in summer	spur blight **dieback**
	b	Other	go to 27
27	a	Stems with greyish, elliptical, purple-bordered spots	cane **spot** or purple blotch **spot**
	b	Other	go to 28

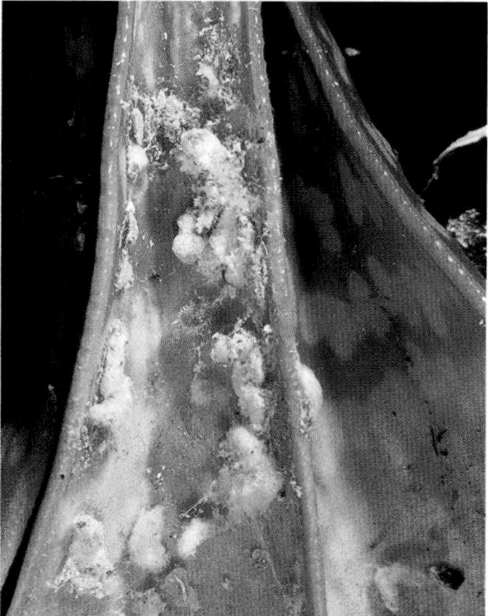

Mealy bug, *Pseudococcus viburni*, on aloe

28	a	Canes with dark, cracked patches close to soil level	cane blight **dieback**
	b	Other	go to 29
29	a	Holes present in bark or wood	go to 30
	b	Other	go to 31
30	a	Hole(s) especially at base of dying back portion; may be tunnelling within; on pines, shoot tips are characteristically twisted	insect (probably **caterpillars**)
	b	Bark tunnelled, especially on dead trees or dead parts of trees, with characteristic radiating galleries	bark **beetles**
31	a	Plant displaying some dying back of branches	go to 32
	b	Other	go to 38
32	a	Leaves silvery, especially on plums	silver leaf **dieback**
	b	Other	go to 33
33	a	Masses of tiny pink pustules present on bark	coral spot **dieback**
	b	Other	go to 34
34	a	Shoots exude slime and die back; flowers and/or leaves shrivelled and appear as if scorched; on woody members of rose family	fireblight or bacterial blossom blight **dieback**
	b	Other	go to 35

Oedema on a succulent

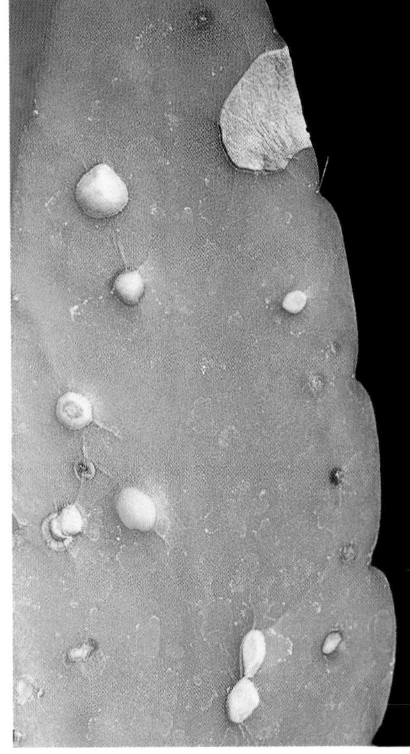

opposite: Mistletoe, *Viscum album*, on black poplar

35	a	Trees have 'stag's head' antler-like appearance, especially on oak and ash	**dieback** of unknown cause, sometimes the result of a change in the water table
	b	Other	go to 36
36	a	On beech, bark peels to reveal sooty mass	sooty bark disease **dieback**
	b	Other	go to 37
37	a	Leaves sparse and yellowed (conifer foliage browned, often in characteristic triangular patches); some death of roots, especially older roots close to stem	root damage, probably phytophthora root **rot**
	b	Other	go to 38
38	a	Large fungal growth present, arising from part of the plant	go to 39
	b	Other	go to 41
39	a	Fungal growth usually bracket- or hoof-shaped, at base or part-way along branch or trunk; rot revealed when branch cut through below position of growth	fungal **rot**
	b	Fungal growth, toadstool-like, usually at stem base	go to 40
40	a	Toadstools brown with scaly caps and/or bootlace-like strands in soil and beneath bark nearby; roots close to stem may be rotted and branches die back	honey fungus (**rot**)
	b	Toadstools otherwise, no other obvious symptoms	non-parasitic (harmless) fungus
41	a	Unusual plant or other growth beneath and close to base of plant but not obviously arising from it	go to 42
	b	Other	go to 43
42	a	Brown or purple, scaly or leafy plant	toothwort or broomrape (**harmful plants**)
	b	Fungal toadstools	non-parasitic (harmless) fungus; probably mycorrhizal
43	a	Abnormal flattening, twisting or deep fluting of bark	genetic abnormality **disorder** such as winged cork
	b	Other	go to 44

44	a	Branches with bark stripped, buds eaten and/or fruits damaged	**squirrels**, **deer** or, if close to ground level, **rabbits** or **voles**
	b	Other	go to 45
45	a	Shoot tips distorted with bunches of small leaves or appearing miniature cabbage-like, especially on yew and hawthorn	midge (**flies**) or **gall** mite
	b	Other	go to 46
46	a	Stems and/or branches broken off	wind or snow (climatic **disorder**)
	b	Stems shattered, often for total height of tree	lightning (climatic **disorder**)
47	a	Overall growth stunted, bloated or otherwise distorted, especially on bulbous plants	stem **eelworm** (this is difficult to diagnose; check Key D and Key J, too)
	b	Other	go to 48
48	a	Stems severed or almost severed, close to soil level, no mould growth	go to 49
	b	Other	go to 51
49	a	Slime trails present	**slugs** or **snails**
	b	Other	go to 50
50	a	Stems eaten through at ground level; plants wilt and die, especially on lettuce and other vegetables	cutworm **caterpillars**
	b	Shoots eaten off, commonly carried away	**squirrels**
	c	Shoots grazed	**rabbits**, **mice** or **voles**
51	a	Distinct spots or scabby warts	go to 52
	b	Other	go to 53
52	a	Rough, warty or scabby protuberance	oedema **disorder**
	b	Flat or finely velvety spots or lesions	go to 54
53	a	Brown, yellow, orange or black powdery pustules	**rust**
	b	Other	go to 55
54	a	Discrete spots, variously shaped, commonly with concentric patterning; usually no mould; shoots may die back	leaf and stem blights (**spots**)
	b	Discrete spots, variously shaped; commonly with concentric patterning; usually some mould and rot; shoots may die back	stem **rot** and stem blights (**spots**)
55	a	Mould growth at stem base; stem may be severed	go to 56
	b	Other	go to 58
56	a	Fluffy grey mould growth	botrytis grey mould **rot**
	b	Other	go to 58
57	a	Cottony, white mould present, often containing small, black bodies	sclerotinia **rot** disease (or, on onions, white **rot**)
	b	Stem base and/or roots rotted; plant not growing well	root and foot **rot**
58	a	On potatoes, stem base black and slimy; tubers may be rotten and leaves rolled	black leg **rot**
	b	Other	go to 59
59	a	On other plants, stem, especially of cuttings, pinched and shrivelled just above ground level	black leg **rot**
	b	Other	go to 60
60	a	Stem and/or other parts with soft and slimy rot; no mould growth	bacterial soft **rot**
	b	Other	go to 61
61	a	Unusual brown or purple, scaly or leafy plant beneath and close to base of plant but not obviously arising from it	toothwort or broomrape (**harmful plants**)
	b	Stem with swelling or other growth distortion	go to 62
62	a	Masses of short or thickened shoots, especially near ground level	**leafy gall**
	b	Other	go to 63
63	a	Firm, irregular swellings	**gall**
	b	Stem and/or other parts thickened, twisted, distorted, especially on tomatoes	hormone weedkiller damage **disorder**

Key F flowers

1	a	On bulbous plants, flowers sparse, growth otherwise normal	blindness, usually the result of shallow planting, lack of fertilizer or inappropriate variety for the location
	b	Other	go to 2
2	a	Insects present	go to 3
	b	No insects present (minute mites may occur)	go to 9
3	a	Colonies of small, yellow, green, pink or dark-coloured winged and wingless insects; foliage sticky and sooty	**aphids**
	b	Insects other	go to 4
4	a	On apples or pears	go to 5
	b	On other plants	go to 6
5	a	Small, flattened insects; foliage often sticky	apple or pear **sucker**
	b	Petals turn brown; small insect larvae sometimes present inside closed flowers	apple blossom **weevil**
6	a	Tough, shiny brown insects, often on dahlias or chrysanthemums	**earwigs**
	b	Insects other	go to 7
7	a	Soft-bodied, sinuous insects	**caterpillars**
	b	Other	go to 8
8	a	Flowers and leaves discoloured, with light flecking, later withering and dying; many small, narrow-bodied insects usually present, especially under leaf bases	**thrips**
	b	Large, often brightly coloured (sometimes 'metallic' or striped) long-legged insects; usually few; may be holes in leaves	**beetles** (including **weevils**)
9	a	Symptoms on cauliflowers or broccoli	go to 10
	b	Other	go to 12
10	a	Curds or flower heads fail to form	blindness **disorder**
	b	Other	go to 11
11	a	Curds with dark internal patches	**downy mildew**
	b	Curds or flower heads with dense, white, cottony mould, often with small, black bodies within	sclerotinia **rot** disease
12	a	Flowers open imperfectly and/or distorted, not merely damaged	go to 13
	b	Other	go to 17
13	a	On strawberries, flowers often killed, leaving rosettes of green calyces; young shoots distorted; lateral buds killed	strawberry **mite**
	b	On other plants	go to 14
14	a	Growth poor; small mites present in buds and growing points	tarsonemid **mites**
	b	Other	go to 15
15	a	Flowers ragged as well as stunted and deformed	**virus** (aspermy)
	b	Other	go to 16
16	a	Flowers malformed; buds sometimes killed	**capsid bugs**
	b	Flowers and leaves grossly distorted; buds killed; stems may be distorted	**eelworms**
17	a	Holes and/or tearing present	go to 19
	b	No holes or tearing	go to 22
18	a	Irregular holes and pieces eaten away; sometimes with silk webbing over damaged parts; no slime trails	**caterpillars**
	b	Other	go to 19
19	a	Large irregular holes; slime trails present	**slugs** or **snails**
	b	Other	go to 20
20	a	Holes eaten in flower bases	bumble **bees**
	b	Irregularly torn and ragged; no slime trails	go to 21
21	a	Holes and ragged petals, especially on dahlias and chrysanthemums	**earwigs**
	b	Petals torn irregularly; no holes	**birds**
22	a	Flowers abnormally and unusually coloured	go to 23
	b	Other	go to 26
23	a	Flowers distorted	go to 24
	b	Other	go to 25

Common earwig, *Forficula auricularia*, on a chrysanthemum flower

24	a	Flowers have brown-black powdery masses in centre	**smut**
	b	On strawberries, flowers green	green petal disease (**virus**)
25	a	Flowers green (especially on chrysanthemums and clematis)	green flower disease (**virus**)
	b	Flowers with streaks or other marks of different colour; leaves may have mottling	virus
26	a	Small, brown spots; usually no mould	botrytis grey mould **spot**
	b	Other	go to 27
27	a	Limp and mouldy	botrytis **rot** diseases: petal blight (**rot**) (chrysanthemum or rhododendron) or ray blight (**rot**) (chrysanthemum)
	b	Other	go to 28
28	a	Brown and shrivelled in spring; often same symptoms on leaves	**frost**
	b	Other	go to 29
29	a	Brown and shrivelled in absence of frost; shoots may exude slime, on woody members of family Rosaceae	fireblight **dieback**
	b	Flowers wilt, then spur leaves wilt (apples, pears, plums, cherries and related fruits)	brown rot blossom wilt **dieback**

Dieback of rose stem caused by *Coniothyrium* sp.

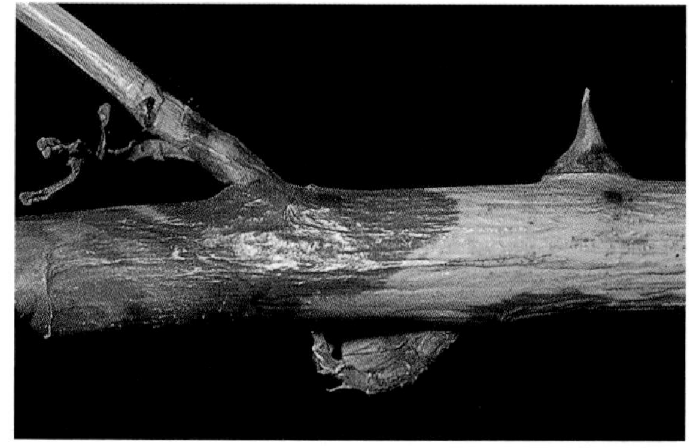

Key G fruit or nuts

for vegetable fruits see Key H

1	a	On apples and pears	go to 2
	b	On plums and other stone fruit	go to 20
	c	On other fruit	go to 28
	d	On nuts	go to 38
2	a	Surface lesions but no holes	go to 3
	b	Other	go to 6
3	a	Mould growth, usually with accompanying rot	go to 4
	b	No obvious fluffy mould growth (may be very thin surface film)	go to 6
4	a	Concentric rings of off-white, mouldy pustules	brown **rot**
	b	Other	go to 5
5	a	Bluish mould	penicillium mould **rot**
	b	Greyish, fluffy mould	botrytis grey mould **rot**
	c	Other	minor fruit **rot** diseases
6	a	More or less rounded, saucer-like depressions	bitter **rot**
	b	Other	go to 7
7	a	Hard, crusty lesions, usually small; accompanied by brown or dark green leaf blotches	**scab**
	b	Other	go to 8
8	a	Large, crusty patches with no leaf symptoms	russetting (a normal feature of some varieties but commonly caused on others by cold wind, drought, chemical spray damage or other factors)
	b	Other	go to 9
9	a	Small, scattered dark spots or patches with no crustiness	go to 10
	b	Other	go to 11
10	a	Surface spots and dark spots within flesh also (especially on apples)	bitter pit (calcium **deficiency**)
	b	Surface spots in small groups with no spots in flesh (on apples)	fly speck (**spot**)
	c	Small, dark green surface film of mould patches that wipe off (on apples)	sooty blotch (**spot**)
11	a	Sinuous, ribbon-like scars (on apples)	apple **sawflies**
	b	Other	go to 12

No.		Symptom	Cause / next step
12	a	Dimples with hard tissue at base of dimple (on pears)	stony pit **virus**
	b	Other	go to 13
13	a	Small holes in immature fruitlets, which commonly drop (on apples)	apple **sawflies**
	b	Other	go to 14
14	a	Small hole close to fruit stalk; core tunnelled; larva may be present in core (on apples)	codling moth **caterpillars**
	b	Other	go to 15
15	a	Leaves adhere to fruit by fine webbing; shallow tunnels in flesh beneath	tortrix moth **caterpillars**
	b	Other	go to 16
16	a	Young fruitlets distorted, often drop and contain small larvae in cavities(on pears)	pear midge (**flies**)
	b	Other	go to 17
17	a	Fruit with irregular bumps	**capsid bugs**
	b	Other	go to 18
18	a	Fruits abnormally small and red	nitrogen **deficiency**
	b	Other	go to 19
19	a	Fruit in store with small pieces removed	**mice** or **voles**
	b	Fruit on tree with holes or cracks	go to 36
20	a	On plums and related stone fruits	go to 21
	b	On other fruit	go to 29
21	a	Fruits with internal tunnelling; brown debris often extruded; larva may be present within	plum **sawflies**
	b	Other	go to 22
22	a	Mature fruit with internal tunnelling; usually also fungal rot; larva often present within	plum fruit moth **caterpillars**
	b	Other	go to 23
23	a	Green-brown, rather crusty lesions on surface	**scab**
	b	Other	go to 24
24	a	Fruit distorted, like small bananas	pocket plums (**galls**)
	b	Other	go to 25
25	a	Red fruits show dark lines and streaks; pale and darker types may have surface grooves and pitting	plum pox **virus**
	b	Other	go to 26
26	a	Mould growth present	go to 27
	b	No mould; holes or cracks present; stone fruits may exude gum	go to 36
27	a	White, velvety mould	**powdery mildew**
	b	Other mould	go to 4
28	a	On raspberries	go to 29
	b	On other fruit	go to 30
29	a	Small, white larva within	raspberry **beetle**
	b	Fruit small and dry	**virus**, **drought** and/or imperfect pollination
30	a	On gooseberries and currants	go to 31
	b	On other fruit	go to 32
31	a	Brown and white, felt-like mould	American **mildew**
	b	Greyish, fluffy mould	botrytis grey mould **rot**
32	a	On strawberries	go to 33
	b	On tree fruit	go to 35
33	a	Mould growth present	go to 4
	b	Small holes present	go to 34
34	a	Black beetles present nearby	strawberry **beetle**
	b	No black beetles	**millepedes**, **woodlice**, **slugs**
35	a	Mould growth present	go to 5
	b	No mould; fruit split or holed	go to 36
36	a	Stab-like holes (often quickly extended by insects or fungal rot)	**birds**
	b	Other	go to 37
37	a	Irregular holes extending beneath skin	**wasps**
	b	Fruit split in absence of insect attack or fungal rot	irregular water availability
38	a	Larva within nuts or small, regular holes in shell	nut **weevil**
	b	Rotted	fungal nut **rot**
	c	Cracked open and contents removed	**squirrels**

Brown rot on a 'Conference' pear

opposite: Greenback on tomato

Key H vegetable fruit

1	a	On tomatoes or peppers	go to 2
	b	On peas or beans	go to 10
	c	On other crops	go to 18
2	a	Abnormal coloration; no lesions	go to 3
	b	Other	go to 4
3	a	Hard, dark green or sometimes yellow patches when remainder ripens	greenback (high temperature injury **disorder**, some varieties especially prone)
	b	Irregular patches of ripe and unripe tissue	**virus** or potassium **deficiency**
4	a	Dark, scabby lesion at blossom end	calcium **deficiency**/ water shortage (blossom end rot)
	b	Other	go to 5
5	a	Mould growth present	go to 6
	b	No mould growth	go to 7
6	a	Greyish, fluffy mould	botrytis grey mould **rot**
	b	Black, soot-like mould; aphids or whiteflies often present	**sooty mould**
7	a	Small, rounded, white spots, especially late in season	ghost **spot** (botrytis grey mould)
	b	Other	go to 8
8	a	Tough, brown patches (tomatoes only, especially outdoors)	potato/tomato blight (**rot**)
	b	Other	go to 9
9	a	Split	water shortage (**drought disorder**)
	b	Hollow	water shortage (**drought disorder**), potassium **deficiency** or weedkiller damage **disorder**
10	a	On peas	go to 11
	b	On broad beans	go to 15
	c	On runner and French beans	go to 17
11	a	Pods and leaves with silvery surface and flecking; small, narrow-bodied insects present	pea **thrips**
	b	Other	go to 12
12	a	Pods with tiny caterpillars inside; holes in peas; brown debris present	pea moth **caterpillars**
	b	Other	go to 13
13	a	Brown-yellow, sunken spots; also on stems and leaves	leaf and pod **spot**
	b	Other	go to 14
14	a	Seeds within pod dry and chalky in texture	botrytis grey mould **rot**
	b	Seeds within pod with dark internal spots	manganese **deficiency**
15	a	Pods with dense colonies of small, black insects, especially along edges	**aphids**
	b	Other	go to 16
16	a	Pods with triangular pieces and beans removed	**birds**
	b	Pods rotted, usually at flower end, and with greyish, fluffy mould growth	botrytis grey mould **rot**
17	a	Pods with rounded, greasy spots	halo blight (**spot**)
	b	Pods with rounded, reddish spots; reddish veins on undersides of leaves	**anthracnose**
18	a	On peppers	go to 19
	b	On other fruit	go to 20
19	a	Dark, scabby lesion at blossom end	blossom end rot (calcium **deficiency**/ water shortage)
	b	Black, soot-like mould; aphids or whiteflies often present on plants	**sooty mould**
20	a	On sweet corn	go to 21
	b	On cucumbers, marrows and related plants	go to 22

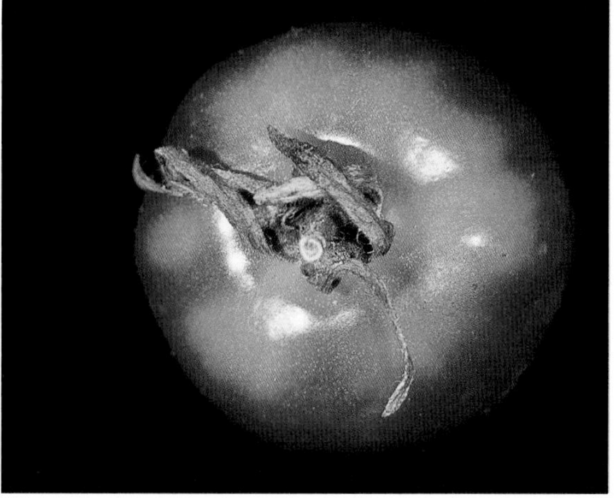

21	a	Cobs fail to develop normally; whitish stripes on leaves; no insect larvae present	boron **deficiency**
	b	Cobs and entire plants stunted; whitish stripes on leaves; insect larvae at stem and leaf base	frit **flies**
	c	Cobs malformed and containing black, dusty matter	**smut**
22	a	Rotted	go to 23
	b	Not rotted	go to 25
23	a	Greyish, fluffy mould growth, especially at blossom end	botrytis grey mould **rot**
	b	Other	go to 24
24	a	Soft and slimy rot, usually when stored	bacterial soft **rot**
	b	Otherwise rotted, especially in store	minor **rot**
25	a	Fruit warty, malformed, often abnormally dark green or with yellow streaks	**virus**
	b	Other	go to 26
26	a	Sunken lesions	**anthracnose**
	b	Other	go to 27
27	a	Hollow or split	water shortage (**drought disorder**) or irregular water supply
	b	Other	go to 28
28	a	Large pieces eaten out; slime trails present on and near plants	**slugs** and **snails**
	b	Small, greyish spots oozing liquid; later a dark green mould	gummosis **disorder**

Adult cockchafer, *Melolontha melolontha*

Key I bulbs, tubers, corms or rhizomes

1	a	Invertebrate pests on affected parts or close by	go to 2
	b	No pests present	go to 13
2	a	Insects (six legs) present	go to 7
	b	Other pests present or legs cannot be counted	go to 3
3	a	Snake-like black or pink pests with many (up to 100) legs	**millepedes**
	b	Other	go to 4
4	a	Ovoid, usually greyish pests with 14 legs	**woodlice**
	b	Other	go to 5
5	a	Brown or black, slimy, legless pests, slime trails present	**slugs**
	b	Other	go to 6
6	a	Wounds on plant parts (especially ornamental bulbs) infested by small, shining white mites with long hairs	bulb **mite**
	b	Other	go to 7
7	a	On bulbs (especially tulips) in store, colonies of yellow or brown wingless insects	tulip bulb **aphid**
	b	Other	go to 8
8	a	Soil-inhabiting caterpillars present; plants partly eaten	go to 9
	b	No caterpillars present	go to 10
9	a	Caterpillars grey-brown; usually close to soil surface	cutworm **caterpillars**
	b	Caterpillars white; below soil surface	swift moth **caterpillars**
10	a	On bulbs, especially narcissi, soft and rotten, grey-brown legless maggots present	large narcissus **flies**
	b	Other	go to 11
11	a	Plant parts eaten; small C-shaped, legless, white larvae present	vine **weevil**
	b	Other	go to 12
12	a	Plant parts with pieces eaten from surface; large, C-shaped, six-legged, white larvae present	chafer **beetles**
	b	Plant parts with small, round holes; long, narrow, yellow larvae present	wireworms (**flies**)
13	a	Plant parts with areas eaten away or holed	go to 14
	b	Other	go to 18
14	a	In store, large pieces eaten; corms often eaten entirely to leave skin only; tiny teeth marks visible on damaged parts	**voles** or **mice**
	b	Other	go to 15
15	a	In soil, many circular holes, 2-3mm diameter	wireworms (**beetles**)
	b	Other	go to 16

16	a	In soil, few holes, generally larger than 3mm diameter	**slugs**
	b	Other	go to 17
17	a	In soil, especially on potatoes, large pieces eaten from surface	chafer **beetles**
	b	In soil, plant parts dug up and at least partially eaten	**squirrels**, **voles** or **badgers**
18	a	On potato tubers	go to 19
	b	On other plants	go to 38
19	a	Mould growth present	go to 20
	b	No mould growth	go to 22
20	a	In store, soft, brown rot and fluffy, grey mould growth	grey mould **rot**
	b	Other	go to 21
21	a	Shrunken or wrinkled, cracks or cavities lined with fluffy, white, blue or pink mould	dry **rot**
	b	Rotted and with matted dark fungal strands	violet root **rot**
22	a	Rotted	go to 23
	b	No obvious rot	go to 24
23	a	Soft and rotten; stem has black and slimy area close to base	black leg **rot**
	b	Especially in store, soft and slimy rot, often foul-smelling	bacterial soft **rot**
24	a	Surface malformation	go to 25
	b	No surface malformation	go to 33
25	a	Warty or scabby patches on surface	go to 26
	b	Other abnormal surface features or coloration	go to 29
26	a	Large, rough and warty white outgrowths or excrescences (rare)	wart (**gall**)
	b	Other	go to 27
27	a	Rough, scabby surface, may be abnormal warty swellings (common)	powdery **scab**
	b	Other	go to 28
28	a	Fairly small, scabby spots or craters of corky tissue	common **scab**
	b	Small, black, scurfy patches	black scurf (**spot**)
29	a	Abnormal coloration	go to 30
	b	Other surface features	go to 31
30	a	Silvery sheen; usually only apparent in store	silver scurf (**spot**)
	b	At least partially green	exposure to light
31	a	Small, brownish pimples	skin **spot**
	b	Other	go to 32
32	a	Small, dark lesions which ooze liquid when touched	watery wound **rot**
	b	Small, thumb-print-like lesions from which rot extends	gangrene **rot**

33	a	Tubers feel soft	go to 34
	b	Other	go to 35
34	a	Soft and rubbery when lifted	**drought**
	b	Rubbery when cut; tissues turn pink within half an hour	pink **rot**
35	a	Cracked or split; no unusual marks in flesh	go to 36
	b	Unusual marks within flesh	go to 37
36	a	Cracked and wrinkled; tissues dry out and have mealy consistency	potato tuber **eelworm**
	b	Split or with internal hollows, not usually rooted and no mould growth	mechanical injury
37	a	Indefinite dark patches within	often caused by chilling, especially during storage, but there are several other causes including **viruses**
	b	More or less definite dark lines or crescent patterns	**viruses**
38	a	Mould growth present	go to 39
	b	No mould growth	go to 44
39	a	Rot and blue-green surface mould	penicillium blue mould **rot**
	b	Other	go to 40
40	a	Rot and fluffy, grey-white mould	botrytis grey mould **rot**
	b	Other	go to 41
41	a	On onions	go to 42
	b	On other plants	go to 43
42	a	In store, soft rot from neck downwards; fluffy grey mould	neck **rot**
	b	In soil, mass of white, cottony mould containing tiny, black bodies	white **rot**
43	a	Plant parts rotted with matted, dark fungal strands	violet root **rot**
	b	Brown rot and strands of thin, white mould between scales or outer tissues of ornamental bulbs and corms	white root **rot**
44	a	On bulbous irises, black patches or streaks; may be extensive rot	ink disease **rot**
	b	Other	go to 45
45	a	On gladioli, less commonly freesias, crocuses and other related plants	go to 46
	b	On other plants	go to 50
46	a	Small, sunken surface lesions, visible when scales removed	gladiolus dry **rot**
	b	Other	go to 47

47	a	Rounded, pale yellow spots	gladiolus **scab**
	b	Other	go to 48
48	a	Central soft rot; centre may fall out	core rot
	b	Other	go to 49
49	a	Dark brown, concentrically ridged, surface lesions	corm **rot** and yellows **rot**
	b	Rounded, pale yellow spots	**scab** and neck **rot**
50	a	Plant parts feel soft; discoloured patterns within	go to 51
	b	No discoloured patterns	go to 52
51	a	Circles of brown, discoloured tissue	stem **eelworm**
	b	Internal, red discoloration of bulb scales and red marks around neck externally	tarsonemid **mites**
52	a	Bright yellow slime when bulbs cut through; plants fail to emerge or are stunted with brownish blotches, especially on hyacinth; not on onions	yellows **rot**
	b	Other	go to 53
53	a	On onions, yellow internal stain; small, black bodies beneath outer bulb scales	smudge (**spot**)
	b	Other	go to 54
54	a	Red-brown rot spreading from basal ring, especially on narcissi	basal **rot**
	b	Other	go to 55
55	a	Soft and slimy rot	bacterial soft **rot**
	b	On onions, roots and leaves shrivelled	shanking (**rot**)

Damage caused by carrot fly, *Psila rosae*

Key J roots

In many cases, you will have been directed to this key from one of the other keys to examine roots because of the presence of some above-ground symptom. Note that this key deals strictly with symptoms on normal roots – not on rhizomes, tubers, bulbs or other underground parts although these may be affected too; see Key I.

1	a	On woody plants	go to 2
	b	On other plants	go to 5
2	a	Roots and stem base rotted; tall brown, scaly-capped toadstools (in autumn) and bootlace-like strands may be present and branches die back	honey fungus **rot**
	b	Other	go to 3
3	a	Roots close to stem blackened and dead; patches of dead bark on stem; shoots may die back and leaves become yellowed and sparse	phytophthora root **rot**
	b	Other	go to 4
4	a	Roots with hard, irregular swellings	crown **gall**
	b	Roots rotted; fungal growths may be present; stem unaffected	fungal root **rot**
5	a	Plant grown in water culture covered with pale yellowish, slimy mass	**slime mould**
	b	Other	go to 6
6	a	Roots with small, hard irregular swellings	root knot **eelworm** (but on family Papilionaceae, see also 8b)
	b	Other	go to 7
7	a	On members of Papilionaceae (pea and bean family) only	go to 8
	b	Other	go to 9
8	a	On peas or broad beans, plant growth poor; tiny, yellow or brown cysts	pea cyst **eelworm**
	b	On all members of Papilionaceae, many small, hard, brown swellings; plant growth normal	root nodules (normal for these plants; beneficial, not harmful)
9	a	On carrots and related plants in family Apiaceae only	go to 10
	b	On other plants	go to 19
10	a	On parsnips, roots with black or orange-brown rot, especially around crown	**canker**
	b	Other	go to 11
11	a	Holes and/or maggots present; foliage discoloured; growth stunted	carrot **flies**
	b	Other	go to 12

12	a	Mould growth present	go to 13
	b	No obvious mould growth	go to 17
13	a	Especially in store, brown rot and cottony, white mould; mainly around crown	sclerotinia **rot** disease
	b	Other	go to 14
14	a	In store, soft rot and grey fluffy mould growth	grey mould **rot**
	b	Other	go to 15
15	a	Rot and matted dark strands to which soil adheres	violet root **rot**
	b	Other	go to 16
16	a	In store, mealy sometimes grey-green rot	black **rot**
	b	In store or overwintering in ground, black sunken lesions on crown	liquorice **rot**
17	a	Soft and slimy rot	bacterial soft **rot**
	b	Other	go to 18
18	a	Elongated, crater-like spots (cavity spot)	calcium **deficiency**
	b	Split vertically	irregular watering
19	a	On members of Brassicaceae (cabbage family) only	go to 20
	b	Other	go to 31
20	a	Unusual swellings present	go to 21
	b	No unusual swellings	go to 23
21	a	Irregular, fairly soft swellings not containing larvae or discrete holes	clubroot (**gall**)
	b	Other	go to 22
22	a	Especially on swede, small, hard nodules not containing larvae	hybridization nodules (genetic, not harmful)
	b	Especially on turnip and swede, small, hard swellings, usually with a small hole and containing a larva	turnip gall **weevil**
23	a	Insect larvae present on or close to roots	go to 24
	b	No insect larvae	go to 26
24	a	Small, off-white maggots	cabbage root **flies**
	b	Other	go to 26
25	a	Large, six-legged, C-shaped, white larvae eating roots	chafer **beetles**
	b	Grey-brown caterpillars present; stems commonly severed at soil level	cutworm **caterpillars**
26	a	Surface of roots extensively eroded and tunnelled (especially on turnips and swedes)	cabbage root **flies**
	b	Other	go to 27
27	a	Soft and slimy rot	bacterial soft **rot**
	b	Other	go to 28
28	a	Shiny, black areas and red-brown rot beneath	black leg **rot** and dry **rot**
	b	Other	go to 29
29	a	Scab-like patches of corky tissue	common **scab**
	b	Other	go to 30
30	a	Split but not usually rotted	irregular watering
	b	In store, soft rot and grey, fluffy mould growth	grey mould **rot**
31	a	On beetroot only	go to 32
	b	Other	go to 36
32	a	Scabby surface patches	go to 33
	b	No scabby patches	go to 34
33	a	Dark patches or rings within flesh	boron **deficiency**
	b	No dark patches within flesh	common **scab**
34	a	Shiny, black areas and red-brown rot beneath	black leg **rot** and dry **rot**
	b	Other	go to 35
35	a	Split but not usually rotted	irregular watering
	b	In store, soft rot and grey fluffy mould growth	grey mould **rot**
36	a	Insect larvae present on or close to roots	go to 37
	b	No insect larvae	go to 43
37	a	On chrysanthemums, roots, stems and shoot tunnelled by maggots	chrysanthemum stool miner (**flies**)
	b	Other	go to 38
38	a	Roots and other underground parts eaten by C-shaped, white larvae	go to 39
	b	Other	go to 40
39	a	Larvae large, six-legged	chafer **beetles**
	b	Larvae small, legless	vine **weevil**
40	a	Soil-inhabiting caterpillars present	go to 41
	b	No caterpillars present	go to 42
41	a	Caterpillars grey-brown; usually close to soil surface; stems sometimes severed at soil level	cutworm **caterpillars**
	b	Caterpillars white; below soil surface	swift moth **caterpillars**
42	a	Infested by small, white insects, often with white, mould-like matter in soil; plants growing feebly	root **aphids**, root **mealy bugs** or **springtails**
	b	Eaten by thin, long, wiry, white or yellow larvae; corms, tubers and rhizomes often with small, cylindrical holes and tunnels	wireworms (**beetles**)

43	a	On stored vegetables	go to 44
	b	On growing plants	go to 46
44	a	Soft rot and grey, fluffy mould growth	grey mould **rot**
	b	Other	go to 45
45	a	White, cottony mould growth	sclerotinia **rot** disease
	b	Soft and slimy rot	bacterial soft **rot**
46	a	Mould growth present	go to 47
	b	No mould growth	go to 48
47	a	Brown rot and cottony, white mould; mainly around crown	sclerotinia **rot** disease
	b	Rotted and with matted, dark strands to which soil adheres	violet root **rot**
48	a	Soft and slimy rot	bacterial soft **rot**
	b	Other	go to 49
49	a	Roots blackened and/or rotted; plants growing feebly	root and foot **rot**
	b	Other	go to 50
50	a	Hard, irregular swellings	crown **gall**
	b	Other	go to 51
51	a	On strawberries, roots with central red core	red core disease (**rot**)
	b	On potatoes, tiny spherical white or brown cysts	potato cyst **eelworm**

Honey fungus, *Armillaria mellea*

Weeds Key K

Use this key in conjunction with the leaf silhouettes on page 213.

1	a	Grass weed	go to 2
	b	Other	go to 7
2	a	Small, tufted, pale green leaves, hairless; flower head loose, open, pyramidal; **annual** or short-lived **perennial**	annual meadow grass
	b	Other	go to 3
3	a	Leaves flat, slightly hairy underneath; many creeping underground stems; flower head slender with upward-pointing flowers; **invasive perennial**	couch
	b	Other	go to 4
4	a	Leaves soft, hairy; flowers with long bristles, pendent from wide, loose heads; **annual**	barren brome
	b	Other	go to 5
5	a	Leaves soft, hairy; flower heads spreading; flowers white, pink-tinged; **perennial**	Yorkshire fog
	b	Other	go to 6
6	a	Leaves softly hairy; flower heads fairly compact; flowers green; stem joints hairy; roots creeping; **perennial**	creeping soft grass
	b	Leaves smooth; plant tufted with stiff-stalked flower heads, stalks persist on lawns when mowing; **lawn perennial**	rye grass
7	a	Leaves divided into very fine segments, sometimes giving a ferny appearance	go to 8
	b	Other	go to 10
8	a	Usually on lawns, pink underground stems; tiny, white or pink flowers in flattish heads; **lawn perennial**	yarrow
	b	Other	go to 9
9	a	Smelling of pineapple when crushed; tiny, tubular, yellow-green flowers in domed heads; **annual**	pineapple weed
	b	Stem ridged and jointed with many rough, narrow branches arising in whorls; creeping underground stems; no flowers; **invasive perennial**	horsetail
10	a	Leaves divided into three or more separate leaflets	go to 11
	b	Other	go to 19
11	a	Three, more or less rounded leaflets	go to 12
	b	Other	go to 16
12	a	Each leaflet with white, crescent-shaped mark; small white or pink flowers in rounded heads; **lawn perennial**	white clover
	b	Other	go to 13

13	a	Small weed, flattened to the soil surface, often on lawns; tiny, yellow flowers in spherical heads	go to 14
	b	Other	go to 15
14	a	Each leaflet with a small point at the tip; **annual**/short-lived **perennial** and **lawn perennial**	black medick
	b	Each leaflet lacking a small point at the tip, annual and lawn annual	lesser trefoil
15	a	Leaves downy, three-lobed and clover-like, often closing up at night	go to 16
	b	Other	go to 17
16	a	Cluster of leaves, spotted pale orange on undersides; many underground bulbils, trumpet-shaped, pink flowers in loose heads; **bulbil perennial**	large-flowered, pink sorrel
	b	Stems creeping along surface; leaves often purplish; no bulbils, small yellow flowers in leaf axils, **perennial** and **lawn perennial**	procumbent yellow sorrel
17	a	Leaves in small, compact rosettes, one terminal leaflet, up to seven pairs along the stalk; tiny, white flowers; needle-like, upward-pointing fruit, often in plant containers; **annual**	hairy bittercress
	b	Other	go to 18
18	a	Large weed with large leaves with several more or less oval, toothed leaflets; white, creeping underground stems; tiny, white flowers in umbrella-like heads; **invasive perennial**	ground elder
	b	Other	go to 19
19	a	Surface-creeping stems forming a mat; leaves with more or less triangular leaflets, each subdivided; flowers cup-shaped, bright yellow; **invasive perennial** and **lawn perennial**	creeping buttercup
	b	Lower leaves in loose rosette with large, terminal lobe and several smaller ones on each side of the stalk; flowers small, yellow, in heads on tall, slender stems; **annual**	nipplewort
20	a	Lower leaves deeply divided into lobes but no obvious distinct leaflets	go to 21
	b	Other	go to 35
21	a	Leaves with pronounced, pointed teeth	go to 22
	b	Other	go to 25
22	a	Leaves very sharply prickly; **perennial** with creeping roots; purple flowers; **invasive perennial**	creeping thistle
	b	Other	go to 23
23	a	Leaves softly spiny, glossy, bright green, exudes milky juice when damaged; small, yellow flowers; **annual** or **biennial**	spiny sow thistle
	b	Other	go to 24
24	a	Leaves blue-green with large, soft teeth; flower stems tall with sticky hairs and exuding milky juice; fairly large, flat, yellow flowers in loose heads, superficially like a large dandelion; **invasive perennial**	perennial sow thistle
	b	Leaves blue-green, not spiny; small, yellow flowers; **annual** or **biennial**	annual sow thistle
25	a	Lower leaves with a large, terminal lobe with smaller, finger-like lobes on either side of the stalk; flowers stems tall (to 120cm) and slender; flowers small, yellow; **annual**	nipplewort
	b	Other	go to 26
26	a	Leaves coarsely toothed; entire plant appearing ragged; stems rather fleshy and pliable; small, tubular, green-yellow flowers in heads; **annual**	groundsel
	b	Other	go to 27
27	a	Leaves green-yellow, deeply divided, strongly scented and spicy when crushed; white daisy flowers with yellow centres; **perennial**	feverfew
	b	Other	go to 28
28	a	Leaves deeply and coarsely toothed, in a rosette; often on lawns; bright yellow flowers in flat heads on short hollow stalks that exude staining white juice; **perennial** and **lawn perennial**	dandelion
	b	Other	go to 29

Groundsel, *Senecio vulgaris*

29	a	Leaves appear deeply lobed and divided, in reality have three leaflets; surface-creeping stems; often on lawns; bright yellow flowers; **invasive perennial** and **lawn perennial**	creeping buttercup
	b	Other	go to 30
30	a	Leaves deeply divided, often more less olive-green, in small rosette; creeping roots; yellow flowers; **invasive perennial**	creeping yellow cress
	b	Other	go to 31
31	a	Leaves blue-green, finely toothed; creeping underground stems; tall (to 150cm) flower stems with pale blue flowers; **invasive perennial**	blue sow thistle
	b	Other	go to 32
32	a	Low, bushy plant; leaves fine and repeatedly divided, blue-green, waxy; flowers small, tubular, pink with dark purple tips, in elongated heads; **annual**	fumitory
	b	Other	go to 33
33	a	Leaves elongated, deeply divided, generally hairy/bristly; large, cup-shaped, bright red flowers borne singly; club-shaped fruits; **annual**	field poppy
	b	Other	go to 34
34	a	Leaves deeply divided and ferny, dark green, like parsley; tiny, white flowers in flat heads with a downward-pointing green fringe; **annual**	fool's parsley
	b	Very variable; leaves usually hairy in a rosette, ranging from very deeply divided to almost entire; tiny white flowers in small heads; characteristic triangular fruits; **annual** or **biennial**	shepherd's purse
35	a	Margins of lower leaves shallowly toothed, indented or wavy	go to 36
	b	Margins of lower leaves entire and undivided	go to 71
36	a	Leaves more or less prickly	go to 37
	b	Other	go to 41
37	a	Leaves blue-green with large teeth; flower stems tall with sticky hairs, yellow flowers; **invasive perennial**	perennial sow thistle
	b	Other	go to 38
38	a	Leaves softly prickly; plant exudes milky juice when damaged, yellow flowers	go to 39
	b	Other	go to 40
39	a	Leaves softly spiny, glossy, bright green; exudes milky juice when damaged; small yellow flowers; **annual** or **biennial**	spiny sow thistle
	b	Leaves blue-green, not spiny; small yellow flowers; **annual** or **biennial**	annual sow thistle
40	a	Leaves very sharply prickly; creeping roots; purple flowers; **invasive perennial**	creeping thistle
	b	Other	go to 41
41	a	Leaves with stinging hairs	go to 42
	b	Other	go to 43
42	a	Leaves large, pointed; up to 120cm tall; roots thick and yellow; purple creeping stems, green tassel-like flowers; **perennial**	stinging nettle
	b	Leaves small; up to 60cm tall; roots white; no creeping stems; green short tassel-like flowers; **annual**	annual nettle
43	a	Plant with twining stems, arrow-shaped leaves	go to 44
	b	Other	go to 45
44	a	Climber, usually among shrubs and in beds, sometimes along ground; flowers large, bell-shaped, cream-white; **invasive perennial** and **lawn perennial**	field bindweed
	b	Vigorous climber, usually on fences, wire netting and in hedges; flowers large, white or pink, bell-shaped; **invasive perennial**	hedge bindweed
45	a	Stems square in cross-section with markedly stiff angular corners, not bristly	go to 46
	b	Other	go to 47
46	a	Leaves heart-shaped, stalked, overall purple tinge; red-purple flowers at top of stem; **annual**	red deadnettle
	b	Leaves irregularly circular, lower very long-stalked, upper stalkless; red-purple flowers at top of stem; **annual**	henbit deadnettle
	c	Leaves in opposite pairs, coarsely toothed; creeping underground stems; white flowers in leaf axils; **perennial**	white deadnettle
47	a	Leaves in pronounced rosettes	go to 48
	b	Other	go to 57
48	a	Leaves large, broadly oval, often red-tinged, basal only in rosette; roots thick, yellow-brown; flowers small, green-red on tall stems; **perennial**	docks
	b	Other	go to 50
49	a	Leaves broad; flowers tiny, white in densely packed, poker-like heads; **perennial** and **lawn perennial**	hoary plantain and greater plantain
	b	Leaves dark green, closely pressed together; white daisy flowers with yellow centres, usually on lawns; **lawn perennial**	daisy
50	a	Leaves elongated, heart-shaped; white, pink-tinged, creeping underground stems; flowers tiny, white in delicate long loose heads; **perennial**	enchanter's nightshade
	b	Other	go to 51

51	a	Leaves elongated, narrow; among unmown grass; flowers tiny, white, in club-like heads on slender stems; **perennial**	ribwort plantain
	b	Other	go to 52
52	a	Leaves more or less rounded, more than 15cm diameter when mature	go to 53
	b	Other	go to 54
53	a	Leaves with scalloped margins; appearing in spring after the flowers and dying down in autumn; flowers yellow, dandelion-like; **invasive perennial**	coltsfoot
	b	Leaves rounded, persisting through the year; pale mauve, sweetly fragrant, in heads; **invasive perennial**	winter heliotrope
54	a	Leaves heart-shaped, dark green, very shiny; small tubers among roots; single, cup-shaped, glossy yellow flowers; **perennial**	lesser celandine
	b	Other	go to 55
55	a	Leaves grey-green, lobed; plant exudes orange juice when damaged; small, yellow, poppy-like flowers on stems up to 90cm; **perennial**	greater celandine
	b	Other	go to 56
56	a	Leaves deeply and coarsely toothed in a rosette; bright yellow flowers in flat heads on short hollow stalks that exude staining white juice; often on lawns; **perennial** and **lawn perennial**	dandelion
	b	Other	go to 57
57	a	Leaves opposite, toothed; flowers small, bright blue; in lawns or on bare soil	go to 59
	b	Other	go to 60
58	a	On soil, flowering stems erect with flowers towards apex; **annual**	wall speedwell
	b	On soil, slender trailing flowering stems; **annual**	field speedwell
	c	Mainly on lawns, slender, creeping stems forming mats; **lawn perennial**	slender speedwell
59	a	Flowers entirely white	go to 60
	b	Other	go to 61
60	a	Very variable; leaves usually hairy in a rosette, ranging from very deeply divided to almost entire; usually less than 30cm tall, tiny white flowers in small heads with characteristic triangular fruits; **annual** or **biennial**	shepherd's purse
	b	Leaves oval, grey-green, clasping stem; up to 60cm tall; extensive creeping roots; flowers white in rather large, dense heads; **perennial**	hoary cress
61	a	Leaves opposite; flower stalks arising in leaf axils, up to 80cm tall; flowers small, white with yellow centres; **annual**	gallant soldier
	b	Other	go to 62
62	a	Bushy plant up to 60cm tall; leaves more or less diamond-shaped; potato-like white flowers with yellow centres; green, pea-like fruit that turn black; **annual**	black nightshade
	b	Other	go to 63
63	a	Very narrow leaves with bristle-like marginal hairs, up to 1m tall; tiny flowers in small heads; parachute-like seeds; **annual**	Canadian fleabane
	b	Other	go to 64
64	a	Plant exudes milky sap when damaged	go to 65
	b	Other	go to 66
65	a	Leaves golden green, finely toothed at tip; up to 50cm tall; usually unbranched; flowers green and yellow in flat head; **annual**	sun spurge
	b	Leaves green, smooth at tips; bushy plant, usually less than 30cm; flowers green; **annual**	petty spurge

Dock, *Rumex* sp.

66	a	Leaves elongated oval, dark green, opposite; tiny, green flowers on long stalks arising in leaf axils; **annual**	annual mercury
	b	Other	go to 67
67	a	Leaves variable but usually more or less diamond-shaped and slightly silvery because of a mealy surface; stem often slightly red-purple, usually unbranched and up to 1.5m tall; tiny, green flowers in dense clusters at stem apex and on stalks in leaf axils; **annual**	fat hen
	b	Other	go to 68
68	a	Narrow, elongated, toothed leaves; upright flower stems to 80cm tall; roots fleshy, creeping white; flowers bell-shaped, violet-purple; **invasive perennial**	creeping bellflower
	b	Other	go to 69
69	a	Leaves elongated-oval; upright **perennial** with small, purple flowers and feathery seeds	go to 70
	b	Other	go to 71
70	a	Up to 1.5m tall; leaves arranged alternately; flowers bright purple; **perennial**	rosebay willowherb
	b	Up to 75cm tall; leaves opposite; flowers pink-purple; **perennial**	broad-leaved willowherb
71	a	Plant with twining stems, arrow-shaped leaves	go to 72
	b	Other	go to 73
72	a	Climber, usually among shrubs and in beds, sometimes along ground; flowers large, bell-shaped, cream-white; **invasive perennial** and **lawn perennial**	field bindweed
	b	Vigorous climber, usually on fences, wire netting and in hedges; flowers large, white or pink, bell-shaped; **perennial**	hedge bindweed
73	a	Very stout, tall plant (to 2m) with bamboo-like stems; pale to rust-brown underground creeping stems; tiny cream flowers in large feathery heads; **invasive perennial**	Japanese knotweed
	b	Other	go to 74
74	a	Leaves in rosettes	go to 76
	b	Other	go to 75
75	a	Leaves large, often red-tinged; roots thick, yellow-brown; flowers small green-red on tall stems; **perennial**	docks
	b	Other	go to 76
76	a	Very variable; leaves usually hairy in a rosette, ranging from very deeply divided to almost entire; tiny white flowers in small heads; characteristic triangular fruits; **annual** or **biennial**	shepherd's purse
	b	Other	go to77
77	a	Bright green, spreading, mat-forming, moss-like plant; flowers minute white; **perennial**	procumbent pearlwort
	b	Other	go to 78
78	a	Leaves fleshy with long stalks, curving upwards to form a cup-shaped bush; flowers tiny, white, arising from a cup formed from two leaves; **annual**	spring beauty
	b	Other	go to 79
79	a	Leaves broad; flowers tiny, white in densely packed, poker-like heads; **perennial** and **lawn perennial**	hoary and greater plantain
	b	Leaves elongated, narrow; flowers tiny, white, in club-like heads on slender stems; among unmown grass; **perennial**	ribwort plantain
80	a	Very variable, leaves usually hairy in a rosette, ranging from very deeply divided to almost entire; tiny, white flowers in small heads; characteristic triangular fruits; **annual** or **biennial**	shepherd's purse
	b	Other	go to 81
81	a	Leaves in whorls of 5–8; stem bristly hairy, clinging, climbing; flowers tiny, white; round, bristly clinging seeds; **annual**	cleavers
	b	Other	go to 82
82	a	Leaves golden-green, finely toothed at tip; up to 50cm tall; usually unbranched; flowers green and yellow in flat head; **annual**	sun spurge
	b	Other	go to 83
83	a	Plants up to 50cm tall; small, oval leaves; flowers tiny, white	go to 84
	b	Other	go to 85
84	a	Pale green leaves; spreading, straggly, branched, rather fragile plant; flowers tiny, white; **annual**	common chickweed
	b	Densely silvery hairy plants; slender, trailing stems; tiny, white flowers; **perennial**	common mouse ear
85	a	Very narrow leaves with bristle-like marginal hairs; up to 1m tall; tiny flowers in small heads, producing parachute-like seeds; **annual**	Canadian fleabane
	b	Other	go to 86
86	a	Up to 1.5m tall; leaves arranged alternately; flowers bright purple; **perennial**	rosebay willowherb
	b	Leaves heart-shaped, dark green; very shiny, small tubers among roots; single, cup-shaped glossy yellow flowers; **perennial**	lesser celandine

Weeds These leaf silhouettes will help in the identification of many garden weeds. Grasses and some very familiar weeds have not been included.

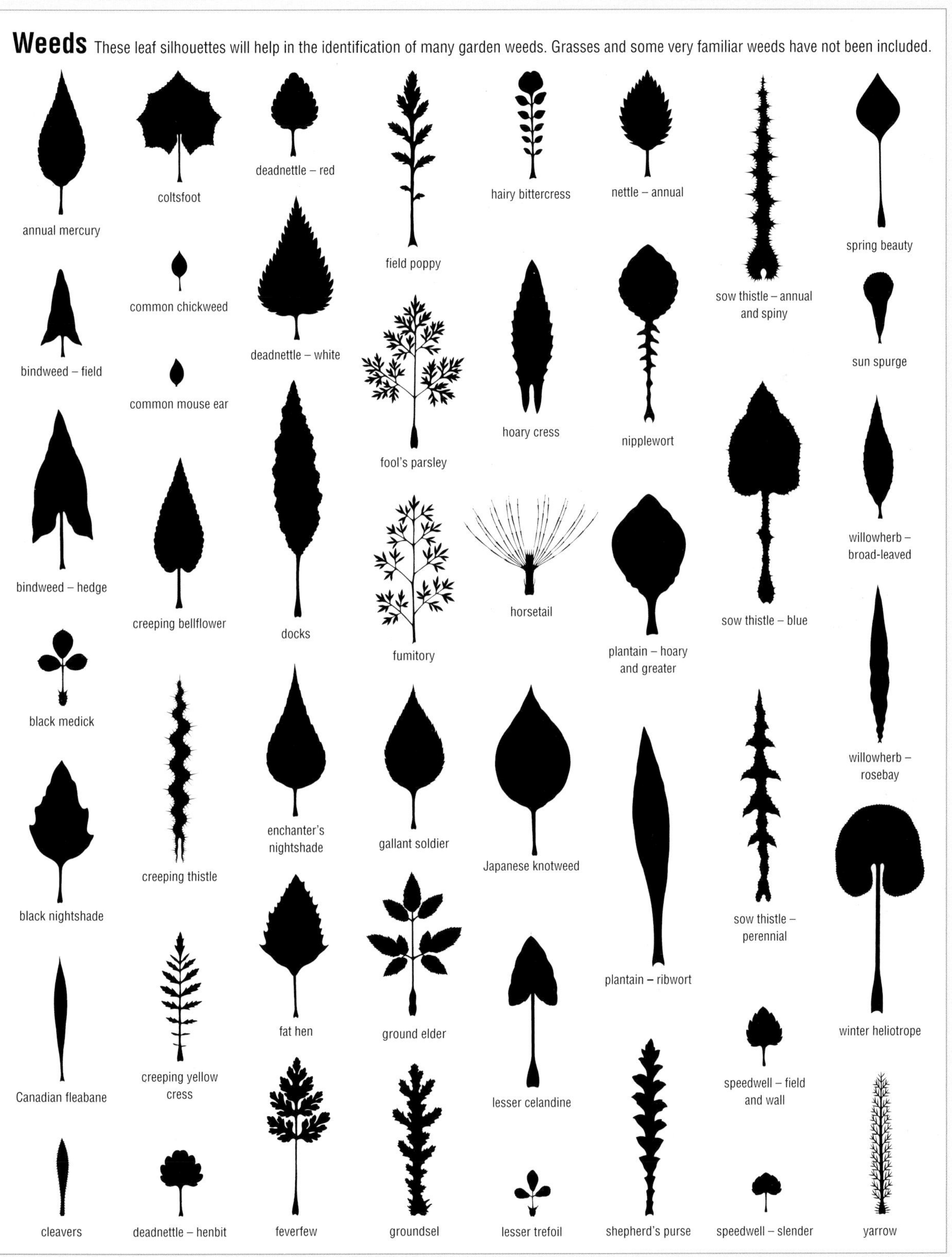

Indexes to plant problems

Pests, diseases and disorders

Adelgids: sap-sucking insects, related to aphids but only occurring on conifers, sometimes causing characteristic galls. Difficult to control but some contact insecticides are effective. The galls should be pruned out if disfiguring on ornamentals.

Algae: primitive uni- or multi-cellular plants differing from other simple organisms, such as fungi, in possessing chlorophyll. Chemical control is not recommended and algae are best controlled by physical removal (blanket weed) or by improving the ability of grass to compete on lawns by additional feeding. Unicellular green algal slime is best controlled with proprietary path care chemicals.

Anthracnose: literally 'charcoal-like'; a type of plant disease characterized by black, sunken lesions. Most anthracnose diseases in gardens cannot easily be controlled and some degree of disfigurement may have to be tolerated.

Ants: small, social insects related to bees and wasps. Ants do not cause direct damage to plants but their mining activities can disturb roots. Chemical ant baits and contact insecticides offer some control but very often improving conditions to ensure a more humus-rich and moisture-retentive soil is the best solution.

Aphids: small, sap-sucking insects, existing as winged and wingless individuals; probably the most important plant pests in temperate climates. Damage is caused directly and also by encouraging sooty moulds, which feed on honeydew secreted by the aphids. They are also the major means by which plant viruses are transmitted in temperate regions. May be treated very effectively with contact and systemic insecticides although, very often, simply pinching out tender young shoot tips (as with broad beans) will effect reliable control.

Badgers: large, mainly nocturnal mammals that are surprisingly common in Britain. They tend to cause damage indirectly through their activities when searching for insects, although they will uproot and eat bulbs and other plants. Badgers are legally protected but can effectively be excluded from gardens with low-voltage electric fencing.

Bees: important pollinating insects, although some types of bee (leaf-cutter bees, burrowing bees and bumble bees especially) can cause some damage to plants. They are too erratic in their appearance to be effectively controlled.

Beetles: the largest group of insects, numbering many thousands of species. In gardens, **weevils** (see below) are the most important pest species but individual plants are attacked by many other types of beetles. Asparagus beetles, flea beetles, lily beetles, strawberry beetles and waterlily beetles are among the commonest. They seldom justify chemical control but are, nonetheless, susceptible to many contact insecticides.

Birds: all species of birds likely to be found in gardens are legally protected and using netting or other physical protection is the only defence for such susceptible crops as soft fruit.

Canker: a disease of woody plants where there is localized and gradually extending death of the cambium beneath the bark resulting in a characteristic target-like lesion. The name is occasionally also used for other types of disease, as in parsnip canker, a form of rot. Cankers must be tolerated on large old trees although isolated lesions on fruit and ornamental trees may be pruned out.

Capsid bugs: sap-feeding insects that are common but elusive pests of plants causing ragged holes in leaves and sometimes, as with apples, distortion of the fruit. Difficult to control because they are so erratic in their occurrence; damage must usually be tolerated.

Caterpillars: the larvae of butterflies or moths; superficially similar larvae occur in some other insect groups, especially sawflies. Individual caterpillars may be picked off by hand; larger infestations are best treated by biological control or contact insecticide, although more sophisticated pheromone traps are available for some caterpillar pests, such as codling and plum moths on fruit trees.

Cats: cause damage through their incidental scratching activities. Never forget that a cat in your garden will be someone's pet and they should not be harmed in any way. Various proprietary exclusion devices are available but deterrents that emit a high-pitched sound are particularly effective.

Deer: several species of deer cause significant damage in rural gardens through physically breaking down plants and feeding on young shoots. Deer fencing, 2m high, is needed to exclude them although various devices, including bags of human hair, are claimed to be effective deterrents.

Deficiency: a shortage (real or induced) of a specific plant nutrient. Avoidance by regular and correct fertilizer application is much the best solution; deficiencies of most individual chemicals can be corrected by application of specific fertilizers with a high content of the relevant substance.

Dieback: a disease, especially of woody plants, in which there is progressive death of the shoots from the tips downwards. Causes are varied and may occur directly, where shoots die because of some airborne infection, or indirectly, as the result, for instance, of the girdling action of a canker, insect activity or root damage. Directly caused diebacks must generally be tolerated; induced diebacks can often be corrected by identifying and treating the underlying cause.

Disorders: all problems that are not caused by a pest or pathogen are called disorders. Nutrient **deficiencies** (see above) form one discrete group and climatic problems (drought, hail, sun scorch, wind damage) another. Injury to plants from these causes is erratic and fairly unpredictable, and employing commonsense to avoid the effects is generally the only possible action. **Frost** (see below) is dealt with separately because it is more predictable and its effects more avoidable. Among other common and sometimes significant disorders are those resulting from chemical or other pollution injury and from mechanical injury. Yet another group embraces those problems that are manifested by some abnormal growth: splitting, bolting, fasciation or spiral growth, for example. In very few cases are these types of disorders either avoidable or curable.

Downy mildew: plant diseases caused by certain obligately biotrophic fungi in the group Oomycetes. Less important overall than the unrelated powdery mildews and controlled by a different range of fungicides, those based on copper being particularly effective.

Drought disorder: plants suffer from water shortage during drought periods but this can be ameliorated if the soil has previously been mulched while moist. Physiological drought is a condition in which water may be present in the soil but plants are unable to make use of it; when it is frozen, for example.

Earwigs: common pests, superficially like elongated, brown beetles. Can cause significant damage to flowers and young plants and best controlled by using homemade traps of hay or straw.

Eelworm: microscopic eel-like animals, usually 1-2mm long, known more correctly as nematodes. Many species live in water, soil and as parasites in plants and animals. A small number cause important garden plant problems and are also significant in transmitting plant viruses. Chemical control is not possible in gardens; affected plants are best destroyed and fresh stock planted on a different area.

Flies: insects belonging to the group Diptera, which includes the house fly and a number of important garden pests, such as carrot fly, cabbage root fly and many midges. (Other flying insects with the suffix fly – whiteflies, greenflies, blackflies, craneflies, sawflies, for instance – belong to other insect groups.) It is the larvae of flies that cause damage and it is at them that control measures are generally directed, although sometimes, as with barriers to exclude carrot flies, narcissus flies and cabbage root flies, it is possible to deter the females from their egg-laying activities. One discrete group of flies are the leaf miners, which tunnel in the tissues between upper and lower leaf surfaces, causing disfiguring but generally harmless sinuous or blotch-like lesions.

Froghoppers: small, sap-feeding insects capable of making huge leaps; familiar garden species produce harmless cuckoo spit on plants. No treatment is necessary.

Frost: while winter frost can be tolerated by correct choice of plants, late spring frosts can be very damaging and underlying principles of avoidance are given on page 87–88.

Gall mites: group of **mites** (see below) that cause characteristic swollen galls. Rarely serious although can be disfiguring and damaged parts should be cut out. Significant exceptions are some bud gall mites, like that causing blackcurrant big bud, which transmit virus diseases and are an indication that the plants should be replaced.

Gall wasp: small, wasp-like insect that stimulates gall development in plant tissues as a result of its egg-laying activities. Generally too erratic in appearance to justify control measures, although the effects can be dramatic and sometimes, as in spangle galls on oak leaves, distinctly beautiful.

Galls: excrescences on plants brought about through disturbance of the plant-growth regulating mechanism, usually as a result of attack by pest or disease organisms.

Harmful plants: among common types are ivy, honeysuckle and clematis, which can swamp or strangle their supporting hosts. They should be removed from all except fully grown trees. A few semi-parasitic plants (mistletoe, broomrape and toothwort) occur occasionally but are more curious than troublesome.

Leaf hoppers: sap-feeding insects, related to froghoppers, causing characteristic mottling on leaf surface of roses and other plants; control is difficult but rarely necessary.

Lichen: unique dual organisms, comprising an alga and fungus in close association. Usually harmless but extensive development on trees and shrubs may limit plant vigour. Lichen on lawns should be taken as an indication that the grass is undernourished and neglected.

Mealybug: small, sap-feeding insects related to scales. Usually most troublesome on houseplants and in greenhouses, and difficult to control. Systemic insecticides are sometimes effective but severely affected plants are best destroyed.

Mice: common small rodents, the wood mouse especially being troublesome in the autumn in stored garden produce. Trapping is seldom effective outdoors because populations are so large, and birds and other animals may be harmed. The best solution is to ensure that stores where fruit, vegetables and planting material are kept are rendered rodent-proof.

Millepede: segmented arthropods of which some species are important plant pests, feeding on bulbs and other fleshy material. Can be discouraged by careful hygiene, removing plant debris promptly.

Mite: small or tiny arthropods with eight legs, unlike the six of insects. Most are general scavengers but a few species, such as the web-forming red spider mites, are important garden plant pests. Very difficult to control as most are not susceptible to insecticides. Improvement of growing conditions often helps; red spider mites especially are most troublesome in hot, dry conditions.

Moles: very common subterranean insectivorous mammals which cause much trouble in gardens through their tunnelling activities; they do not directly damage plants. Many homespun remedies are claimed to discourage them but trapping (by an expert) is often the only remedy.

Powdery mildew: disease caused by fungi of the group Ascomycetes, characterized by velvety, generally off-white growth over leaves and other plant parts. Seriously debilitating and very common diseases, especially troublesome in hot, dry conditions (improvement of moisture will help) and fairly effectively controlled with systemic fungicides or sulphur.

Rabbits: exceedingly common and troublesome mammals and only effectively controlled by exclusion with small-mesh wire netting, either buried at the base or turned outwards over the soil surface.

Rot (see also **turf rots**): more garden plant diseases involve some form of rotting than any other symptom. Once a rot, either by fungal or bacterial action, has become established, it is usually impossible to reverse. Nonetheless, where the rot affects a long-term perennial plant, either woody or herbaceous, physical cutting out of the decayed area may allow natural healing to take place. Where the rot affects soft leaf, flower, fruit or other tissues, especially on annuals or short-term vegetable crops, there is much less that can be done and destruction of the affected plant in its entirety is usually necessary. Almost all types of rot are encouraged, both in initiation and spread, by wet conditions.

Rust: relatively few rust diseases are serious on garden plants; however, although many may be checked by treatment with an appropriate fungicide, long-term prognosis for the affected plants is poor.

Sawfly: small insects, related to wasps and bees. Larvae resemble caterpillars and many species are significant plant pests, the larvae feeding voraciously and causing serious damage in a very short time. Hand-picking is seldom effective as they are present in large numbers and spraying with a contact insecticide is often necessary.

Scab: form of plant disease in which rough and corky lesions form on affected parts. Caused by a range of different organisms, especially Ascomycete fungi. Where the symptoms are merely disfiguring leaf or fruit spots, scab may be tolerated. If serious disfiguring occurs on ornamentals, use a systemic fungicide; for scab on young fruit trees, use systemic fungicides according to the manufacturers' instructions.

Scale insects: small, sap-feeding insects that produce characteristic dull-coloured scales, relatively immobile in the adult stage. Many are serious plant pests, causing general debilitation and also fouling foliage by their honeydew secretions. Difficult to control; systemic insecticides may be effective during the growing season, while affected deciduous plants may be treated with tar-oil sprays during the dormant season.

Slime mould: non-parasitic organisms that, despite their name, are unrelated to fungi. They cause no real harm although extensive growths may smother tender plants. No treatment is necessary and they usually disappear within a few days.

Slugs: soft-bodied, non-segmented gastropod molluscs, closely related to snails but lacking a large hard shell. Some species cause much damage in gardens by feeding on soft plant parts; subterranean species are especially troublesome on potatoes and other root crops. Chemical molluscicides are available as pellets or other formulations, but must be used carefully because of the risk that wild animals and pets may consume them. Liquid formulations are generally thought safer. There are, however, many proprietary and home-spun methods for trapping slugs, such as upturned grapefruit skins or jars filled with beer, most utilizing their preference for hiding in dark, damp places.

Smuts: obligately biotrophic fungi, serious on some commercial crops although few are significant in gardens. Named after their characteristic black sooty mass of spores. Occurrence in gardens is too infrequent to justify control measures but badly affected plants should be destroyed.

Snails: soft-bodied, non-segmented gastropod molluscs, closely related to slugs but possessing a large hard shell; there are species that span the boundary between the two. Usually cause less damage to garden plants than slugs although some plants, such as hostas, are very seriously affected. May be controlled in similar ways to slugs; hand picking at night is also effective.

Sooty mould: fungal growth over leaves and other plant parts, encouraged by the presence of sugary honeydew secreted by aphids and other sap-sucking insects. Control is through elimination of these insects.

Spots: spotting, primarily of leaves but also other plant parts may be one symptom of diseases such as some cankers and scabs. There is also, however, a very large group of problems in which spotting is the sole visible effect. Few are serious enough to affect the growth of the plant although some may induce premature defoliation, which, if repeated annually, can be debilitating. Some can also be disfiguring on ornamentals. A number of proprietary products are effective, most notably those marketed for the control of black spot on roses.

Springtails: wingless terrestrial arthropods, related to insects. They are common in soil, especially among leaf litter and other plant debris and a few species cause damage to plant roots, particularly in containers where the compost has become too wet. Improvement of compost quality is the best solution.

Squirrels: important in gardens with trees

nearby. The pest species is the introduced North American grey squirrel which has moved into areas vacated by the native red squirrel. Control is very difficult and netting susceptible plants is the only effective solution.

Suckers: small, sap-feeding insects, the immature forms of a group called psyllids. They are rather common on indoor plants. Control is difficult because of the protective covering possessed by adults although systemic insecticides may be effective.

Symphylids: small arthropods related to millepedes and centipedes; live in soil and may cause damage to plant roots, especially in greenhouses. As with springtails, improvement of growing conditions is generally the best approach.

Thrips: tiny, elongated insects, commonly called thunderflies. Larvae and adults of many species feed on plant tissues and can cause mottling damage to surfaces. Some are important virus vectors. Control is seldom justified but, as with red spider mites, lower temperatures and more moist conditions will often deter them.

Turf rots: grouped here are the various rot diseases that affect leaves and/or roots of lawn grasses. They are unrelated to each other and in most instances, careful attention to lawn feeding and the passage of time should eliminate them. Fairy rings will continue to appear and cannot be eliminated, however.

Virus: effects and control of viruses and related problems are discussed at length on pages 66–69.

Voles: small rodents, distinguished from mice by their blunt faces; can cause serious problems in gardens, especially by their fondness for corms and stored vegetables. Treatment is as for mice (see above).

Wasps: often maligned as garden pests, wasps only cause damage at fruit-harvest time and this is counter-balanced by their role in feeding their young on other insects, including many pests. Except where they or their nests present a threat to children or people with serious allergies to stings, wasps should not be destroyed.

Weevils: very large group (over 50,000 species worldwide) of long-snouted beetles. Include numerous plant pests of which the vine weevil is the most important in gardens and for which biological control using nematodes is the most acceptable remedy. Careful scrutiny of new plant purchases (especially of greenhouse plants) for the presence of vine weevil adults or larvae is also important. Other weevils may be controlled if necessary by contact insecticides.

White blister: disease caused by a small group of Oomycete fungi; sometimes a problem on brassicas and related plants in gardens but seldom enough to justify control measures.

Whiteflies: small, sap-feeding insects, related to suckers and psyllids among other garden pests. The glasshouse whitefly and the brassica whitefly are the most important garden pest species. They are very difficult to control with chemicals because their immature stages are little affected, but the glasshouse whitefly can be combated very effectively with biological control using *Encarsia.*

Wilt: a group of diseases in which fungal or bacterial attack is the cause of the obstruction of the water-conducting tissues. Impossible to control; treatment, where possible, should comprise the replacement of contaminated compost or soil and the use of crop rotation.

Woodlice: terrestrial crustaceans with up to seven pairs of legs. Live in and feed on rotting wood and other plant debris and can cause damage to plants by nibbling soft fleshy parts. Easily controlled with most insecticides once their hiding places are located. Garden hygiene is also important to avoid accumulations of plant and other debris.

Weeds

Annuals: best controlled in permanent plantings by early season mulching. In vegetable and annual flowerbeds, hoeing or hand weeding is most effective. Chemical control should not be necessary unless growth is very extensive and the soil very wet.

Biennials: as Annuals.

Bulbil perennials: almost impossible to control. Careful removal of plants as soon as they are detected, together with a substantial area of surrounding soil is as much as can usually be achieved. Translocated weedkillers may have some effect.

Invasive perennials: digging out is possible with some types on light soils but broken root or rhizome fragments mean that some regrowth is almost inevitable. Translocated weedkiller will usually give good results although several repeat applications in optimum conditions are needed. Where time and space allows, mulching with black plastic sheet for at least 12 months will also generally be reliable.

Lawn perennials: isolated individual plants may be removed by hand tool but most will re-grow from broken root fragments. Selective lawn weedkillers should be used in optimal conditions and products with different ingredients tried in rotation for stubborn patches.

Perennials: digging out, if done carefully and thoroughly, is usually effective on all except very heavy soils. Extensive growth, especially on difficult sites, justifies the use of translocated weedkiller.

Index

Page numbers in *italic* type refer to picture captions: **bold** page numbers refer to main identification and treatment entries.

acaricides 150
accidental damage 56, 106, 140
Acer 111, *111*, 181
Acrolepiopsis assectella, *see* leek moth
actinomycete 8
adelgids 29, 78, **164**, 188, 190, 196, **214**
Aegopodium podagraria, *see* ground elder
aerobic organisms 128
Aethusa cynapium, *see* fool's parsley
African violet 136
Agropyron repens, *see* couch grass
Agrostemma githago, *see* corncockle
albinos 109, *110*
aldehydes 107
alder sucker 190
algae 28, 189, 197, **214**
  from rainbutts 140
alkalinity 13, 100–2
Alliaria petiolata, *see* hedge mustard
Allium 142
almond 175
alpines 34
Alsophila aescularia 145
aluminium ammonium sulphate 161
Amblyseius cucumeris 149
American gooseberry mildew **164**
American powdery mildew 191, 202
amitrole 157, 159
ammonia 107
ammonium carbonate 160
ammonium hydroxide 160
ammonium thiocyanate 157
Anacyclus 62
anaerobic organisms 128
Angiospermae 28
annual meadow grass 114, 208
  annuals 35
  see also weeds
anthracnose 196, 203, 204, **214**
antibiotics 158
antirrhinum 43
  rust 43, **164**
ants 77, 160, **164**, **214**
Aphidius matricariae 149
Aphidoletes aphidimyza 149
aphids *9*, *11*, 28, 34, 62, 72, 73–4, 78, 118, *121*, 153, **164**, 189, 190, 191, 196, 200, 203, 204, 207, **214**
  beech 80, *80*
  biological control 149
  blackcurrant 142
  cabbage 190
  chemical control 152, 160, 161
  leaf curling **172**
  lettuce root 43
  migration 119
  organic gardening 152
  peach-potato 133
  predicting infestations 127
  red currant blister **177**
  rose **178**
  as vectors 68–9
  woolly **183**, 190
apple *16*, 17, 43, 109, *128*
  blossom weevil 200
  brown rot **165**
  canker 43, 56, *58*, 60, **165**
  capsid bug **168**
  codling moth **169**
  misletoe 122
  powdery mildew 58, 60, **165**
  russetting 97, 201
  sawfly 43, **165**, 201, 202
  scab 43, 91, 92, 127, 160
  storing apples 143
  sun scald 90
  woolly aphids **183**
aquilegia *9*, 109
Arabis mosaic virus 67
Armillaria, *see* honey fungi
arsenic 156
arsine 107
Artemisia 62
Ascomycotina (ascomycetes) 44
asparagus beetle 29
aspermy 200
asphyxiation 106, 128
aster wilt **166**
Asteraceae 27, 62
Athalia rosae, *see* turnip sawfly
atrazine 157, 159
Austrian pine 109
Autographa gamma, *see* silver Y moth
avoidance practices 128
azalea, rhododendron bud blast 29, **178**
azalea gall 121, 193

Bacillus thuringiensis 149
bacteria 8, 49, 55
  aerobic 128
  chemical control 158
bactericides 158
badgers 76, 145, 205, **214**
balling 189
bamboos 17
bark 18
bark beetle 121, 198
barren brome 208
barriers 144
basal buds 113, 116
basal rot 206
Basidiomycotina (basidiomycetes) 46
bats 76
bay sucker **166**, 190
BCH 156
beans
  crop rotation 133
  root and foot rot **166**
  see also individual types
Beaumont period 126
beech 17, *17*, 90
  aphid 80, *80*
bees 121, 144–5, **214**
  bumble 200
  leaf cutter **172**, 195
beetles 72, 74, 78, 144, 189, 190, 194, 198, 200, **214**
beetroot 23, 110
Begonia 111, 139
bellflower 117, 212
bendiocarb 160
beneficial insects 147, 152
benomyl 155
berries 118
bifenthrin 155, 160
big bud **166**
bindweed 113, 153, *153*, 210, 212
binomials 26–7
bioallethrin 160
biological control 146–9
biotrophic fungi 53, 141
birch 183
birds 73, 74, 78, *78*, 80–1, 118, 145, 161, **166**, 188, 200, 202, 203, **214**
  diseases transported by 121–2
  weed seeds 123
bishop weed, *see* ground elder
bitter pit 201
bitter rot 201
bitumen 64–5, *64*
black leg rot 188, 194, 196, 199, 207
black medick 209
black rot 207
black rust 31
black scurf 205
blackberry *22*, 102
blackcurrant 164, 166
  aphid 142
  gall mite 188
blackfly, cherry **168**
blanching 130, *130*
bleached tissue 107
blight 160, 191, 193, 197, 199
  blossom 198
  cane **177**, 197, 198
  fireblight 29, 121, **171**, 198
  halo 203
  leaf 193
  petal 201
  potato, *see* potato
  raspberry cane blight 43, **177**
  ray 201
  spur 197
blindness 109–10, 135, 200
blood, fish and bone 104
blossom blight 198
blossom end rot *9*, 94, **181**, 203
blue mold rot 205
bluebell *23*
bolting 94, *107*, 110
bonemeal 105
borax 105, 160
Bordeaux Mixture 154
boron deficiency 102, 103, 105, 192, 195, 204, 207
Botrytis
  B. allii, *see* onion neck rot
  B. cinerea, *see* grey mould rot
  B. tulipae 52
box *88*
Braconid wasp 119
branches
  dead 141
  symptoms **196–9**
Brassica oleracea 27, 82, *83*
brassicas
  bolting 94, 110
  cabbage root fly **168**
  caterpillars **167**
  clubroot, *see* clubroot
  crop rotation 133
  leaf spot **167**
  nitrogen deficiency *193*
  oedema 111
  powdery mildew **167**
  ring spot *52*
  whitefly **183**
breeding 36–41, 82
Bremia lactucae, *see* lettuce downy mildew
brimstone butterfly *79*
bristlecone pine, *see Pinus aristata*
broad bean
  chocolate spot **167**
  rust **167**
broccoli 82, 110
brodifacoum 161
broom gall mite 188
broomrape 198, 199
brown rot 50, *50*, 53, **165**, 201, *202*
browning, marginal 107, 108
Brussels sprout 27, 80–2, 109
Bryophyta *30*
bud blast 29, **178**, 189
bud scales 21
buddleia 21
buds 21, **188–9**
buff tip moth *61*
bulbils 116, 117, 219
bulbs 17, 18, 23, *23*
  blindness 110, 135
  bulb mite 204
  bulb rot **168**, 192, 196
  buying 134
  herbicides 151
  lifting and storing 90, 110, 143, *143*
  planting 135
  scorch 90
  smut 60
  symptoms **204–6**
bupirimate 160
burnt lime 101
butoxycarboxim 160
buttercup 17, 19, 209, 210
butterflies 74, 76, *79*, 119

cabbage 27, 109
  aphid 190

clubroot, *see* clubroot
moth *195*
root fly 154, **168**, 207
see also brassicas
Cacoecimorpha pronubana, *see* carnation tortrix moth
cacti *14*, 15, 111
calcifuges 101
calcioles 101
calcium 101
deficiency *9*, 94, 180, 191, 192, 193, 194, 195, 201, 203, 207
calcium carbonate, *see* ground limestone (chalk)
calcium deficiency 102, 103
calcium hydroxide, *see* slaked lime
calcium oxide, *see* quicklime
calcium sulphate, *see* gypsum
calomel 154, 155
camellia 111
Campanula, *see* bellflower
cane blight **177**, 197, 198
cane midge **177**, 197
cane spot 196, 197
canker 30, 46, 55, 56, 60, 65, 111, 137, 140, 194, 196, *196*, 197, 206, **214**
apple and pear 43, 56, *58*, 60, **165**
heat 90
parsnip **175**
plum and cherry 30, 56, **176**
sweet chestnut canker 121
caps 98, 128–9
Capsella bursa-pastoris, *see* shepherd's purse
capsicum 111
capsid bugs 78, **168**, 200, 202, **214**
captan 154, 160
carbaryl 155
carbendazim 155, 157, 160
carbohydrate 23
carbon monoxide 107
Cardamine
C. hirsuta, *see* hairy bittercress
C. pratensis, *see* lady's smock
Carduus tenuiflorus 157
Carex 142
carnation 40, 43, 136
rust 43
tortrix moth 145
viruses 68
carrot 18, *18*, 23, 124, 143
fly 29, 36–7, 144, **168**, 193, 206, *206*
caterpillars *61*, 62, 74, 75, 79, 80–1, 119, 147, 189, 190, 194, 195, 197, 198, 199, 200, 202, 207, **214–15**
biological control 149
cats 145, 161, 187, 188, **215**
cauliflower 27, 82, 104, 105, 110, *161*
celandine 18, *116*, 117, 132, 211, 212
celery 110, 130–1
cells 12, 13, 14
cellulose 12, 54, 62
centipedes 72
Ceratocystis 121, *see also* Dutch elm disease
chafer beetle 189, 204, *204*, 205, 207
chalk 101
chemical control 150–61
bacteria 158
persistent chemicals 157
resistance 157–8
viruses 158
see also fungicides; herbicides; pesticides
chemical damage 107–9
chemical-tolerant plants 109
Chenopodium album, *see* fat hen
cherry 90, 137
blackfly 43, **168**
canker 30, 56, **176**
chickweed *113*, 114, 117, 212
chilling injury 89, *89*
Chinese cabbage 110
chitin 54
chlorides 107
chlorine 102
chlorophyll 13, 94, 109
chloroplasts 13
chloropyrifos 160
chlorosis 13, *101*, **174**
chlorpyralid 159
Chondrostereum purpureum, *see* silver leaf disease
chrysalis *120*
chrysanthemum *11*, 43, 62, 85, 96, *121*, 144, 201
eelworm 43
leaf miner 43
rust 43
stool miner 43, 207
Chrysoperla carnea, *see* lacewing
cineraria 84, *84*
Cirsium, *see* thistle
classification, plant 28
cleavers 117, 212
clematis 43, 101, 197
wilt/dieback 43
Clepsis spectrana, see cyclamen tortrix moth
climate 86–7
clover 208
clubmosses 28, *30*
clubroot 6, 8, 19, 29, 43, 48, 133, 142, 146, 154, 155, 160, **169**, 207
coastal gardens 97
salt-tolerant plants 109
cockchafer 204, *204*
codling moth 145, **169**, 202
Colchicum 27
collars, blanching 130, *130*
Colletotrichum 44
Colorado beetle 29, 74, 119–20
coltsfoot 211
companion planting 147–8
compartmentalization 64
composite flowers *20*
compost
making 52, 53, 142
mulching 132
concrete, laying 106
conidia 44
conifers *14*, 15, 17, *31*, 164
contact 152
container-grown plants 134, 135
containerized plants 134
Convolvulus, *see* bindweed
copper 102, 158
deficiency 103, 193
copper oxychloride 160
copper sulphate 160
coral spot 29, 46, 141, 198
core rot 206
corms 18, 23, *23*, 74
bulb rot **168**
buying 134
lifting and storing 143
rot 206
symptoms **204–6**
corncockle 112
Corynespora cassiicola 62
cotoneaster *89*
couch 116, 142, 144, 208
coumatetralyl 161
cranefly 74, *75*, 189
creeping soft grass 208
creosote 108
Crioceris asparagi, *see* asparagus beetle
crocus 28
rust 121
see also bulbs
crop rotation 51, 132–4
crown gall **169**, 197, 206, 208
crown rot 194
Cryphonectria parasitica, *see* sweet chestnut canker
Cryptolaemus montrouzieri 148, *148*, 149
Cryptomyzus galeopsidis, *see* blackcurrant aphid
Cryptostroma corticale, *see* sooty bark disease
cucumber 43, 91, 111
mosaic virus 29, **169**
cultivars 24–5, 27, 36–40
cultivation 128–34
currant 43, 120
leaf spot 63, **170**
red currant blister aphid **177**
sawfly **170**
cuticle 15, 16
cutin 62
cuttings 59, 136–7, *136*
cutworm **170**, 188, 207
cyclamen *23*
mite 29
tortrix moth 145
Cydia
C. funebrana, *see* plum fruit moth
C. nigricana, *see* pea moth
C. pomonella, *see* codling moth
cypermethrin 160
cyst eelworm 70, 134, *191*, 206, 208
cytoplasm 13
daffodil *27*, 28, 110
herbicides 151
see also bulbs
dahlia 18, 23, 40, 85, 144
albino 109, *110*
mosaic virus 124, *124*
propagation 136
viruses 68
daisy 210
dalapon 159
damping off 30, *46*, 48, **170**, 188
dandelion 113, 116, *116*, 122, 209, 211
Darwin, Charles 26–7
day length 95–6
DDT 157
deadnettle 114, *114*, 142, 210
decay 186
deciduous plants 15–16
deer 34, 70, 76, 118, 144, 145, 199, **215**
defences 61–5
deficiencies 102–5, 188, 193, **215**
Deilephila elpenor, *see* elephant hawk moth
Delia antiqua, *see* carrot fly
Delphastus pusillus 149
deltamethrin 160
derris 62, 152, 155, 161
desiccation 17
deterrents 145
Deuteromycotina 44
dicamba 151
dichlobenil 159
dichlorophen 159, 160
dichlorprop 151, 159
dicotyledons 27–8
dieback 111, **170**, 193, 194, 198, 201, **215**
difenacoum 161
digging 128–30
diquat 151, 157, 159
discoloration 186
diseases 8, 118
disorders 8, 9, **215**
distorted growth 108, *109*
disturbed growth disorder 188
dithiocarbamates 154
diuron 159
division 137
DNA (deoxyribonucleic acid) analysis 28
dock 116, 153, 210, *211*, 212
dodder 197
dogs 161
dollar spot 189
dormancy 17
epicormic shoot growth 110–11
seeds 114–15, 125
dormice 76
double-digging 130
downy mildew 43, 48, 126, *127*, 154, **173**, 188, 192, 200, **215**
drawn 94
dropsy 111
drought 17, 93–4, 98, 189, 191, 192, 194, 202–4, 205, **215**
bolting 94, 110

physiological 93
dry air disorder 194
dry climates 16
dry rot 43, 51, 205
Dutch elm disease *57*, 60, 121

earthworms 187
earwigs 144, 200, **215**
Echinacea 62
ecology 80–5
eelworms 19, 60, 72, 75, 137, 188, 200, **215**
chrysanthemum 43
cyst 70, 134, *191*, 206, 208
potato 43, 134, 205, 208
root knot **178**, 206
stem 191, 199, 206
tomato 137
as vectors 68
electronic scarers 145
elephant hawk moth 79
elm *57*, 60, *61*, 111
Encarsia formosa 148, 149
Endelomyia aethiops, *see* rose slugworm sawfly
Eotetranychus tiliarum, *see* lime mite
epicormic shoot growth 110–11
epidermis 15, 16
Epilobium angustifolium, *see* willowherb
epiphytes 98
Equisetophyta 28, *30*
Equisetum arvense, *see* horsetail
eradicant 152
Erannis defoliaria 145
erica 109
Erwinia salicis, *see* fireblight; watermark disease
escallonia 109
ethylene 107
etiolation 94
eucalypts 17
Euphorbia, *see* spurge
evergreen plants 15, 18, 74, *88*, *89*
evolution, theory of 26–7, 30–1, 84
Exobasidium vaccinii, see azalea gall; rhododendron gall

F1 hybrids 36, 39–40, *39*
fairy rings 50, **171**, 189
families 27, 28
fasciation 111
fat hen 117, 212
fenitrothion 156, 160
ferns 7, 28, *30*, 107
ferrous sulphate 159
fertilizers 104–5, 108
application 135–6
nitrogenous 110, 135–6
potassium 135–6
feverfew 209
fire disease rot 191
fireblight 29, 121, **171**, 198
flea beetle **171**, 188, *188*, 190, 195
fleabane 211, 212
fleece, horticultural 144
flies 147, **215**
flower breaking **171**
flowers 14, 19–21
blindness 109–10, 200
symptoms **200–1**
watering 110
fluorides 107
fly speck 201
food chain 12, 70, 157
food storage 18, 23
fool's parsley 117, 210
forking 129–30
forsythia 111
foxes 76
French bean rust **179**
frit fly 204
froghoppers 78, 190, 196, **216**
frogs 71, *72*
frost 86–90, 189, 194, 201, **216**
glazed 93
mulching 132
frost heaving 89
frost lift 89
fruit 22–3, *22*
handling 106, 143
splitting **180**, 202
storing 143
sun scald 90
symptoms **201–2**
see also fruit trees; soft fruit
fruit cages 108, *142*, 144
fruit trees
canker, *see* canker
capsid bug **168**
frost 88
grease bands 145
leaf curling aphid **172**
peach leaf curl **175**
plum rust **176**
powdery mildew 154, **165**
silver leaf **179**
woolly aphids **183**
Fuchsia 79, 107
rust 142
Fumaria officinalis, *see* fumitory
fumitory 117, 210
fungi 8, 12, 28, 34, 44–9, 56, 68
aerobic 128
bracket *45*, *54*, 60
feeding habits 53–4
growth and reproduction 50–3, 91–2, 118, 120–1
fungicides 108, 127, 150, 154–5
eradicant 152
listed 160
persistent chemicals 157
protectant 152
selective 151–2
systemic and non-systemic 59–60, 152, 153
fungus gnat 149
Fusarium 56, 58, 60

Galium aparine, *see* cleavers
gall mites 193, *193*, 199, **216**
gall wasp 193, **216**
gallant soldier 211
galls 199, 205, **216**
blackcurrant 188
broom 188
crown **169**, 197, 206, 208
leafy 199
nut gall 188
pocket plum 202
rhododendron and azalea gall 121, 193
spangle **180**
turnip 207
walnut leaf *193*
witches' broom **183**, 197
galvanized wire 108, 144
gangrene 205
Ganoderma applanatum 54
gas exchange 14–15
gas leaks 108
genetic abnormalities 109–10, 198, 207
genetic engineering 38
genetic modification (GM) 41–2
Genista hirsuta 12
gentian 101
Geranium 26
G. pratense, *see* meadow cranesbill
G. robertianum, *see* herb Robert
geranium rust 80
gerera 24–5, 26, 27
ghost spot 203
gladiolus 109
dry rot 205
scab 206
Globodera rostochiensis 70
glyphosate 151, 153, 157, 159
goat moth 194
gooseberry
leaf spot **170**
mildew, American **164**
rust 142
sawfly 120, *122*, **170**
sun scald 90
grafting 137, *137*
grapevine, *see* vine
grass
growth 14
leatherjackets 74
roots 18
see also lawns
grease bands 145
green petal disease 201
green-veined white butterfly *120*
greenback 90, *202*, 203
greenhouses
biological controls 146, 149
humidity 111
insect traps 145
painting 108
shade 90
smokes (pyrotechnic mixtures) 158
ventilation 90
watering 111
whitefly **183**
grey mould rot 28–9, 44, 53, 54, 56, 133, 141, 157, **171**, 188, 189, 191, 192, 199, 201–5, 207, 208
ground beetle 147
ground elder 113, 116, 117, 144, 209
groundsel 82, 84, 114, 117, 131, 209, *209*
Growmore 104
growth 14
disturbed growth disorder 188
problems with 109–11
restricting 106
growth points, *see* meristems
gummosis 204
gunnera 87
Gymnospermae 28
gypsum 101

hail 93
hairiness 16, 62
hairy bittercress 117, 122–3, 139, 209
hairy rock cress 67
halo blight 203
hard pans 128–9, 130
Harry Lauder's walking stick, *see* hazel, twisted
haustoria 58
hazel *21*
twisted 111
HCH 156
hebe 109
hedge mustard 80
hedgehogs 76, *76*
hedges, roadside 108
Helenium 20
Heliopsis 62
heptenophos 160
herb Robert 26
herbicides 107, 108, 150–1, 156–7, 203
contact 152, 156–7
hormone 108–9, *109*, 156, 194
listed 159
persistent chemicals 157
post-emergence 152
pre-emergence 152
resistance 157
selective 151, 157
translocated 152, 153
Heterobasidion annosum 146
Heterorhabditis megadis 149
hoary cress 211
hoeing 131, *131*
holly 108, *108*, 118
hollyhock 43
rust 43, **172**
holozoic nutrition 70
honey fungi 50–1, *53*, 141, 144, **172**, 198, 206, *208*
honeysuckle 197
hormone rooting powder 137
hormone weedkillers 108–9, *109*
hormones 6
hornbeam 109
horsetail 28, *30*, 116, 132, 208
Hosta 7, 79
houseplants
scale insects **179**
watering 136

hoverfly 120, 147, *147*
humidity 91–2, 94, 97, 111
humus 99
hybrid vigour 40
hybridization 36–41
hybridization nodules 111, 207
hydrangea 56, 109
hydrocarbons 107
hygiene 69
Hypoaspis miles 149

icheumonid fly 147
imidacloporid 160
imported plants 84
infection focus 91
inflorescence 21, *21*
ink disease 193, 205
insect pollination 21
insecticides, *see* pesticides
integrated pest management (IPM) 42
intumescence 111
inulin 23
iris 28
iron 13
  deficiency 102, 103, 192, 193
  sequestered 105
ivy 197

Japanese knotweed 122, 153, 212
Japanese spindle 109
Jerusalem artichoke 23

kale 82
keeled slug 43, 126
kholrabi 82
kniphofia 87

laburnum 109
lace bugs 78, 190
lacewings 147, 148, 149
Lachnellula 46, *64*
ladybird 120, *121*, 147, 149
lady's smock 80
Lamium, *see* deadnettle
lammas shoots 111
Lapsana communis, *see* nipplewort
larch 111
  Siberian 89, *89*
large white butterfly 29, 75, 79, 80–1, 119, 144, **167**
Larix sibirica, *see* Siberian larch
lawns
  fairy rings **171**, 189
  fertilzers 105
  herbicides 151, 157
  lawn mowers 108
  oil and petrol damage 108
  red thread **178**, 189
  scorched 96
  turf rots **218**
  urine damage 108, 189
  see also grass
layering 137
leaching 104
leaf blight 193
leaf buds 21
leaf curl 193
leaf curling aphid **172**
leaf cutter bees **172**, 195
leaf holes 185–6
leaf hoppers **216**
leaf miner **173**, *194*, 195
leaf mould rot 43, 192
leaf roll virus 194
leaf rolling sawfly 194
leaf scars 16, 63, *64*
leaf scorch 194
leaf spot 44, 93, **173**, 194, 196, 203
  brassica **167**
  currant **170**
  gooseberry **170**
  raspberry 43
  strawberry **181**
leafhoppers 78, 93, **172**, 190, 191, 195
leafy gall 199
leatherjacket 74, *74*, 189
leaves 14–16, *14*, *15*
  symptoms **189–96**
leek
  blanching 130, *130*
  moth 75
  rust 142, **173**
leopard moth 194
Leptinotarsa decemlineata, *see* Colorado beetle
lethal mutations 109, *110*
lettuce 43, *107*, 110
  downy mildew 43, 63, *63*, **173**
  mosaic virus 43
  root aphid 43
lichen **173**, 189, *189*, 197, **216**
life forms 16, 32–4
light 16, 94–6
lightning 96, 199
lignin 17, *17*, 54, 62, 70–1
lilac *21*, 109, 144
Lilioceris liliae, *see* lily beetle
Liliopsida 27–8, *27*
lily 111
  beetle 29
  see also bulbs
lime 101–2, 109
lime mite 29
lime sulphur 154
lime-induced chlorosis *101*, **174**
limestone 101
lindane 156, 160
linkage 37
Linnaeus (Carl von Linné) 26
liquorice rot 207
liverworts 28, *30*, 134
lobelia 139
locusts *77*
Lonchocarpus 62
long-day plants 95
Loranthus europaeus 122
lupin *15*, *20*, *22*
Lycopodiophyta 28, *30*

magnesian limestone 101
magnesium deficiency 102, 103, 193
Magnolia 15
Magnoliophyta 28, *31*
Magnoliopsida 27–8, *27*
Mahonia aquifolium 27
mail order, buying by 134
maize, *see* sweet corn
malathion 156, 161
mancozeb 154, 160
manganese deficiency 101, 102, 103, 105, 193, 194, 203
manure
  mulching 132
  straw content 109
maple 90, 141
  field 111
marginal conditions 34
marrow 91
Matricaria matricarioides, *see* mayweed, rayless
mayweed, rayless 117
MCPA 151, 156, 157, 159
meadow cranesbill 80
mealybug 78, *148*, 149, **174**, 190, 196, *197*, 207, **216**
mecoprop 151, 159
medlar 165
Meloidogyne, *see* eelworm
melon *62*, 91
mercury 154
mercury, annual 212
meristems 14
metaldehyde 161
Metaphycus helvolus 149
methiocarb 161
mice 76, 78, 144, 161, 187, 188, 202, 204, **216**
Microsphaera alphitoides, *see* oak mildew
midges 148, 149, 199
mignonette 29
migrating pests 32
mildew 53, 120, 124, 140
  American gooseberry **164**
  downy, *see* downy mildew
  powdery, *see* powdery mildew
millepedes 72, *73*, 74, **174**, 191, 202, 204, **216**
mind-your-own-business 117
mint 43
  rust 59, *59*
misletoes 122, *123*, 197, *198*
mites 150, 193, *193*, 200, 204, 206, **216**
moles 77, 161, **174**, **217**
molluscicides 150, 161
molybdenum 102, 104
  deficiency 103, 105, 195
monocotyledons 17, 27–8
monoculture 85, *85*
Monterey cypress 109
Monterey pine 109
mosaic virus 69
  cucumber **169**
mosses 28, *30*, 134
moths 74, 76, 119
mould 34, 185
  grey, *see* grey mould rot
  leaf mould rot 43, 192
  slime 189, 206, **217**
  snow 189
  sooty **180**, 203, **218**
mouse ear 212
mulching 91, 132
mustard oils 30
mutations 40, 109, *110*, 111
myclobutanil 155, 160
mycoplasma-like organisms (MLOs) 49
mycoplasmas 49
Mycosphaerella
  M. brassicicola, *see* brassica ring spot
  M. ribis 63
Myzus persicae, *see* peach-potato aphid

names, plant 25–8
naphthalene 161
narcissus 43
  fly 110, 204
  leaf scorch 192
nasturtium 29, 80–2, 167
natural selection 84
neck rot 205
necrotrophic fungi 53
nectarine 175
Nectria
  N. cinnabarina, *see* coral spot
  N. galligena, *see* apple canker
Nematus ribesii, *see* gooseberry sawfly
netting 144
nettle 114, *115*, 117, 210
nightshade
  black 117, 211
  enchanter's 210
nipplewort 117, 209
nitrogen deficiency 102, 103, 192, *193*, 202
nitrogen oxides 107
nuclei 12
nut gall mite 188
nut rot 202
nut weevil 202
nuts **201–2**

oak *22*, 122, 180
  holm 109
  mildew 80, *82*
oedema 111, 195, *198*, 199
oil and petrol damage 108
olearia 109
onion 23, 93, 110
  neck rot 138, *138*, **174**
  seed 138
  sets 138–9
  white rot 51, 133, *133*, 142, **175**
Oomycetes 46
Operophtera brumata 145
ophiobolus patch 189
Orchidaceae 27
orchids, propagation 136
organic gardening 152
organic matter, degradation 92, 128, 142
organochlorine 155–6, 157
organophosphorus insecticides

156
Otiorhynchus sulcatus, *see* vine weevil
Oxalis 117
ozone 107

paint 108
palms 17
pans 128–9, 130
Papilionaceae 27
paraquat 151, 156–7, 159
parasitic wasps 148, 149
parsley 168
parsnip 143, 168
canker **175**
pathogens 8, 44–55
migration 120–2
pathology, plant 6
pathovars (pv) 49
pea
crop rotation 133
moth 42, 75, 126, *126*, 145, **175**, 203
root and foot rot **166**
thrip 203
pea sticks 141
peach leaf curl **175**
peach-potato aphid 133
pear
brown rot 50, *50*, 53, **165**
canker **165**
capsid bug **168**
codling moth **169**
leaf blister mite **175**
midge 202
powdery mildew **165**
stony pit virus *160*, 202
storing pears 143
sun scald 90
pearlwort 122, 212
peat-based compost 139
pectin 54
pelargonium 111
rust *58*, 59, **176**
penconazole 155, 160
Peniophora gigantea 146
peony grey mould rot 192
peperomia 111
pepper dust 161
peppers 94, **181**
perennials
buying 134
division 137
planting 134–5
see also weeds
Pericallis ¥ *hybrida*, *see* cineraria
permethrin 155, 161
pesticides 107–8, 147, 150, 155–6
contact 152
listed 160–1
persistent chemicals 157
resistance 157
selective 151–2
systemic and non-systemic 152, 153
pests 8, 9, 63, 70–9
migration 118–20
reproduction 118
spread 118–20
petal blight 201
petals 14, 21
pets 161
urine damage 108, 189
pH 100–2
Phasmarhabditis hermaphroditica 149
pheromone traps 145
phosphine 107
phosphorus deficiency 102, 103
photosynthesis 13, 15
Phyllaphis fagi, *see* beech aphid
phylloxera 43
phytochrome 96
Phytonemus pallidus, *see* cyclamen mite
Phytophthora infestans, *see* potato blight
phytoplasmas 8, 49
Phytoseiulus persimilis 149
phytotoxicity 107
Pieris
P. brassicae, *see* large white butterfly
P. napi, *see* green-veined white butterfly
P. rapa, *see* small white butterfly
pigments 13–14
pine, *see Pinus*
pineapple weed 208
pink rot 205
Pinophyta 28, *31*
Pinus 14, 17
piperonyl butoxide 161
pirimicarb 152, 155, 161
pirimiphosmethyl 156, 161
plane 109
plant, definition 12
plant structure 13–23
plantain 210, 211, 212
planting 106, 134–6
Plasmodiophora 14, 48
P. brassicae, *see* clubroot
Plasmopara viticola, *see* downy mildew
Pleurotus osteatus 60
plum 94, 97, 165
canker 56, **176**
capsid bug **168**
fruit moth 145, 202
leaf curling aphids **172**
pox 202
rust **176**
sawfly 202
silver leaf **179**
Poa annua, *see* annual meadow grass
Poaceae 27
pocket plum 202
Podosphaera leucotricha, *see* apple powdery mildew
pollination 19, 21
pollution
airborne 97, 107–8, *108*
chemical-tolerant plants 109
polyphyletic 44
Polyporus squamosus 45
poplar 60, 90, 122
poppy, field 117, 210
pores, *see* stomata
potassium deficiency 102, 103, 105, 193, 195, 203
potato *22*, 23, 40, 43, 119
aphids 62
blight 43, 48, 92, 124, 126, *126–7*, 133, **176**, 203, 206
chilling injury 89, *89*
Colorado beetle 29, 119–20
common scab 43, **176**
cyst eelworm 43, 134, 208
dry rot 43
earthing up 131
Fusarium 56, 58
greening 94
keeled slug 126
leatherjacket 74
peach-potato aphid 133
propagation 136
skin spot 43
storage 94
tuber eelworm 205
viruses 68
wart 43, 48
powdery mildew 43, 46, 48, 53, 58, 60, *82*, 91, 111, 154, **177**, 189, 191, 202, **217**
American 191, 202
apple and pear 58, 60, **165**
brassica **167**
rhododendron 192
rose 43, 48, *150*, **179**
powdery scab 205
precipitation 91–4
predicting problems 124–7
primula 94
privet 109
Prokaryotes 49
propagation 68, 136–40
propagators*138*, 139
protectant 152
pruning 64–5, *64*, 106, *128*, 140–1
Prunus 43, 63, 109, 137
Pseudomonas syringe 30, 56, 137
Psila rosae, *see* carrot fly
psyllids 78
Pteridophyta 28, *30*
Puccinia
P. caricina var. *pringsheimiana*, *see* gooseberry rust
P. graminis 31, 58
P. horiana, *see* white rust
P. lagenophorae 82, 84
P. menthae, *see* mint rust
P. pelargonii-zonalis, *see* pelargonium rust
purchasing plants 122–3, 134
purple blotch spot 196, 197
Pycnostysanus azaleae, *see* bud blast
pyracantha scab **177**
pyracanthus 118
pyrethrin 155, 161
pyrethrum 62, 152, 155, 161
pyrotechnic mixtures 158
quassia 161
quicklime 101
quince 165

rabbits 34, 76, 118, 144, 199, **217**
rain 91–3
rainbutts 140
raking 131
Ranunculus, *see* buttercup; celandine
raspberry 43
beetle 202
cane blight and midge 43, **177**
cane and leaf spot 43
lime-induced chlorosis *101*, **174**
mosaic virus 43
moth 197
rats 161
ray blight 201
red core disease 208
red currant blister aphid **177**
red spider mite 91, 149, 160, **177**, 190, *190*
red thread **178**, 189
repellents 161
reproduction 19, 21
resistance 8
resistant varieties 43, 49, 82
wild varieties 80–4
resmethrin 155, 161
Reynoutria japonica, *see* Japanese knotweed
Rhizoctoniz solani 30
rhizomes 23, 116, 122, 130
bulb rot **168**
symptoms **204–6**
rhododendron 43, 201
bud blast 29, **178**, 189
bug 43, 190
gall 121
leafhopper 190
powdery mildew 192
whitefly 43
ridging 131
Rigidiporus ulmarius 60
ringspot 95
rodenticides 150
rodents 145, *145*, 150, 161
rogueing 134
root crops
crop rotation 133
wireworm **183**
root knot eelworm **178**, 206
root vegetables
potato common scab **176**
root knot eelworm **178**, 206
soft rot *55*
strangles 91
rooting powder 137
roots 18–19, *18*, 185
adventitious 18
asphyxiation 106, 128
creeping 116–17
planting 106
root hairs *18*, 19
rot **166**, 188, 192, 194, 196, 198, 199, 208
symptoms **206–8**

taproots 18, *18*, 116
trenching and ridging 130–1
waterlogged soil 92–3
see also root vegetables
rootstock 137
Rosaceae 27
rose 19, *36*, 40, 43, *48*, 49, 85, *85*, 109, 160
aphids **178**
black spot *8*, 43, 91, 92, 108, 140–1, **178**
fertilizers 105
fireblight **171**
grafting 137
hybrid tea *21*
leaf cutter bees **172**
leaf rolling sawfly 43, 194
lime-induced chlorosis **174**
powdery mildew 43, 48, *150*, **179**
pruning 141
rust 43, **179**
slugworm sawfly *159*
rot 188, 189, 192, 201, 205, **217**
bitter 201
black 207
black leg 188, 194, 196, 199, 207
blossom end *9*, 94, **181**, 203
blue mould 205
brown 50, *50*, 53, **165**, 201, *202*
bulb **168**, 192, 196
corm 206
crown 194
damping off, *see* damping off
fire disease 191
leaf mould 192
nut 202
onion neck 138, *138*, **174**
onion white 133, *133*, 142, **175**
root and foot **166**, 188, 194, 196, 198, 199, 208
sclerotinia 188, 192, 199, 200, 207, 208
soft **180**, 188, 192, 199, 204, 207, 208
strawberry fruit 91, **181**
tree stem **182**
turf 189, **218**
white tip 192
wirestem 188
rotary cultivators 130, *130*
rotation, crop 51, 132–4
rotenone 155, 161
Rumex, *see* dock
runner bean 130
rust **179**
russetting 97, 201
rust 46, 48, 53, 58, 82, 84, 121, 140, 160, 189, 191, 192, 195, 199, **217**
antirrhinum 43, **164**
black 31
broad bean **167**
carnation 43
chrysanthemum 43
crocus 121
French bean **179**
fuchsia 142
geranium 80
gooseberry 142
hollyhock 43, **172**
leek 142, **173**
mint 59, *59*
pelargonium *58*, 59, **176**
plum **176**
rose 43, **179**
runner bean **179**
spread 120–1
twisting 197
white *11*, *121*
rye grass 208

Saginaprocumbens, *see* pearlwort
saintpaulia 95, 136
salt, *see* sodium chloride
salvia 95
sap-sucking insects 29, 78, 153, 161, 190, 191, 200
saprotrophic fungi 53–4, 141
sawflies 120, 190, 195, 215, **217**
apple 43, **165**, 201, 202
currant **170**
gooseberry 120, *122*, **170**
leaf rolling 194
plum 202
rose slugworm *159*
turnip 120
scab 196, 201, 202, **217**
apple 43, 91, 92, 127, 160
common 205, 207
potato 43, **176**
powdery 205
pyracantha **177**
scale insects 70, *71*, 78, 149, 153, 160, **179**, 190, 191, 196, **217**
scarecrows 145
scars 16, 63, *64*
see also wounds
sciarid 160
scion 137
sclerotinia rot 50, *50*, 188, 192, 199, 200, 207, 208
Sclerotium cepivorum, *see* onion white rot
Scolytus 60
scorching 96, 97
sculla 60
sedge, *see Carex*
seedlings
damping off 30, *46*, **170**, 188
millepedes **174**
symptoms **188**
woodlice **183**
seeds 22–3, *22*
dispersal 22, 115
dormancy 114–15
light and germination 94
propagation by 138–40, *138*
Senecio vulgaris, *see* groundsel
Septoria 50
Serpula lacrymans, *see* dry rot
shanking 206
shepherd's purse 114, 117, 210, 211, 212
shoots **196–9**
short-day plants 95–6
shrubs
accidental damage 106, 140
dead twigs and branches 141
planting 135
snow 93
silver leaf 137, **179**, 193, 198
silver scurf 205
silver Y moth 76, 119
silvering 111
simazine 157, 159
skin spot 205
slaked lime 101
slime flux 197
slime mould 189, 206, **217**
slugs 72, 79, 144, 149, 150, 161, **180**, 188, 189, 190, 195, 199, 200, 202, 204, 205, **217**
black *73*
collars 130–1
keeled 43, 126
slugworms *159*, 190
small white butterfly 79, 119, 144, **167**
smokes 158
smoking tobacco 69
smudge 206
smut 46, 59–60, *90*, 91, 125, 192, 201, 204, **218**
snails 72, 79, 144, 150, *152*, 161, **180**, 188, 189, 190, 195, 199, 200, 204, **218**
snow 15, 93, 199
snow mould 189
soaps, horticultural 155, 160
sodium 102
sodium chlorate 156, 159
sodium chloride 107, 108, *108*
salt-tolerant plants 109
soft fruit
birds 166
lime-induced chlorosis **174**
propagation 136
soft rot **180**
see also individual types; fruit; fruit cages
soft rot *55*, **180**, 188, 192, 199, 204, 205, 206, 207, 208
soil 98–105
compaction 92, 98, 128–9
drainage 128
dry 88
frozen 86–7, 93
nutrients 102–5
pests 149, 160
pH 100–2
seed propagation 139
sterilization 139
symptoms present in **187**
waterlogged 92–3, 98
Solanum 111
see also nightshade
Soleirolia soleirolii, *see* mind-your-own-business
Solytus, *see* bark beetle
Sonchus, *see* thistle, sow
sooty bark disease 91, 125, 198
sooty blotch 201
sooty mould **180**, 203, **218**
sorrel 209
spangle gall **180**
specialization and evolution 30–1
species and subspecies 24–6
speedwell 117, 211
Sphaerotheca pannosa, *see* powdery mildew, rose
spiders 72, *72*
spinach 110
spiral growth 111
splitting **180**, 202
sporicidal 62
sporostatic 62
spots 186, 194, 196, 197, 199, 203, **218**
see also leaf spot
spring beauty 212
springtails 187, 188, 207, **218**
spur blight 197
spurge 24–5, 27, 117, 142, 211, 212
squirrels 76, **181**, 199, 202, 205, **218**
Stachys 142
starch 23
Steinernema carpocapsae 149
Stellaria see chickweed
stem eelworm 191, 199, 206
stems 16–18, *16–17*
creeping 116
symptoms **196–9**
sterilization, compost 139
stomata 14, 56
stony pit virus *160*, 202
strangles 91
straw 109
strawberry 29, 43, 91, 144, 193
beetle 202
fruit rot 91, **181**
leaf blotch **181**
leaf scorch **181**
leaf spot **181**
lime-induced chlorosis **174**
mite 200
powdery mildew 43
streptocarpus 136
succulents 174
suckers 144, 189, **218**
sugar maple 109
sugars 23
sulphate of potash 105
sulphur 102, 103, 108, 154, 160, 161
sulphur chips 101–2
sulphur dioxide 107
sun scald 90
superphosphate 105
swede 43, 111, 143
soft rot *55*
sweet chestnut canker 121
sweet corn *18*
smut disease *90*, 91, 125
sweet pea 130
swift moth 207
sycamore *22*, 109, 181
sooty bark disease 91, 125
symphylids 187, **218**
symptoms and host plant 30

Syrphid, see hoverfly
systemic and non-systemic
infections 59–60, *59*, 67, 152, 153

tamarisk 109
Tanacetum cinerariifolium 62
tar oils 161
tar spot **181**
Taraxacum offinale, see dandelion
tarsonemid mite 200, 206
taxonomy 25, 27
temperature 86–91, 97
tertamethrin 161
thiophanate-methyl 155, 160
thistle *22*, 113, *147*, 153, *157*
creeping 117, 209, 210
sow 117, 122, 209, 210
thrips 78, 91, 149, 190, 195, 200, 203, **218**
thuja 109
toads 71
tobacco mosaic virus 69
tomato 43
blossom end rot *9*, 94, **181**
chemical injury **182**
composting seeds 142
distorted growth 108, *109*
eelworm 137
fertilizers 105
greenback 90
grey mould 53, 56
leaf mould 43
mosaic virus 43, 69
oedema 111
potato blight 124, 126, *126–7*, **176**, 203
silvering 111
sun scald 90
wilt 137
toothwort 198, 199
tortrix moth 145, 202
training *128*
translaminar 152
translocated 152, 153
transplanting 19
traps 144–5, *145*
tree stem rot **182**
trees 17–18
accidental damage 106, 140
canker lesions 65
dead twigs and branches 141
fruit, *see* fruit trees
fungi *53*, 54–5, 60, 6405
honey fungi 50–1, 141, 144, **172**, 198, *208*
lightning damage 96
planting 135
pruning, *see* pruning
roadside 108
roots 18, 106
silver leaf **179**
snow 93
suckers 144, 189, **218**
sun scald 90
training *128*
viruses 67
wind damage 96, *96*, *97*
witches' broom **183**, 197
wound response 63, 64–5, *64*, *65*
see also pruning
trefoil 209
trenching 130–1
Trialeurodes vaporariorum, see whitefly
trichlophon 161
triforine 155, 160
Tropaeolum majus, see nasturtium
trunks 17, *17*, **196–9**
tsuga 109
tubers 17, *22*, 23, *23*, 74
bulb rot **168**
storing 143
symptoms **204–6**
tulip 93, 171
Botrytis tulipae 52
bulb aphid 204
see also bulbs
turf rots 189, **218**
turnip 111
gall weevil 207
sawfly 120
twigs
dead 141
symptoms **196–9**
twisting rust 197
2,4-D 151, 156, 159

unidirectional symptoms 185–6
uniformity 40
Uromyces geranii, see geranium rust
Urtica, see nettle
Ustilago, see smut

varieties 24–5, 27
vectors 68–9, 78, 121, 158
vegetables
bolting 94, *107*, 110
companion planting 147–8
handling 106, 143
protective cages 144
soft rot **180**
splitting **180**
storing 143
symptoms **203–4**
see also root vegetables
vegetative propagation 68, 136–7
Veronica, see speedwell
Verticillium, see wilt
vine 43, 111
downy mildew 126, *127*, 154
phylloxera 43
scale insects **179**
vine weevil 72, 74, 139, 149, 160, **182**, 190, 195, 204, 207
violet root rot 205, 207, 208
viruses 8, 29, 66–9, 193–5, 200–3, 205, **218**
chemical control 158
spread 67–9
symptomless 69
vectors 68–9, 78, 121
Viscum album 122, *123*
voles 76, 78, 187, 188, 199, 202, 204, 205, **218**

wallflower 169, 171
walnut leaf gall mite *193*
warts 205
wasps 144, **182**, 202, **218**
gall 193, **216**
parasitic 148, 149
water lily *20*
water loss 16
watering 136
and flowering 110
houseplants 136
overwatering 111
seeds 140
watermark disease 121
weeding 141–2
weedkillers, *see* herbicides
weeds 112–13, 122–3, **208–13**
annual 114–15, 122–3, 125, 129, 131, 219
biennial 219
introduced 117
leaf silhouettes **213**
mulching 132
perennial 115–16, 122, 130, 219
and viruses 69
weevils 195, 200, **219**
apple blossom 200
nut 202
turnip gall 207
vine, *see* vine weevil
wet wood disorder 197
white blister **182**, 195, **219**
white rot 205
white rust *11*, *121*
white tip 192
whitefly 78, 142, 145, *148*, 149, 153, *154*, 158, 160, **183**, 190, **219**
as vectors 68
willow
twisted or corkscrew 111
watermark disease 121
willowherb *18*, 122, 142, 212
wilt 44, *57*, 60–1, 191, 194
aster **166**, **219**
tomato 137
wind 15, 93, 96–7, *96*, *97*, 199
wind pollination 21
windborne pests and diseases 185
winged cork 111, *111*, 198
winter heliotrope 211
winter moth 145
wire, damage caused by 106
wirestem rot 188
wireworm **183**, 204, 207
wisteria 21
witches' broom **183**, 197
wood 14, *16*, 17–18, *17*
woodlice 28, 74, **183**, 187, *187*, 191, 202, 204, **219**
woolly aphid **183**, 190, 196
worms 72, 74, 92
wound response 63–5, *64*, *65*
wounds 56, 58, 197
accidental 106, 140
hail damage 93
healing 140
see also scars

Xanthomonas populi 60

yarrow 208
yellow cards 145
yellow cress, creeping 210
yellow edge disease 193
yellows 49, 206
Yorkshire fog 208

zinc 102, 108, 144
zone-lines 64

Author's acknowledgements

This book is based on my personal experiences but many friends and colleagues have contributed to them over the years and for this I am extremely grateful. I owe a special debt to my friend Dr Keith Harris who has taught me much about crawling things and I have drawn on our jointly published key in constructing the new keys in this book. I am also most grateful to Richard Chancellor who has kindly allowed me to base my weeds key on his; and also to Hilary Broad whose weed leaf silhouettes contribute so much to the ease of identification.

Photography acknowledgements

All photographs © Professor Stefan Buczacki, except pages 7 and 24 bottom right (Mayer/Le Scanff/Garden Picture Library); page 24 bottom left (J.S. Sira/GPL); page 24–25 (Jacqui Hurst/GPL); page 25 bottom right (Christopher Fairweather/GPL) and pages 25 bottom left and 30 top right (Mark Bolton/GPL).